THE IRISH SOUL: IN DIALOGUE

The Irish Soul

In Dialogue

Stephen J. Costello

The Liffey Press
Dublin

the
liffey
press

307 Clontarf Road,
Dublin 3, Ireland.

© 2001 Stephen J. Costello

A catalogue record of this book is
available from the British Library.

ISBN 1-904148-00-X
Originally published under ISBN 1-86076-212-3

The painting on the cover is entitled *The Irish Soul* and is the copyright of the artist,
© Graham Knuttel. Reproduced here with kind permission.

While every effort has been made to trace copyright of photographs, the Publishers
will be happy to correct any omissions in future printings of this book.

Printed in the Republic of Ireland by Colour Books Ltd.

Contents

Acknowledgements

There are a number of people I would like to thank, without whom this book would not have been written.

Firstly, my deep gratitude to all of those who consented to being interviewed for this book and who gave of their time generously and graciously and from whom I learnt so much: Gerry Adams, Dr Ivor Browne, Catherine Comerford, His Eminence Most Reverend Desmond Connell, Brendan Dowling, Roddy Doyle, His Grace Most Reverend Walton Empey, Brother Mark Patrick Hederman, Professor Richard Kearney, Graham Knuttel, Alice Leahy, Dr Josephine Newman, Senator David Norris, Daniel O'Donnell, Micheál Ó Muircheartaigh, and Dana Rosemary Scallon. The strengths (if such there be) in this book are theirs, the weaknesses present my own.

My gratitude also goes to my publishers, especially David Givens and Brian Langan for seeing the potential in this publication.

I would like to thank Richard McCauley, of the Sinn Féin office in Belfast, for arranging the interview with Gerry Adams.

My special thanks to my parents Val and Johnny Costello who were a source of constant encouragement to me throughout the writing of this book and to my late grandfather, Jimmy Doyle. This book is dedicated to them.

I would like to express my sincere gratitude to my brother, Simon, to my sisters Suzanne and Sarah and my uncle Graham Doyle for their interest and advice throughout all the stages of the book.

Thanks also to my friends, especially Oisín and Elva Quinn, John Rice, Helen and Garrett Sheehan, Katharine Maurer, Tomas O'Connor, Alan Dodd, Stephen McCoy, Hugh Cummins, Fionnuala MacAodh and Tommy McDonagh for their enthusiasm, understanding, constructive comments and, above all, for their loyal friendship over the years. Thanks also to Luke Sheehan for his helpful comments and suggestions. To Jesus Reyes who has sustained me through his letters and e-mails from Puerto Rico. Thanks also to Abbot Celestine Cullen, OSB, Fr Terence Hartley, OSB, Fr John Harris, OP, and Fr Derek Smyth for their emotional and intellectual support over many years. My heartfelt thanks to you all for your firm and fruitful friendship.

A particular word of thanks has to go to my two Aikido instructors and friends who taught me how to dance, Brendan Dowling and Brigid Ruane. The *dojo* has become a family of friends for me, and the gathering afterwards a kind of therapy and philosophical instruction. To my fellow Aikidokas in the Whitefriar Aikido Club, I feel honoured to know you all.

I am especially grateful to Ronan Sheehan for his invaluable advice and enthusiastic support. My profuse thanks.

Finally, a considerable word of thanks must go to Mészáros István, my *anam cara*, who has sustained and supported me in many ways. Thanks Mosze.

I dedicate this book to my parents Val and Johnny Costello and to my beloved grandfather, Jimmy Doyle, in memoriam

"It's all about soul
It's all about faith and a deeper devotion
It's all about soul."

— Billy Joel, *All About Soul*

Preface

James Joyce coined a neologism "lugly", conjoining "lovely" and "ugly", to describe Dublin. I was born and bred in Dublin. Certainly the Dublin of Joyce is far removed from the Dublin of the 2000s and the Ireland of the Celtic Tiger. Where Joyce talked about forging "in the smithy of my soul the uncreated conscience of my race", Ireland, for many people, seems to have become a soulless entity.

The question is: in our contemporary cultural climate, does soul still exist and if so, what is it? By "soul", I mean depth and passion, sensitivity and "simple" spirituality. Soul points to the spiritual dimension of life. I believe that, despite the unprecedented economic success of our small country and the rampant commercialism and materialism that is seeping in and strangling Ireland's spirit, and despite Official Ireland's smug, complacent consensus, certain outstanding individuals have worked wonder with their words, music, ideas and ideals.

In my opinion, the Irish are still a soulful people. It is soul that permits us to "see into the life of things", into "the still, sad music of humanity", as Wordsworth wrote. The yearning for ultimate meaning is becoming more and more intense. When people's basic material needs have been met, as Maslow recognised, they yearn for something more, for something other. Having lost faith in dogmas, systems and failed and faded ideologies, one is thrown back on the resources of one's own soul, where alone resides living truth.

Contact with transcendence, in whatever form it may take, can alleviate suffering, can provide an overwhelming sense of reality, can soothe the spirit. The divine reality can dissolve the closure of soul, of a soul that seeks to commit suicide out of disgust with life. Camus was right when he said that the only truly philosophical question is whether one should commit suicide. The choice is stark but simple: an act of suicide in despair, in the dark, or an act of worship on bended knees before the God who made us. It is a choice, ultimately, of closure (chaos) or of a rediscovery of the spiritual order of existence (cosmos). Closure of soul is the suffering of one cut off from all contact with transcendent reality. It is to elect the darkness of disorder over the divine Ground of being. Yeats said that "man is but a paltry thing . . . unless / Soul clap its hands and sing, and louder sing / For every tatter in its mortal dress". Soul is the essence of man, for it is the receptacle of spirit. Soul alone endures. But soul is also intimately connected to darkness — "the dark night of the soul", described so vividly by St. John of the Cross.

Both soul and depression concern depth. As Yeats asked: "Who can distinguish darkness from the soul?" It was another great, soulful Irishman, Samuel Beckett, who pondered on the mystery but concluded that he hadn't "the strength to go on or the courage to end". The hope is that life and love will triumph over despair and hate. Such a struggle is surely Sisyphean — it is enough to fill a man's soul.

In the contemporary spiritual wasteland of our civilisational crisis and in the disintegration of spiritual order, only the divine reality can dissolve the closure of soul and combat the calamity of a despiritualised humanistic consciousness. Contemporary consciousness is marked and marred by the relentless drive toward self-divinisation, which is nothing short of a metaphysical revolt. It is Gnostic through and through with its "immanentisation of the eschaton", to use Eric Voegelin's felicitous phrase. This Promethean hubris aims to divinise human nature and humanise the divine. A resacralisation is required to counter the entrenched secularisation of the age. The divine presence is encountered in the depths of the soul and in the cosmos. True divinisation, then, necessitates the opening of the soul to the God who is the beginning and the beyond. Divinity is encountered in the hidden depths and dark recesses of the soul and in society, where the pneumatic centre draws us beyond and is the source of all our eschatological expectations and the cipher of our eternal destiny.

Where better to begin than in Ireland, the land once known as the isle of saints and scholars? There are some lone voices in this country who are deconstructing the dominant paradigm. But they are few and far-between. I have had the privilege of meeting some of them.

The people portrayed in these pages have painted darkness as well as light. The book presents us with a detour through varying cultural landscapes, permitting a truly panoramic vision. The dialogical explorations that follow deserve reflection because they are concerned with (creative) imagination and (critical) intellect. These Irishmen and women share certain common characteristics of Irish soul. The interviews contained within these covers are expressions of soul. This book adumbrates a survey of contemporary Irish history under the rubrics of philosophy, psychology, politics, painting, music, religion, literature and sport.

As to my criteria for selection: I chose these representatives of Irish soul because I either knew them personally and counted them among my friends and mentors or I respected and admired them and acknowledged their contributions, their character and their calling. Needless to say, I assume full responsibility for any errors I may have unwittingly caused involving the transcription of these interviews from tape to written word.

The personalities encountered in these pages, with their passions and prejudices will, I know, inspire, interest and intrigue you. It is my hope that there is something in this eccentrically eclectic compilation for everyone. Our trajectory provides a plethora of divergent positions and standpoints, pointing to a rich and fascinating tapestry of contemporary Irish life. The people it was my pleasure to interview come from all walks of life, representing a cross-section of the community. They are: Gerry Adams (President of Sinn Féin), Ivor Browne (psychiatrist), Catherine Comerford (Assistant Governor of Mountjoy Women's Prison), Desmond Connell (Catholic Cardinal), Brendan Dowling (martial artist), Roddy Doyle (writer), Walton Empey (Archbishop of the Church of Ireland), Mark Patrick Hederman (monk), Richard Kearney (philosopher), Graham Knuttel (painter), Alice Leahy (Director of Trust), Josephine Newman (psychotherapist), David Norris (Senator), Daniel O'Donnell (singer), Micheál Ó Muircheartaigh (broadcaster) and Dana Rosemary Scallon (MEP).

An interview is an interrogation of soul; these cameo-reliefs, these snapshots show us a plurality of personal perspectives and possibilities. It began as a very personal, philosophical search on my part. Probably I am present on every page as much as my "subjects" are. I never pretended to be objective or journalistic. I was frank and forthright, personal and passionate. The questions I put and the answers my interviewees provided mattered much to me. For each questioning involves, at an intimate level, a questing after something, for nobody is completely at home in himself or his world. The very act and art of questioning involves the being of the questioner, because we are not stoical spectators but passionate participators in the drama of being. We *care*. We ask why and wherefore, we wonder, we despair and we hope.

Searching still and sometimes succeeding. Remembering and recording, rhapsodically. The Irish soul, then, in dialogue with itself.

Stephen J. Costello,
Dublin,
September 2001

GERRY ADAMS
President of Sinn Féin

Gerry Adams is President of Sinn Féin, a member of the Northern Ireland Assembly and MP for West Belfast. The eldest of ten children, he grew up in working class West Belfast where he worked as a bartender and became involved in the civil rights movement. He was interned in 1972 on the Maidstone, a British prison ship. He participated in peace talks with the British that resulted in a truce, which was broken later. He was arrested and interned without trial, spending four years, from 1973 to 1977, in prison. In 1983, Mr Adams was elected President of Sinn Féin and as a Member of Parliament for West Belfast, a position he regained in the recent Westminster elections. In 1993, together with John Hume, he played a pivotal part in the Irish peace initiative, which led to the Downing Street Declaration and the Joint Framework Document. The subsequent talks eventually led to the Good Friday Agreement in 1998. He has published several books, including an autobiography. Despite censorship and the demonisation of his personality and his party, Mr Adams remains for some the most controversial figure in contemporary Irish politics while for others he is an international statesman of huge renown.

SJC: You have been active in politics from an early age, growing up in working-class West Belfast, eventually becoming President of Sinn Féin. You have written a number of books, including *Falls Memories*, *The Street*, *Cage Eleven*, *Free Ireland* and your autobiography, *Before the Dawn*. I want to know where you get all your energy from, what keeps you going, and do you ever get depressed with the situation in the North?

GA: I am influenced by a wide range of people and experiences. Those I work closely with are very important; as is the wealth of experience I have accumulated over 30 years of political activism. I am also a keen observer of human experience and behaviour, whether here in Ireland or when I travel overseas to the USA, or South Africa or England. I read widely, listen as often as I can to the radio and occasionally watch television. All of these events, people, cultures, and languages affect me as a human being and influence what I write. One conclusion I have drawn from all of this is that the Irish people are no better than any other, but we are no worse. We are as unique as they are and our uniqueness arises from the island we inhabit, the languages we speak — Irish and English — the influence that our nearest neighbour has had on us, our sense of ourselves as Irish, as well as our music, dance, literature and *craic*. And somewhere deep in all of that is our soul — the Irish soul — which brings all of this together and makes us, for better or worse, what we are. And ultimately it is that which gives me strength. I believe absolutely that the Irish people are good people who don't want to exploit our neighbours, who aren't racist and who want to build a better life for themselves and their families, and neighbours and friends. What we are today, as a people, as a nation, is also hugely influenced by the English colonisation of us as an island people and our historic response to that in all its forms. In many ways, the Irish are the survivors. And when the political situation deteriorates and another crisis looks like pushing us back, it is all of these marvels, and our republican vision of a better future, which brings me back to earth and reinvigorates me, recharges my batteries.

SJC: The IRA have signed up for peace. To a large extent, you have been responsible for and successful in bringing the IRA leadership to the brink of peace. But what about the Real and Continuity IRA? How dangerous are these dissidents?

GA: The rejectionist republican groups have no popular support. They are unrepresentative and have no moral or political centre of gravity. But as we saw at Omagh, they do have a capacity to hurt and kill and damage the efforts for peace. Martin McGuinness long ago argued his thesis that it is only by making politics work, by building trust and confidence, that these people can really be defeated; and then it will be the people — not some repressive policy — who achieve that.

SJC: What do you think is the greatest obstacle to the peace process?

GA: There are many dangers and threats to the peace process. It would be wrong to single any one out and raise it above the others. If we take our eye off the prize of peace; if loyalist death squads and the British securocrats increase their attacks on Catholics and on the process; if the pro-Agreement forces in the 26 counties lose interest, or worse revert back to the policies of the past because of the threat Sinn Féin poses electorally to them; if the British government continues to devalue the Good Friday Agreement and tries to sell it short by not delivering on issues like policing and demilitarisation and human rights and justice matters; then the process will continue to be at risk. And in these circumstances we must remain vigilant and stay focused on the needs of the peace process. That is why every day is a battle, everyday is filled with negotiations, everyday is part of that greater struggle for freedom, justice and peace in Ireland.

SJC: Who has done the greatest disservice to the cause of republicanism and nationalism?

GA: There is no simple answer to this. Many people, many parties and groups failed to live up to the ideals of Tone and Pearse and Connolly. Many have failed to implement the ideals enshrined in the 1916 Proclamation. Our task is to ensure that we don't make that mistake. Each generation of activists have to update republican strategy so that republican principles and objectives are relevant to contemporary conditions and to the people's needs. That is what Tone, Connolly and Pearse did. That is what we have to do.

SJC: What exactly is the difference, in your opinion, between nationalism and republicanism?

GA: That is a question that would take a book to answer — and I haven't time to do that now. In short, there are those who define both too narrowly and consequently do both a disservice. Each is complementary and in Ireland we draw upon overlapping and merging experiences. I am both a nationalist and a republican. My nationalism and republicanism is rooted in the best of Tone, Pearse and Connolly. Republicanism entails a particular form of society in which the people are sovereign. In the Irish context, that involves a national — that is, 32-county — republic, independent and democratic with an inclusive ethos based upon equality and justice. I believe the interests of our people will be best served by a new economic dispensation based on socialist principles and democratically agreed, in which a citizen's rights to a home, to work and care from the cradle to the grave are central to society's ethos. I believe the nation's resources should be used to end poverty and create equality. I also believe in decentralisation and I would be very flexible about devolving political institutions. The Good Friday Agreement gives a good example of how this could work. Nationalism in the Irish context is another word for patriotism, an allegiance to the people of Ireland, to the nation and to the country. I believe that the people of Ireland have the right to determine our own future, our own destiny. But it must be a future for all as equals shaped by a republican philosophy which is democratic, radical and socialist.

SJC: In 1967, Cathal Goulding, then Chief-of-Staff of the IRA, made a landmark speech in Bodenstown attacking the armed struggle and favouring socialist policies. You said you had mixed feelings at the time. When exactly did you abandon the physical force tradition in Irish republicanism and come to believe that the ballot box rather than the bomb was the way forward?

GA: Stephen, this is a question that would need more time to answer than I have available at the moment.

SJC: With whom in the 1916 Rising would you have the most affinity?

GA: James Connolly.

SJC: Who before and since then has influenced you the most, both in Ireland and internationally?

GA: Many, many people. Some of them I have already mentioned — Tone, Connolly, Pearse — but also for this period Bobby Sands and his comrades, my friend Cleaky Clarke who died last year, Martin McGuinness, Nelson Mandela, Martin Luther King, Rosa Parkes, and every republican I have ever met. But they all share one attribute — their courage and determination in the face of adversity and their commitment to humanity.

SJC: James Connolly once said: "The cause of Labour is the cause of Ireland. The cause of Ireland is the cause of Labour." And in *Free Ireland*, you say: "If you want to talk about socialism in the Irish context, you cannot divorce the socialist aspiration from the aspiration of national independence." Are you a socialist in the tradition of

James Connolly? You also say that one cannot be a socialist and not be a republican; but can one be a republican without being a socialist?

GA: James Connolly was and continues to be an inspiration. But even he acknowledged that his writings should not be viewed as dogma. It's about constantly growing, thinking and learning, and applying that to the circumstances in which we live. Yes, I would like to think I am in the tradition of Connolly, adapting my politics to the political conditions in which I live to advance the republican goals of independence and sovereignty. I believe Connolly was absolutely right when he described republicanism and socialism as opposite sides of the same coin. They are complementary. But equally, it has to be acknowledged that there are many varieties of both in this world and even here on this small island of ours. Consequently, we have to thoughtfully define our politics and what our republicanism and socialism means for citizens. You cannot divorce the socialist aspiration from the aspiration of national independence. This is the big lesson of the Connolly experience. To use Connolly's phrase, this requires the reconquest of Ireland by the Irish people, which means the establishment of a real Irish republic. You cannot be a socialist in Ireland without being a republican. That is clear. Of course, you can be a republican without being a socialist. As I have outlined earlier, republicanism is a form of society — a republic.

SJC: Fianna Fáil calls itself the Republican Party — is it? If not, why not?

GA: There are other parties on this island, including Fianna Fáil, who would describe themselves as "republican". Fianna Fáil and those other parties, all of whom have enjoyed political power, some for generations, have failed to live up to the ideals and goals that should guide a republican party. Their policies until recently were partitionist. They are big business oriented. The revelations of sleaze and corruption are evidence of the way in which elements of the party have perverted the Irish republican tradition of Tone and others. I believe the vast majority of people on this island are instinctively republican. But a political party has to be judged on its policies and its achievements, especially if it has been in power.

SJC: On that, how do you view politics in the Republic and why do you think Sinn Féin here only stands at between 1 and 5 per cent of the vote? Has that something to do with what used to be Section 31 of the Broadcasting Act?

GA: Sinn Féin's vote is on the increase in the South. Recent opinion polls, which must always be treated with caution, have indicated growing support for Sinn Féin. I believe that that is because our party activists are working hard at grassroots level on those issues that affect people on a day-to-day basis, whether it's unemployment, poverty, drug abuse, waste management, racism, people's rights or other issues. Regrettably, at this time we still have to develop the organisation or the organisational skills needed to maximise our potential but I am confident that we will get there. It is certainly true that censorship in the past meant that citizens had a less-than-accurate view of Sinn Féin politics. And even today there remains an inherent bias among sections of the media. But all of that is changing and people are increasingly able to see beyond the misreporting.

SJC: Do you fault the IRA for any of the policies it pursued? Is there anything in or about the IRA with which you disagree?

GA: The IRA is a fallible organisation made up of ordinary people. Yes, it has made mistakes but it is equally certain that without its courageous decision of August 1994 to call a complete cessation, there would be no peace process and no Good Friday Agreement.

SJC: You were on the run for over a year, interned without trial and spent, all-in-all, four and a half years in prison. What were those difficult years like for you?

GA: My experience was not unique. It is estimated that there are 6,000 ex-prisoners in West Belfast alone. That is a phenomenal number of families affected directly by the conflict. So while those years were difficult ones for me and for my family, they were equally difficult for many other families. One thing we must strive to ensure is that no other young people have to live through that experience again.

SJC: I know the hunger strikes affected you deeply, especially the death of Bobby Sands. Was this a landmark event for changing public perceptions?

GA: The hunger strikes, but especially the second in which Bobby and his nine comrades died, was a watershed in contemporary Irish history, as well as within Irish republicanism. Its effect on each of us individually, as well as collectively, is as strong today as it was 20 years ago.

SJC: In your autobiography, you describe the torture that was carried out by the British in Long Kesh. It was horrific reading. Do you agree with me that we in the South just haven't a clue what's going on in the occupied statelet and what our fellow citizens have had to endure at the hands of the RUC, the Special Branch and the British Army?

GA: Section 31, as well as successive governments in Dublin who saw the conflict in the North as a British issue for a British government to sort out, contributed enormously to the lack of public knowledge. It created a climate in which citizens, including human rights lawyers, could be killed by British intelligence agencies using loyalist death squads, and with little or no challenge from the establishment in the South. The hunger strike of 1981, more than any other event, unmasked the unwillingness of the South's political establishment to do anything for the hunger strikers, or indeed anything to challenge British rule in a part of Ireland. But while the Dublin establishment vacillated and tried to ignore events in the North, the people were sound. The people had stripped away the propaganda and lies. They saw beyond censorship and they were willing to stand up for right against wrong. We must remember that lesson every day. We must remember that when ten Irishmen stood against the British, ten of thousands of their fellow citizens from the 26 counties stood with them. We must remember over the years of the peace process, when Irish governments have not been as strong as they should have been, ordinary people have stood firm and governments have been moved. We must not forget that the shape of British policy in Ireland and its aims and objectives is dependent on how prepared an Irish government is to uphold Irish national interests and to influence British policy in this direction. The attitude of southern politicians and the policies they pursued undoubtedly added significantly to the years of conflict. Unfortunately, that mindset is still not far below the surface among certain sections.

SJC: You describe my uncle, Seamus Costello, as "an extremely competent leader and a formidable personality". I'm interested in what you thought of him and why you didn't join either of his organisations — the IRSP or the INLA?

GA: I met Seamus Costello many times as part of the audience of meetings he addressed up until 1970. I was in my early twenties at that time and I had no direct relationship with him. I was very impressed by his analytical powers, his ability to make a good case for his argument and his obvious leadership qualities. I consider the split of 1970 and the subsequent feuding to be huge setbacks for the republican and democratic cause. While I could identify with the founding statement of the IRSP, which was established following yet another schism, I saw no reason to leave Sinn Féin. I would encourage alliances between all political groups with common objectives; but once Seamus was assassinated, the IRSP lost any possibility of long-term development as a mainstream political party.

SJC: Do you think "our day will come" ("*tiocfaidh ár lá*") and you will achieve that for which you most crave — equality, justice, freedom and peace?

GA: I am absolutely certain that we will achieve our goals. I can't give you a calendar date by which it will be done but as surely as day follows night we will see the British out of Ireland and the Irish people deciding how we will live together on this island.

SJC: What's your view of contemporary Ireland and the Celtic Tiger?

GA: I commend those who have created the conditions for the greater prosperity that is enjoyed by many people today. It is good that there is greater wealth but that wealth needs to be utilised for the greater good. Too many have not benefited. The gap between the poor and the rest of us is growing wider. The Celtic Tiger has failed a significant number of people in the South. Too many live below the poverty line, or in poor housing, or scrape a living in low-paid jobs. Moreover, the Celtic Tiger is partitionist. It stops at the border. Sinn Féin wants to change all of that. We want to see the wealth of this island shared more equally among its people. That's why we have developed policies to achieve that.

SJC: What are your interests outside politics?

GA: I like to walk, to write, to walk the dog, to think about gardening, to read and listen to music. I have a large music collection that I like to dip into frequently.

SJC: Are you a spiritual person, a believer, a practising Catholic, and if so what's your opinion of the Church's decision to excommunicate (in the past) members of the IRA?

GA: Yes. The Catholic hierarchy's excommunication of IRA volunteers in the past is a mark of the Church at that time. It was wrong, as were the Magdalen laundries, the official Church attitude to courtship, dancing, poitín-making and other churches. It was an abuse of power and about control. It was nothing to do with God or the teachings of Christ.

SJC: Does Ireland still have soul and what do you think soul is?

GA: Yes. Ireland has a soul. It is what underpins our humanity. It is our humanity. It is also universal and it exists in all people, of all races and creeds and nations everywhere.

SJC: Finally, Mr Gerry Adams, are you happy? Are you hopeful?

GA: Yes, basically I am a happy person. And I believe in hope. It is essential to happiness and to life.

IVOR BROWNE
Psychiatrist

Dr Ivor Browne is not what might be described as an "orthodox" psychiatrist. He has always followed his own light. He is an independent thinker. Formerly Professor of Psychiatry in University College Dublin and chief psychiatrist of the Eastern Health Board, he was involved, prior to his retirement, in innovative psychiatric pro-grammes in St Brendan's Hospital and in countless community projects. Extremely helpful, courteous and charming, we had a fascinating chat in his home in Ranelagh, where innumerable topics were covered from psychotherapy to politics, soul to spirituality.

SJC: What attracted you to psychiatry in the first place?

IB: Nothing very strong. My ambition at the time was to become a jazz musician. But I had to keep my parents quiet so I took up medicine. I had a vague interest in what makes people tick, especially what made me tick. Then I got TB half way through studying medicine. I had still no idea about psychiatry. One day in the staff room in the Richmond after qualifying, the Professor of Medicine, who had a very biting sense of humour, said to me: "You're only fit to be an obstetrician or a psychiatrist!" That had some influence and I certainly didn't fancy being an obstetrician. It was a kind of negative thing. Most people who enter psychiatry do so because they have questions about themselves. They have trouble understanding themselves and I certainly had plenty of that. The sad thing about much psychiatry, about people who take the medical, organic view, is that they end up not studying themselves and so learn nothing and go off into a tunnel. But I certainly didn't follow that direction.

SJC: People come to you with their problems, existential crises and deep-seated personality breakdowns. Do you consult with anyone? How do you cope with the pressures of your life, both personally and professionally?

IB: At present I'm retired. I have a close colleague to whom I often refer cases. I'm only doing one morning a week. I'm doing it from a diagnostic point of view. I'm not taking people on myself unless it's very short term. In the past, when I was working heavily in psychotherapy, we had a whole team and had lots of team meetings and group discussions.

SJC: Unlike psychotherapists, psychiatrists aren't obliged to undergo psychotherapy.

IB: The situation when I took it up was very loosely organised on this side of the Atlantic. In the States, because of the dominance of psychoanalysis, the people who were doing their residency were involved in psychotherapy training and personal supervision. All psychoanalysts would have gone into therapy [*analysis*] but there wasn't the same organisation for psychiatrists, which was very medically oriented. I started to get interested in psychotherapy fortuitously and had a lot of supervision in an informal way. In a job at Oxford, there was an elderly psychoanalyst who took an interest in me, and that started me in that direction. After that, I worked in John of God's, which was very medically oriented, as was the hospital in Oxford; they didn't put any stress on understanding yourself except for that one man I met who had a profound influence on me. In 1959, after another breakdown of TB, I went to the day hospital in Marlborough whose founder was Joshua Bierer, who had been a pupil of Adler's, so I had a direct line back to that. They used to say he was more Bierian than Adlerian. He was a great old character. I did a year of psychoanalysis with him, actually lying on the couch, which wasn't orthodox psychoanalysis, which would be every day; I went twice a week. Also, he was more Adlerian and though I lay on the couch in his office on Harley Street, actually, he was very unorthodox. Most psycho-analyses would go on for four or five years but after one year he said: "That's enough."

SJC: What was psychoanalysis like for you?

IB: I think the Adlerian approach, particularly, has quite an amount of truth in it. All of these have within certain limits. But pure Freudian psychoanalysis is quite out of date now.

SJC: In the realm of psychiatry, you're more exploratory than orthodox. When did that strain of radicalness show itself? Was it when you were at the College of Surgeons, at Harvard or later still?

IB: It started in my first job at Oxford. All the patients there were either students or staff at the university and that was a revelation to me because for the first time I met people who thought independently. I came up in the ordinary school system in Ireland and didn't believe I could think for myself. It was a crisis revelation. Here you were dealing with the top two per cent of academic ability. When a question came up, they didn't think about authority and that approach affected me all my life. To answer your question, it made me ask: "Why can't I think for myself?" The more radical aspect started when I went to the day hospital in London. They were working with LSD and we were treating a lot of people with LSD and I saw people change from ordinary consciousness to childhood conflicts at or near birth. Once you see that, you can no longer accept the medical/clinical view. That put me in a strong position in relation to psychotherapy. Then when I went to Harvard, I was working in the School of Public Health and in the Mass. General and Eric Lindeman was the director of the Mass. General at that time. He was the first to write a paper on unresolved grief. He was a German psychoanalyst and the man in charge of the mental health programme in the part of Harvard I was in was a child psychiatrist and psychoanalyst. He brought in psychotherapy and an ecological approach. I had exposure to epidemiologists as well who had a different view of medicine to the treatment aspect that I had been trained in at the College of Surgeons. That tended to make you think in terms of prevention. It was a completely different view of health from a preventive point of view. The main interest of both Lindeman and Caplan was the handling of crisis, which is an everyday thing now. But when I came back here, nobody had ever heard of it; a person was either depressed or they weren't. But the notion that they hadn't dealt with grief hadn't started. But the pioneers of that were Lindeman and Caplan. Mental health centres were being set up after Kennedy was elected so I was in at the beginning of all that. It's now commonplace. So that's what set me off on a somewhat maverick direction!

SJC: As a psychiatrist, what's your view of man and human nature? What have you learnt after so many years practising?

IB: When you say "man", you mean . . .?

SJC: I mean humans.

IB: I don't like that term "man".

SJC: I use the term generically.

IB: What's my view of human beings?

SJC: Human nature.

IB: It's partly a spiritual view. I would be centred on a spiritual view but I would never have accepted a determinist position from Newtonian science. Freud would have been a determinist. To me, the human being is uniquely rather than totally free in creating his own destiny. That view would have been strengthened by the old man I met in India, Ram Chandra. His view and the general Eastern philosophy view is that it's not God who has programmed us but, having set the creation going, we have created it from the animal stage up so that some of our problems are created by ourselves or by society. We have created the society we live in. It's a different view from a so-called scientific/determinist view or a standard religious view that God decides everything. It's meaningless to pray for things. In a charitable sense he [Chandra] would allow you to pray. It's the same true Christian message in that you're praying for God's will. The central view is that we are creating the mess we're living in. We have the freedom to change. That's the psychotherapeutic view. If you were logical about Freud's view that everything was determined, there would be no sense whatever sitting down and working with someone! There's a complete lack of logic in the determinist position.

SJC: The human being, so, is a biopsychospiritual being? Is that your view?

IB: Yes, very much so.

SJC: And they are all interrelated. So we need to integrate biology, psychology and spirituality into any psychotherapy?

IB: Yes. But when we say three, it's only we who make the three. But there is only one unit. With all the community work I've been involved in, what's come over is a systems view. The more recent aspects of physics would say that everything's interconnected, if you read people like Bohm or Capra.

SJC: And Maturana and Varela?

IB: Yes, people like that. But there is a discontinuity between levels of system. By virtue of my boundedness (although at a deeper level, all may be one), there's a partial separation between different levels. I'm not sure how we got to this! It means while I'll have some control, as a living system, of controlling my boundary, I'm also part of a larger system like the family. And we're all parts of messy systems at the moment, each of which has something of its own life within its boundary. We are parts of groups of other systems, to the whole biosphere. It's a discontinuous interconnection, if you see what I mean.

SJC: Ken Wilber describes systems theory as a monological flatland and accuses it of being a subtle form of reductionism.

IB: What does he mean by that?

SJC: He has a view of the "Great Nest of Being" and that Being is holarchically graded.

IB: I've never read him in detail. But surely a hierarchical Nest of Being is a Nest of different related parts?

SJC: He says that there is no such thing as wholes or parts but that there are only "whole/parts" or "holons", a term he took from Koestler. He talks of the holonic nature of reality.

IB: I would agree with that but that's what I would mean by a different level of living system. To me, a family is a holon, an individual is a holon but they're one within the other so they're only partially separate, but they are separate from one another by virtue of their boundedness. He would talk of that in spiritual terms, in terms of levels of consciousness.

SJC: Yes, from the prepersonal through the personal to the transpersonal.

IB: Or the gross body and the astral body, which is an Eastern idea but that again is aspects of boundedness between those levels that are ultimately all one. I think he must have a different view of systems than I.

SJC: So you came to that view. Was that from your experience in India with Ram Chandra? You spent some time with him?

IB: I spent over twenty years in that system but I'm not strictly related to it anymore. I've gone my own individual way. I felt it was very helpful in dealing with the stress of very disturbed people. There is a great emphasis in that system on cleaning out the impressions, so that every day you are cleaning away stuff.

SJC: You still meditate?

IB: I do, but I left the system. The old man died in 1983. The whole thing grew in numbers and it was time to go back to my original idea, which was to get some form of spiritual path. It was becoming bureaucratic.

SJC: How do you meditate? Which is the "best" (that's the wrong word) way to meditate?

IB: They all have a central ground of agreement. You can't talk about the best; it's really a view of life and there is great wisdom in many forms of Buddhism. What I liked about the system I did was that you were talking about an individual who lived in our time. I feel a great privilege to have known someone of the same calibre as Buddha, rather than dealing with someone who lived two and a half thousand years ago. These messages tend to become more and more corroded with commentaries, which is happening with this system too, which is called "The Natural Path" (*Sahaj Marg*).

SJC: So how do you meditate?

IB: It works through a form of transmission, which is very master-centred. The view is that there is divine energy, a bit like the Divine Light people. There is a minimum of technique in the sense of using mantras and thought control. It's very heart-centred. You simply focus on a light in the heart. I don't think of the light anymore and you open yourself up to the transmission coming in. So that's the form of it.

SJC: How often do you meditate like that?

IB: This morning I did it for forty minutes.

SJC: In your career, you have been associated with Jungian psychology, constructivism, systems theory and some sort of holotropic breathwork at St Brendan's Hospital. Can you take me through these various clinical and intellectual interests?

IB: I met Stan Grof in the early eighties. I had been using LSD with my patients intermittently back in 1959, as a form of therapy. I was in at the beginning. I think I was the first to bring some psychedelics out to the West Coast. I met a disc jockey out there who was smoking a lot of hash but he didn't have any psychedelics. That was 1960. When bad publicity came in and I couldn't get any more LSD, I gave up for a couple of years and then I met Stan Grof and came into contact with his non-drug method of drums and breathing but I wouldn't be considered orthodox by Stan Grof. Nevertheless, it was he who started me on that road. We did a modified version of it with bodywork. Others, who worked with me, such as Marty Boroson, went off and trained with Stan Grof. He introduced me to ketamine, which I used to a limited extent as an alternative to LSD because some people (quite a sizeable minority) won't get into anything with just the breathing. Ketamine is very powerful, about ten times as powerful as LSD but the trouble is it tends to push you beyond your own personal boundary and you go off into outer space. The dosage is critical. It's more difficult to manage. The holotropic thing is too forceful; it's driving the person too much. I now think that traditional psychotherapy is more appropriate.

SJC: What type of therapy?

IB: Well, Vincent Kenny, with whom I worked, was very deeply involved with George Kelly and constructivism but I would never describe myself as a constructivist. I never describe myself as anything. Since I retired, I find there's no such thing as a cognitive or behavioural therapist. The behaviour you find yourself in depends on what the person is bringing. Cognitive aspects may be predominant in one situation whereas in another a person may need to work on a deeper level. I did a little test and watched myself for a morning and I found myself behaving in four or five completely different ways. All therapies have a large common area, whether it's psychosynthesis, gestalt or the holotropic thing. It's more a case of suiting the form of therapy to the person.

SJC: So there's no one particular psychological paradigm that comes closest to the truth about the human condition?

IB: No. I think people come with various kinds of problems and you have to take their constitution into account. If you have some person with an obsessional constitution, which is genetic and environmental, you are not going to deal with them as you would with someone who is cyclothymic. There's the personality type aspect. That would be a Jungian view. It depends on the nature of the person and the kind of problem they're coming with.

SJC: Is a therapy that omits a spiritual perspective lacking?

IB: Yes. Most emotional problems have a spiritual base but not everyone can relate to it in that way or go on to that level. Ethically, you can only take the person to where they want to go.

SJC: What's your view of the fourth force in psychology, which is known as transpersonal psychology and is associated with Grof and Maslow, Wilber and Assagioli?

IB: Yes, I would share a lot of that. I had many people in Brendan's who went into transpersonal states, which would seem to be from former lives. I had no belief system as such but equally I wasn't prepared to explain it away. I found that people tended to have a theme and if they went outside their own individual life the theme continued. So if it was an abusive theme, the experiences from what seemed like former lives would also be abusive. I would tend to search for the theme of this person's life.

SJC: Did your experience of these altered states alter your belief system in any way?

IB: I don't like to use the word "belief". I think the evidence to me suggests that there are past lives, from near death experiences, etc. There is impressive evidence for it. Ram Chandra would see what had happened in some former life. But this is the stage in which we can make change. There is a good reason why we are not normally aware of our previous visits to this planet. If we have had some thousands of lives, the burden we would have to carry if we had to be conscious of all that would be enormous. One view in Eastern philosophy is that when we are out of this reality we can see our long-term destiny more clearly. When we are born into this world we lose that clarity, but the possibility of change comes in.

SJC: It's like Plato's doctrine of *anamnesis* or recollection. For Plato, the soul pre-exists and has knowledge. At birth it loses all the knowledge it once possesses and it's only by degrees through life that it remembers or recalls this knowledge to consciousness.

IB: Yes.

SJC: Who are your mentors in psychiatry and psychology?

IB: Joshua Bierer was a major influence. I remember going to a whole series of lectures on Adlerian psychology and everything was explained in that system but when you left it you could have another explanation from Jungians. These are languages, much of which is saying the same thing. But I tend to share the more transpersonal and positive view of human life, like Assagioli, though I never studied psychosynthesis as such.

SJC: What is your own area of expertise in psychiatry?

IB: I would say I would have a very eclectic view. I would still find the medical basis useful and I see a place for pharmacotherapy but on the whole I would see it as a very temporary place. If anyone's honest who has to deal with the full spectrum, it's hard nowadays to manage without some psychotropic drugs, but I think the long-term use of them is damaging. So I would have a certain medical orientation, perhaps more, a biological orientation but I would feel I'm genuinely biological whereas the so-called biological psychiatrists disconnect our biochemistry from adaptation and interaction, which from the biological view is absolutely crazy. One part of me is a basic biological psychiatrist, in the Maturana systems sense and the other is a broadly transpersonal, spiritually based psychotherapeutic view.

SJC: If we take the psychoses such as manic depression and paranoid schizophrenia, would you see them having an organic base?

IB: Only in the sense that it's a language. It's not a question of whether drugs are good or bad or whether it's organic or functional, it's that everything we do in terms of adaptation and mind alters our biochemistry. The point they miss is that they have an *a priori* assumption: that is, if something is biochemical it's primary and it will cause certain clinical phenomena, but it itself is not caused by anything. Now that to my mind is stupid and non-biological. As we are talking now there are myriad biochemical changes going on within us. For every state of mind there is a biochemical equivalent but I don't think it's limited to that. I would take Sheldrake's theory seriously.

SJC: Yes, Rupert Sheldrake speaks of "morphogenetic fields", which comes close to Jung's theory of a collective unconscious.

IB: Exactly. His theory is the nearest to a scientific explanation because Jung never explained it. If the theory of fields is correct, that would be where the collective unconscious can happen. But it also has profound implications for transmission from generation to generation. What is genetically transmitted is only a very crude basis, like forming proteins. His view, which I think makes a lot of sense, is that much of what we are is transmitted through the fields. I don't know if you've read his *The Presence of the Past*, but that's where he develops his whole theory. There is a great infatuation now with the Genome Project. Undoubtedly, within 50 years they will have mapped the whole genome spectrum but I think they're in for a big surprise, of how little is actually transmitted through, though it will be useful for certain rare genetic disorders (they may be able to transplant genes) but it's not going to be able to explain human personality.

SJC: If I become depressed, psychiatrists will distinguish between reactive and endogenous depression, the latter they say is genetic. Is that just a case of language?

IB: Tragically, though, it's language that has become concretised. While the DSM IV is useful if you take it as a dictionary, to make it a reality and to say that these things actually exist in reality is wrong and this is where American and a lot of British psychiatry has got to. They are actually believing their own delusions, that there is such a thing as axis one depression, as some separate reality. There's a big change coming partly because of the failure of the drugs and the side effects and it's happening in places like Sweden and Finland. If you say to me, "What do you think of schizophrenia?", to me the first statement is that it is a human being who, like every other human being, has disturbances and problems. They may be genetically a bit different but that's a maybe. They're certainly a bit different by the time they reach twenty years of age but all sorts of factors have gone into making them what they are. They are a psychotherapeutic problem to me basically but the type of psychotherapy has to be questioned. I don't find that most schizophrenics have been particularly traumatised (some have) but the majority, if anything, are understressed. To my simple mind, essentially a schizophrenic is a person who hasn't grown into adulthood. It's no use doing holotropic work with people like that; they just get more fragmented and infantile. If a drug helps you momentarily to make contact and diminish the substitutive symptoms the person has developed, then it is of some use. The orthodox view is that they have to have drugs for an indeterminable period but some question that a lot of schizophrenics need drugs at all and if they do, they need them in a low dosage, if you have a proper psychotherapeutic and family input. The core of the therapy will always be a personal relationship. But if a person believes their own delusions and hallucinations, it may be difficult to get them to look at alternatives. I'm not saying you can treat everyone. I also think the longer a person goes into that world of fantasy, the more structural damage they're doing. Our early development and the way in which we live is all the time altering our structure. There's a reaction now to the sociopolitical caucus of big drug companies bribing and colluding with psychiatrists.

SJC: There's much talk of evolutionary psychology.

IB: What do you mean?

SJC: In evolutionary psychology, certain psychopathological syndromes are seen in terms of our alleged ancestral past on the African savannah.

IB: Like most things, there could be an aspect of truth to that but if we have had numerous lives, then they have been crossing cultures (not just a genetic stream) so that's another whole stream of causality, laying down *samsara's* impressions that we carry into this life. And you have genetic learning and learning from day one and habit formation in a field, so there could be four or five interlocking streams of transmission.

SJC: It's complicated!

IB: I think that's the reality. You have others who say it's all in the family tree and I have seen how hidden secrets in a previous generation have affected a person. In fact, I was just reading Anthony Clare's book and he gives a good example in the last chapter of a case he saw who didn't know he was the son of his sister and he didn't know who his father was. It was a secret which had a radical effect on his behaviour. I've seen that also. All of these can hold the truth for that person. I know it's distressing to be broad and not sign up to some certainty but I refuse to sign up to certainties because you have to look at all these influences.

SJC: Lacan stresses the family.

IB: I've never understood him.

SJC: Well, a Lacanian would say that psychosis is a result of the foreclosure of the paternal function. The psychotic has never reached the Oedipus complex and so has nothing to repress.

IB: This is just Freudian bullshit. The psychotic hasn't learnt to create a self and hasn't learnt to grow up. That's a much simpler way of putting it. I don't know what all this jazz about the Oedipus complex is. It seems to me to have been grossly exaggerated in importance. I certainly think psychosis is a family problem.

SJC: There's the individual in the family but also the family in the individual.

IB: And usually they are actually living with their family. I share a lot in common with my old friend Ronnie Laing, but where he went wrong was in demonising parents and he made something sacred of the psychotic. The failure to separate is central in most schizophrenics.

SJC: Margaret Mahler mentions that — separation and individuation.

IB: I don't know her work.

SJC: Do you place any store on psychoanalysis, both as a theory and therapy?

IB: I would in the broad sense, but to me, Jung would make more sense than Freud's narrow view and where he went critically wrong was in putting it back to infantile sexuality and he denied serious trauma, understandably. He was right initially, in certain cases but it's also true you have cases of false memory syndrome. It's a total repeat in the last twenty years of the discourse that went on a hundred years ago. It's only in the last twenty years that Pierre Janet's work has come to the fore. He was closer to the theory I've been trying to work on, which I call "unexperienced experience". His term is "unassimilated happenings". My view is that it's not the trauma that causes problems in rape, abuse or an accident; it's the fact that it hasn't yet happened, it hasn't got into the brain. It's held up, like an island within the person.

SJC: Is it an unmetabolised experience?

IB: Exactly.

SJC: That's just another way of saying repression.

IB: Yes, but I think that's a bad word for it. It's not a repression of something that was integrated; it's the holding out of an experience that hasn't been allowed to happen. We know that for any experience to get in it has to go through that primitive part of the brain.

SJC: Are you referring to MacLean's model of the triune brain?

IB: Yes. Traumatic syndromes are to do with the ancient biological mechanism of freezing. We've heard so much about flight/fight but more equally used in the animal kingdom is playing dead or "freezing". That must have given rise to survival in many instances, even though you are a sitting duck.

SJC: If you had a nervous breakdown, to whom would you go? What would your preferred therapy of choice be?

IB: I would have to answer that by saying that it depended on the nervous breakdown. I couldn't really be more specific than that. There are very few therapists that I would be anxious to trust myself to.

SJC: I'm not looking for names but rather the type of therapy.

IB: I'd imagine that if I had a nervous breakdown it would be more the longer term sorting out therapy. As Jung said about the second half of life, it's more about meaning. I didn't have any particularly traumatic upbringing except for family interaction. I've done a lot of the holotropic thing but never came upon anything very startling, except being crucified.

SJC: You established "The Foundation for Human Development". What was that?

IB: I'm afraid it's a long-winded answer. When I came back from the States in 1962, I didn't find any kindred spirits. One of the first jobs I took on was the newly opened clinic in Ballyfermot, which at that time was like Neilstown or Darndale now. It was 40,000 young families thrown into that wilderness — "Ballyfarout", as Brendan Behan called it. From the very first day, a whole line of women with horrendous social problems presented themselves and I remember being faced with a concrete existential choice, either I put my head down and start to give out Valium or I had to do something to try to address all these problems. The first approach I tried was quite wrong, which was trying to help them solve them. When Sister Francis came in with a person, I used to hide behind the desk because if she couldn't handle it, it was always horrendous, a case of money laundering or not being able to pay the bills or afford the communion dress. I got into this dependency mode of trying to help solve these problems but after a while I realised you didn't get anywhere because they weren't competently able to manage their lives. It was an amazing learning experience. But out of that, I got involved with a lot of professional workers out in Ballyfermot and the first phase of that was the clinic, the second phase was getting involved with all the professionals, the GPs and social workers and so on, and we had meetings and tried to set up a network to help these people but it had a pathologically caring orientation.

That phase lasted up to 1968 (by that time I had become Professor of Psychiatry in UCD) and the big rush of student unrest that began in China had started. The same thing happened to me as happened to Maturana: he was a conventional biologist until the students took over the university in San Diego and then his whole view of biology changed and he started on the whole notion of autopoiesis. In the same way, I got involved with the little revolution in UCD, what Garret FitzGerald called the "gentle revolution", but there were groups of very anarchic radical students. Around the same time, I got a fellowship to go to the States and I went over to a dozen cities, travelled for two months and went right up into Canada. I was in Montreal and playing the whistle — at least, people tell me that but I have no memory of it at all. Anyway, I met all these community people who told me that I had got it completely wrong. They said I was trying to care for them instead of motivating them.

I came back with a different orientation at the same time as the student unrest. I got the notion of empowering people. The Foundation didn't exist. But I began to think that people could be helped to take over and run their own lives as a community. Don Carroll, who was Chairman of the Bank of Ireland at the time, came to UCD to give a talk to a society and he was trying to put forward a picture of enlightened capitalism and the students tore him apart. I was chairperson that night.

After the talk, I told him that I was trying to work with these issues and he said he would help. It was very socialist at the time and very different from your generation. Now the whole socialism thing is gone out the window.

I came to the conclusion that we could get nowhere without a full time organiser, so we hired one. Then we hired other people and a point came when we had a street committee on every street in the area. That was the beginning of the Foundation. But also, I began to see that the internecine local politics had all the same vicious characteristics as Fine Gael and Fianna Fáil. That went on and we were invited to Sean McDermott Street. Instead of going in paternalistically, we started with the people themselves. Not long after that (this would be 1972, after Bloody Sunday), people came down to see the first community association and wondered whether we could set something up in the Bogside in Derry. I went up and met Paddy Docherty and he began the work.

At this point, we had spent half a million from the Bank of Ireland! We had to think of a name so I thought of this grandiose name, the Irish Foundation for Human Development. We had a year of frustrating meetings in the Bank of Ireland; the Governor at the time was a man called Finlay. They wanted to employ a capable businessman and were waiting for Tom Hardiman to finish in RTE. I was struck by the contradiction in these caring community projects between people wanting innovation as well as control. Tom Hardiman is a very fine person but from the day he came in the whole thing began to die. It went out of existence in 1978 but the work in Derry went on. Generally, I think the whole movement failed. The whole thing got top heavy. I was a hopeless administrator and would have needed some training in business management. But it did start the whole community action thing in this country. The main benefit I got out of it was that I developed some notion of systems. I saw the community as a living system.

SJC: So that's how you related your psychological vision to the cultural issues outside the clinic, to socio-political questions?

IB: At the time, I was very interested in the Fifth Province, which Richard Kearney had brought up. Even if it was misplaced, the idealism has all died now. We have reached a totally flat materialistic position.

SJC: I totally agree. I was at a wedding recently and all my age group were talking about "making a killing" and their houses and cars and bank balances. It was very sad.

IB: This Celtic Tiger is quite frightening because the old religion has died and nothing is replacing it. There are no signs of any idealism. I've been reading Tony Clare's book and he is a great communicator. However, he is talking about saving the "family" and does not seem to realise that the nuclear family is itself an artefact, it never existed in any society. It's the tribe and the extended family that got us through a couple of million years.

SJC: In an article you wrote for *Across the Frontiers: Ireland in the 1990s* [Wolfhound Press, 1988], you said: "One cannot really change as an individual unless the society out of which we emerge changes also" and "No part can change unless the whole changes and the whole cannot change unless there is change in the parts". You draw on the work of Capra, Prigogene, Maturana and Varela, all of whom hold that the human being is a living system that is interconnected with all other living systems.

IB: You can begin change at any level and no one is better than another. You could devote your life to helping ten people and be a real help, or you can work in communities. What I found is that it goes out in waves. At one point, about four authorities complained about me: the Eastern Health Board, the police, the Church, the corporation, because we were disturbing all their systems for controlling people.

SJC: You were doing something right then! Do you still see the world through the lens of systems theory?

IB: I would and I think there is an express train now running for the cliff, which is going to destroy itself. One possibility is gradual transformation, but there is not too much sign of that. We thought it was going to happen in 1995, we actually had a date! In fact, Chandra said in 1945 that communism would die in its own homeland in 1990. That was totally unexpected. He said there would be a lot of destruction. All the seeds seem to be there now for a major shake-up and I think it's on the way. Every week you see more signs, the lake in the Polar icecap in the North, the Mediterranean temperatures down through the ice and Antarctic, the pollution. And the scientists are particularly bad at predicting, because they always talk about taking hundreds of years. We could be moving to a point where there will be a sudden crack, it seems to me. If the seas went up suddenly by thirty feet, all European and American cities would go under water. It could happen as easily as that. There is going to be major destruction. My hope is that a simpler, cleaner, spiritual base would come out the other side without the loss of all our technology. If you could get rid of all the shit, we could run a very simple world, which would be focused on being. We only need to produce a tiny proportion of the crap we presently produce, so people would have to work very little. We could therefore set up communities and people would have time to grow things, not because they had to economically but because it's nice to grow things. So we could be in touch with our children again. Anthony Clare misses this completely; he's hoping for a place for men but there's no place for men or women or children in this economic madhouse. All the attempts at solutions at the moment are tinkering with the problem, like trying to manage the traffic. If you had Ireland of Celtic times now, as the basis, with thirty thousand little communities and you could impose our present technology on it, you would have a completely different set-up.

SJC: Yes, but how do you go about doing that?

IB: There have been all sorts of attempts, like the *kibbutz* and the hippie communes but none of them worked because they were all too partial and didn't touch the main economic machine, which is driving on relentlessly. A lot of knowledge is there now that could set up a very different kind of community but there would have to be a radical change of the whole thing, not bits of solutions like bus lanes and all that crap.

SJC: You are in favour of the application of liberation theology to community projects and strengthening the relation between mental health professionals and the community. And judging from what you have just been saying, you're quite political.

IB: Any change at that level has to be political but I also think it has to deal with the management of groups like the Tavistock groups. All the forms of group therapy are about helping the individual in a group setting but the Tavistock conferences are attempts to look at the group as a living system even though they don't realise it because they have Kleinian theory. It's about the primitive behaviour of a primate group. Bion got it wrong; it's not about fantasy but about behaviours in which any group of mammals have to engage in order to survive.

SJC: You have said that in the 1960s you had hopes of reconstructing society in a granular form. What are your hopes now and how do you see Irish society in the year 2001?

IB: Teilhard de Chardin was another influence. I think he was a hundred years ahead of his time. Have you read Capra's *The Web of Life*? It's worth reading. It's a collection of disparate papers that I had to struggle to find. I don't think people like me can do this even though I did have, for a period, this messianic notion. I think it's wonderful that we have broken out of the colonial mode. We still have the revisionists that sicken me, that Murphy fellow and Kevin Myers and Conor Cruise O'Brien and Eoghan Harris but the young people are full of confidence but unfortunately we have moved towards something that's completely materialistic and you have the underbelly. Lemass started this American model and I said at the time that we would end up having all the stuff they have — drugs, rape on the street, and we have it now.

SJC: What is soul?

IB: I would take the Ken Wilber and Eastern view that everything is God. Chandra has made the extraordinary statement that God has no mind because if God had mind he would be subject to *samsaras*. He sees God as an inactive potential out of which activity came and the creation started by a stir around it, which fits in with the Gaia hypothesis, that it is a partnership of us creating the biosphere. All of that is out from God and so part of God but the core of God would be something behind all that, which is beyond any attributes. So talk about God being good and God being love is nonsense.

SJC: So is God spirit?

IB: Ultimate Spirit, but there are no words for describing God. There have been great incarnations in terms of special people who have come into the world, like Christ and Buddha, who try to set us back on track and who are more directly connected to that centre.

SJC: Do you think Christ was the Son of God?

IB: I think he was one of them. Like Mohammed, they were absorbed in the Divine and radiating this divine pure energy. We are all potentially Buddhas but it is very difficult to make that full connection. Only very rare souls do it.

SJC: You're a cradle Catholic. What exactly are your spiritual beliefs? Are you a Buddhist?

IB: It's not Buddhist, but the general Eastern philosophy including China and Taoism. This makes a lot more sense because they don't turn God into an old man with a beard, an anthropomorphic notion. There's some kind of creative core to the universe. This is how the modern physicists conceive it, that there is a great circulation that has come out of this inactive potential and takes on the characteristics of movement and change and then will be reabsorbed back into it again and start all over again. God has no choice but to create.

SJC: Do you have a picture of post-mortem existence?

IB: I would think similarly to the *Tibetan Book of the Dead*, that some souls are lost and wandering and others are progressing towards the Source, but the simple answer is that we just don't know. I'll have some answers in a few years! I don't feel a fear of death. I see it as a transition. If you took an X-ray and told me I had lung cancer tomorrow I might be upset. I feel pretty convinced now, though, that there is a continuity.

SJC: Woody Allen says that he doesn't fear death; he just doesn't want to be around when it happens!

IB: Or like the fellow in a film who said, "If this is dying, I don't think much of it"!

SJC: Are you happy?

IB: No. I don't think so. As John McGahern said, "If there is a heaven, there aren't any writers in it"! I'm probably more contented than at any other period of my life but I don't think this is a situation of happiness, nor do I think it's particularly important. That's where we have gone wrong now, that we are searching for it. This need to be happy is an absurd notion.

CATHERINE COMERFORD
Assistant Governor,
Mountjoy Women's Prison

Photo: © Kinane Studio

Catherine Comerford is Assistant Governor of Mountjoy Women's Prison. I interviewed her in her office in Mountjoy Prison, where we had a fascinating and informative conversation about prison life and her experience in working with and helping those convicted of crime. After lunch in the prison with "the women" ("inmate" or "prisoner" are words not used), I was shown around and met with and talked to the women, including some, such as Catherine Nevin, who had been convicted of murder. Later, I was shown around the men's prison, which was an experience I will not forget. It was an eye-opener, to say the very least. I had the privilege of speaking with more prisoners there. Asked by one man whether I would like a bed for the night, I politely declined the invitation! Catherine Comerford is a kind and courteous lady. She is not only Governor but friend and confidante to the women who reside there and this was apparent throughout my day's visit there. With her hospitable presence in Mountjoy, the women are in capable and caring hands.

SJC: How did you come to work in the prison system?

CC: Through a career guidance teacher. I wanted to join the guards and I was too young so she suggested that I look at the prison service, which had never occurred to me. I wrote away and they wrote back saying they were advertising in the papers and it started from there. I didn't know what I was getting into. I said I would stay for 12 months and then I would go to the guards and I am still here 24 years later!

SJC: How do you find your job as Assistant Governor of the women's prison in Mountjoy?

CC: I worked here for 16 years in the women's prison before I was promoted to the rank of Assistant Governor and I found the women's prison very rewarding, but the women themselves are very demanding and you never know what's going to happen on a daily basis. What you do have to have is time, patience and a good listening ear because they want to talk and if you are not prepared to give of your time, there's no point being here. My whole day could be taken up talking to the women and often when I visit them in the morning I might not get back here till one o'clock and you are only talking about seventy women. Whatever the problem they have on that day is a huge problem for them.

SJC: You're almost a counsellor as well.

CC: You wear many hats here. You have to be a psychologist, psychiatrist, nurse and doctor. They would often ask me to get medication for them and I have to say that I am not qualified — that's up to the doctor. It's all about trust. I find it very rewarding, to sit down and explain something to a woman, something which in her own mind is difficult to sort out. For example, if a woman here has a child and the Health Board have decided that the child has to go into care, her first reaction is to say, "You're not getting the child", without thinking further down the road, that it might be better for the child to go into voluntary care without going through the courts and having her child taken from her. You might have to explain this two or three times before they realise what you are saying. If I don't know the answer to the question, I will tell them. You never promise to do something for them and then not do it. And you never lie to them. They will lie to you. But they don't expect that from me or the staff and you must honour what you say you are going to do for them. That's very important and you treat them the way you yourself expect to be treated and you won't have any problems.

SJC: Did you train for these skills or simply pick them up along the way?

CC: I got five weeks' training. And it was all about the theory and the rules and regulations. I had no training in how to deal or speak with people. I was talking to one of the girls this morning who has a case coming up — she was brutally attacked — and she was telling me of her life in an abusive household and I just said to her, "I didn't know what incest or sexual abuse was until I started this job." She's looking at me and thinking, "Aren't you lucky".

SJC: So is there a huge barrier between your world and their world?

CC: I've never thought of it that way. Yes, I can't feel the pain that they're feeling. I know they're feeling it but I can't feel it. I try and understand. I really try and understand what they're going through. Over the years when you hear these stories, again and again you can't think of them as people who should be locked away. The general public think, "Lock them up and throw away the key." It's much more than that. Women here in general have no self-esteem or confidence in themselves and they believe they are no good and nobody wants to help them. That's where I start from, to try and build up their confidence. It's all about dialogue and we do consult with the women if we want to change things. We have house meetings with them — there are ten in a house and we encourage them to speak in front of each other. That's confidence-building. It's to keep them going because there's no support for them out there and they're back to square one.

SJC: There have been innumerable theories proposed about the root causes of crime: poverty, violent videos, society in general, parents in particular. Some have suggested that the cause of crime is criminals! In your view, what factors contribute to crime? My own view is that emotional rather than social deprivation in early childhood is the key to understanding the structure of the criminal.

CC: I think it's both emotional and social deprivation. The family structure has broken down. I find here that there are mothers and grandmothers who have been through the prison system. I have one girl here whose mother and grandmother were here when I joined and whose father, brothers and cousins are in Mountjoy. It's the chicken and the egg syndrome, and how do you break that cycle? A lot of them would have been in care as well. When they reach the age of 18, they are adults coming into prison. Definitely for the women it's emotional deprivation, because ninety per cent of them are abused coming in here — physical, sexual or emotional. They are in big families and in order to be recognised they have to fight or steal. And it's the areas they come from. Eighty per cent of women here would have a drug problem. Back in 1976, there were twenty women or so in custody and none of them was on drugs — there was no drug culture then. In 1981, when it exploded in this country, they were shoplifting in order to feed their habits and you were talking about 17- to 19-year-old girls. It's very rare you get a woman coming into prison in her 30s or 40s, or even late 20s, who has only been on drugs for twelve months. These kids have been on drugs since the age of nine, in some cases. You can't change a lifetime's experience in twelve months. It's not practical or logical and people expect us to rehabilitate them and send them out as fine decent human beings. They are fine, decent human beings before they get into trouble. They have lost their way. The pushers hit the poorer areas. Cocaine and hash were in the Dublin 4 area, rather than heroin. In some circles it's perfectly acceptable to be smoking hash — there's no problem. But because life was so grim in those poor areas — there was no work, education was poor, family structure had broken down, violence reigned alongside sexual abuse — in order to escape they took drugs to block out all of the scarring that had been done to them. One of the women said to me this morning, "I took heroin to block out all that was horrible in my life. I want to stay here. I'm coming off the detox and I'm now seeing the psychologist and psychiatrist and I have got to face up to all those problems and the only place I can do that safely is here." But they go back out to the same.

SJC: If drugs got eighty per cent of them into crime, what about the other twenty per cent?

CC: The other twenty per cent have committed serious crime. You're talking about manslaughter and murder. You are talking about the mules, people bringing in drugs to the country. And white collar crime.

SJC: Are they housed separately?

CC: No, they are all together. You actually met them. You met two women doing a life sentence but you wouldn't be able to tell me who they were. It wouldn't even have crossed your mind that they were in for murder. They are normal people.

SJC: You would obviously know but would anybody else know, like their fellow prisoners?

CC: Yes, because they would tell them. They wouldn't discuss it but they would ask, "What are you in for?" and the answer would be for shoplifting or murder or manslaughter. But they wouldn't go into great detail unless the media has a hold of their facts, as in murder cases and we get the newspapers here every day, which we supply to every house every day because it's important that they keep in touch with what's going on in the outside world as well. I know they have televisions now in their rooms but I don't know how many would actually watch the news. Some of them would tell, others wouldn't but one would tell the other. It's a great telegraph system around here! They would often know things before we would know it and they would come and tell me.

SJC: There is the view out there, and this probably pertains more to the men's prison, that if you come in and say that you have committed murder you are on the top of the pile. It's almost a boast. Is that perception erroneous?

CC: I have never witnessed that in the women's or men's prison. I'll tell you why. Anybody who has been convicted of a murder offence deeply regrets what they have done and they have great difficulty dealing with it themselves. They don't go around boasting about it. They don't want to talk about it. It takes them about two to three years before they can actually deal with what they have done. We sat night after night for nearly two years with one woman, in the cell, keeping her going, getting her through the night, and today if she could turn the clock back she would. All of them I have met would. Whatever happened on that particular day or night, it got out of hand and somebody lost a life. Unless you are talking about the Generals of the world — maybe those types of guys, but the ordinary person who has murdered as a first offence doesn't go shouting about it. They want to put their head down and serve their sentence.

SJC: What types of criminals are there in Mountjoy?

CC: All sorts of crimes have been committed — embezzlement, fraud, cheques, prostitution and soliciting.

SJC: I would have thought the person soliciting is the man who stops them in his car.

CC: Well, I have yet to meet one. I have never met a man convicted for procuring a prostitute. It seems a bit unfair, because they're not on the streets for fun. It's not a job choice. It's out of necessity. You are talking about 17 or 18 year olds.

SJC: Is there a drugs problem in the prisons?

CC: There are drugs in the prison. It's not as bad, certainly in the women's prison, as people make out. They will try to get drugs and bring them in in their bodies. We don't do internal searches because it's inhumane and degrading. Legally, we can't, which is a godsend, as far as I am concerned. They will kiss the visitor and try to swallow them as well. But we have about twenty women who are on continual maintenance, so the need for them to get drugs in is greatly reduced. The drugs we come upon when we do random urine samples are hash and, in the odd case, heroin.

SJC: Many people don't think hash should incur legal penalties.

CC: They don't see anything wrong with that. And some members of the general public think cannabis is fine but we have to say it's never acceptable in here. If we find them with hash on them we cut them off from their family completely. We take it seriously. Then they say, what about cigarettes, aren't they a drug?

SJC: It does seem a bit arbitrary but I suppose you have to have rules.

CC: You have to have rules and regulations. And if they get caught they get a good talking to. It's hard to motivate them all the time but we have to keep going.

SJC: Now, you were explaining to me earlier, when you were showing me around, that there is no such thing as solitary confinement?

CC: No.

SJC: But there is a three-tier system in that you can be put into a single-roomed flat or . . .

CC: I'll explain it like this. We have a health care unit, where there are four rooms. It was designed for people with general medical problems who needed constant nursing care, but we don't have any solitary rooms. They are all solitary in the sense that they are all single rooms but we don't have a punishment area if that's what you are talking about. Padded cells are there for them if they are a danger to themselves or others and only a senior officer can put them there and only a psychiatrist can approve them to come out. We have no solitary confinement block anywhere because we aren't in the business of locking people into rooms and leaving them there — that is not good for them. You try and get them out to mix with people all day, which is far healthier.

SJC: But they can move into self-contained flats in the prison?

CC: Yes, but that takes a long process. We're talking about very long-term women. They first go into the small secure area where we try to get them stabilised, not only on medication but in terms of health because they are generally undernourished. After a period, they move to the other side of the building where there's a lot more freedom and they can attend workshops and get on with life.

SJC: You have said that those who are convicted of murder aren't placed in a separate section of the prison. You may not be able to comment on individual cases but I'm wondering about Catherine Nevin, who is here.

CC: You met her.

SJC: Yes.

CC: We try to treat them all here the very same. There's not one set of rules for drug addicts and another set of rules for those in for murder. Generally, long-term prisoners don't give you any problems. We want to treat them as human beings because that's what they are.

SJC: Their punishment is the deprivation of liberty.

CC: Their punishment is the deprivation of their liberty. That's it. And I certainly wasn't reared to be cruel and nasty to people.

SJC: So is that another fiction, that prison officers are damaged and sadistic and get jobs in prisons to let off their aggression? I'm thinking of prisons abroad, such as the States for instance.

CC: I wouldn't work in American or English prisons if you paid me all the money in the world. I've been to prisons in England. I'll give you an example. I was in Holloway and there was another officer with me and I was appalled at dinner being served in the wings at 11.30 in the morning; the meal was being slopped out onto plastic plates and I couldn't fathom that at all. The staff didn't appear to talk to the prisoners at all and as we were walking past a number of cells I heard: "Is that you Miss Comerford?" I said: "Yes, who's that?" And it was a girl who had been in Mountjoy and was in remand in Holloway and I asked the senior officer could I go back and talk to her and she said no, and I asked her for only two minutes and she said no, even though we were equivalent rank. They wouldn't even open the cell door. I shouted back to her: "Have you any money?" And she said that she hadn't a penny and I told her I would leave her some money. I took twenty pounds out of my pocket and I was giving it to the senior officer and she said she wouldn't take it. She hadn't even the price of a cigarette and they still refused to take the money off me. I would hate to work like that. That was only eight years ago. Prisoners would tell you that themselves, that they would rather do twenty years in Mountjoy than one year in an English prison or anywhere else. It's the culture. Sometimes they are locked away for 23 hours a day in an English prison. We have them out 15 hours a day here, in the women's prison.

SJC: Are prisons suitable places for certain people who have committed crimes?

CC: No, psychiatric cases shouldn't be here. I don't want to be critical of anybody but I sometimes wonder do people really look to see what's going on in these people's lives. Sometimes, the judge doesn't have a choice but to put them in prison and I wouldn't criticise them for all the tea in China because they have a job to do. Yesterday, we got a woman in here serving five days and she also got a £50 fine with £30 costs — she had no bus ticket. We've had people who here who haven't had a dog licence or a TV licence and you just think that they don't have the money in the first place to buy a TV licence or whatever because they are more interested in feeding their children. If I had their lives I would say I would be in the same situation. I often think that.

SJC: Can you take me through a typical day in the life of a prisoner?

CC: At 8 a.m. she's called in her room. She gets up, has her shower and gets dressed. If she has to collect medication she goes to the health centre. They come back and have breakfast in their house. They clean their house. At 9.30 they go to school or the workshops — French, woodwork, computers, English, photography, home economics, arts and crafts. They are not up running fully yet. We try and keep them occupied all day till 4 p.m. Others might go out to work five days a week and they earn their money and pay their taxes. At 12.30, they go back to their house. At 12.45, lunch is called and they go to the communal dining rooms. Because there is no smoking there, they usually gob it down and are gone within 20 minutes! Between 1.00 and 2.00 they are allowed to watch TV and smoke a cigarette or go to their rooms and listen to music or whatever. At 2.00, they will go back to where they were that morning. The remand women will be getting visits on a daily basis, so their day would be interrupted by visits or by the doctor or psychologist coming in or going to the dentist or whatever. At 4.30 they go back into the house and at 4.45 it's teatime and back to the house. Then it's recreation time. They can go to the gym or watch TV or the library, which will be opened soon. In four of the houses, at 7.30 they are asked to get their supper and they are back in their rooms at eight o'clock at night and their rooms are locked at 8.00, and in two of the houses they are out till 10.00 and 12.00 respectively. They are checked then every half hour. Then you would have court escorts or hospital appointments, etc. They are quite busy all day long, every day, 365 days a year.

SJC: Can they deal with their time here?

CC: They find the loneliness difficult. They are in prison surrounded by people but prisons are the loneliest places on earth. They miss their children greatly. They have an intercom system between their room and the control room and they just have to push the button to talk to the officer at night or they'll ask the supervising officer for somebody to come to their room to talk with them and they'll come. It's not within the rules but you might be preventing something bigger from happening. They miss their freedom, of course. And if the husband or boyfriend doesn't visit they're wondering if they are going off with somebody else. If they've been abused and they have children they worry if they're going to be abused too. We've people here from South Africa and it's very difficult for them to get through on the phone. They have a phone call every day seven days a week to their families, which has been a huge development within the prisons. Sentenced women get a thirty-minute visit every week and the remand women get fifteen minutes a day. Some of them self-mutilate quite badly out of worry.

SJC: And there have been some suicides.

CC: Yes. But why we never know. And it's always the people we least expect. We're expected to know but not even the psychiatrists would know. We've had four suicides through my history here and all of them have been a total shock and I've had many more over in the men's prison. If you can't read or write and you don't have a radio and you're just sitting staring at four walls you would drive yourself crazy. At least the TV is company and staves off loneliness. It's also educational and they will watch the news. I would hate to be locked in a room.

When I'm out talking to transition year students, I always ask them to imagine their own bedroom at home with everything out of it except their bed and then the handle inside their door was taken off. You have no control. Just imagine how that would feel, that you are at the mercy of someone on the other side of the door. The women would say to me: "You don't know what's it like to be locked up" and I would say "I do". The only reason I only got five weeks' training when I first joined was because a woman was sentenced to death and when anyone's sentenced to death they have to be guarded by officers twenty-four hours a day and one of my first duties was the death cell. I had no notion. I asked what the death cell was and I was told by someone who had started six weeks before me, "Shut up and follow me." This cell door was opened and there was this woman sitting on a bed and there were two officers who walked out and we came in and the door was locked and I had to ask permission to use the toilet and I felt humiliated and degraded. Before we had in-cell sanitation, the women also had to ask permission. Now they don't. Nobody should have to. She was one of the last to be sentenced to death by hanging but thankfully it was never carried out. It was commuted to 40 years' life imprisonment with no parole. The victim's family may be of a different view.

SJC: You don't agree, then, with capital punishment?

CC: The thought of going down, when I first joined, and watching someone hanging — I couldn't get my head around that. I would have resigned. You get to know the person. Life is too precious for it to be taken away.

SJC: Not even in cases of "murder most foul", to use the late Lord Denning's expression?

CC: And was it he who said about the Birmingham Six that if there was capital punishment we would have hanged these people and then nobody would have worried about their innocence? And how many mistakes were made in England? I can't go around every day and think: "Oh, she did this and she did that and her crime was heinous and hers was bad." I couldn't work that way. I know they're here and the length of time they're here for and I would know what they've done, but I don't let my mind dwell on it. I have to get on and do my job and get them to face up to what they've done. And I don't do it on my own. It's a team effort.

SJC: I'm interested that you said they have a lot of guilt. Freud said that some (neurotic) criminals have a lot of unconscious guilt and they commit crimes so as to get caught and be punished (this is all unconscious) in order to allay their sense of guilt. Punishment almost comes as a relief to them. What do you make of that?

CC: That's the first time I've heard that one, to be honest. Is he actually saying that they decide to commit a crime in order to get punished for whatever reason?

SJC: To alleviate their sense of unconscious guilt.

CC: I've never thought of it that way. It's turning it all on its head. You may be right or Freud may be right. It's something I've never thought about. Yes, it's quite possible. I'd have to think about that!

SJC: Yes. And gamblers gamble because unconsciously they want to lose money.

CC: Parts of it make sense. You could say that a lot of them come in here as a haven — they subconsciously need to get into a safe place so they commit the crime to get in here; we're not talking about serious crime but about women who smash a window or something.

SJC: Would you agree that a prison system should be both retributive and rehabilitative, incorporating punishment as well as psychotherapy?

CC: The punishment is depriving them of their liberty. Rehabilitation can only be done if they are willing to be rehabilitated. But what are you rehabilitating them to? You could do all the good work in here but when they go out the gate what happens? Back to the same situation they came out of. To rehabilitate someone to what? Who is to say that the life they are living is wrong? It may not be acceptable to you or me but it may be to them. It might sound contradictory here, but I don't know what the word "rehabilitation" means. It's a word that people throw out. But what exactly does it mean? We try to get them to face up to reality here. We have a psychologist and a psychiatrist but no psychotherapist. There's no quick fix — it takes a long time. But everybody can't like everybody. You have all different personalities here and one officer who gets on with somebody would be, unconsciously, their key worker. The women will sit down and discuss their problems with that officer and if it's told in confidence it's never gossiped about among other officers. We're the only ones they really can trust. The general public wouldn't want and don't want to know that. It's not a "them or us" situation. We're the first people they see in the morning and the last people they see at night and during the night. All the other agencies come and go. They see us seven days a week. I would never refuse any of the women a cup of tea. I even smoked a rolled up cigarette and there could be anything in it!

SJC: Do you think the notion of "diminished responsibility" should be introduced into Irish law?

CC: Oh crikey, I'm not a lawyer. I don't think that's a question for me! Here we have the "guilty but insane" law.

SJC: Yes, which should be "not guilty by reason of insanity".

CC: Exactly.

SJC: It's guilty or not here but what about diminished responsibility?

CC: Yes. In France you have "crimes of passion". It's very black or white here. All murders here carry a mandatory life sentence. I would certainly think it might help the judiciary. They use victim impact reports as well and probation and social background reports on the people themselves, which I think is a good thing, rather than sentencing them blindly. The judge is now making an informed decision about someone's life. Someone might also get five years in prison with a review in twelve months' time and in those 12 months she would have had counselling. Sometimes we're asked to give a Governor's report stating what she's done in those 12 months and the report of the urinal analysis would be included. She has a choice: she can do nothing or focus in on her life and I have yet to see them do nothing. They will take up every option available to them. But we're not all saints.

SJC: Indeed. We have all committed some crimes.

CC: We speed, we go through red lights, we don't stop at amber lights, we take a glass home with us, which is stealing. They get caught — we don't.

SJC: Aristotle said that one act of thievery doesn't make a man a thief.

CC: That's right.

SJC: But there are some criminals who continue to commit crimes. What can one do with recidivism and recidivistic criminals?

CC: It's like an addiction until they get to a certain age. In women it's around 25. They can't do time anymore. They may have met someone or got married or had children. For a number of years, you will not see them and then suddenly they'll pop out of the woodwork. Men seem to continue on with their crimes, sentence after sentence after sentence. It's only by them admitting that it's not working that anything can be done for them. Maybe they can't help themselves. It's when they've decided they have had enough, and some never decide that. They try to get a skill while they're in prisons and we have employers every day looking for people to work.

SJC: That's great.

CC: It was a problem in the days of unemployment. They're not monsters.

SJC: Would you say that a great deal of crime could be curbed if the potential criminal had experienced the voice of the law, embodied traditionally by the father in the family, the law that prohibits desire?

CC: I don't know if it's the voice of law. I think it's about respect and caring for each other. A lot of prisoners come from fatherless families or the fathers have been in prison when they were growing up. The biggest upset for me is to sit in my office and look at wives and girlfriends coming up to visit their fathers in prison. And there are babes in arms so you would wonder what effect it is having on the child. It's not positive. They're growing up coming to see mum or dad in prison. The idea of prison as a deterrent for them doesn't exist because they have been used to prison all their life. It's just another place to go. You have also people here who have wonderful parents and they've gone off the rails completely. They will tell you it's because they got in with the wrong crowd.

SJC: There has been an alarming increase in incidents of personal assaults and murder in Ireland, and Dublin especially. What do you think that's about? Is it connected to the increased prosperity that the Celtic Tiger has brought?

CC: I'd say that's a factor. I think society has become a bit more violent anyway. I don't know why that's the case. I think drink has a lot to do with it, and drugs. The culture is such now in this country that if you want something you have to fight for it. People don't really respect each other as much as they should. They don't respect your view or even where you live. But I haven't suffered the way the women here have suffered in their personal lives. They're not as violent as men generally but you would get the odd case that would shock you. I know men here have cried in front of the male officers but my male colleagues would be uneasy about that. It's because of the whole macho thing. One man isn't going to throw his arms around another man to console him. And if they do cry in front of me, I make sure their eyes are dried before sending them out, because there may be twenty guys outside and they would give him a terrible slagging.

SJC: Jung said that evil "is lodged in human nature itself". Do you believe that some people are simply evil?

CC: I have never met a totally evil person nor have I met a totally good person. I don't know of any child who's born evil. They are born innocent. If they're evil, you would wonder how they got to be so evil. They have to learn it from somewhere.

SJC: Jung said that that "we are all potential murderers" and "every one of us contains a criminal who wants to commit crime though we don't know it". He also said that "everybody has done something or is planning to do something which is not right, which is criminal". Would you agree with his sentiments?

CC: I would agree with him. I don't think there's anyone outside these walls who could say, "I will never end up in prison." You don't know the hour or the day. You might hit somebody who could fall and hit their head off the pavement and be charged with manslaughter in the morning. It's a very thin line. You're at home in the kitchen and pick up a knife when you're having a row and you go at somebody. They could be dead in two minutes. It could happen to any one of us tomorrow. You could have three pints and get into your car and kill somebody. You are a killer. Or you have a drink and think that's a nice glass and put it into your handbag — you're a thief.

SJC: A couple of years ago, we had the Sheedy affair. Was he treated differently because he was middle-class and professional?

CC: No. If you come to Mountjoy, you're lobbed in with the rest of them. It doesn't matter who you are.

SJC: What about "white collar" crime? I mean, Haughey's not going to end up in prison?

CC: I can't speak for the judges, but if he's found guilty and if he was sentenced, there's only one place to go and that's to Mountjoy.

SJC: Presumably some people just can't cope?

CC: Absolutely. To find the gates closing behind you and to know you can't open them again has a touch of reality about it. You were apprehensive coming here today — can you imagine if I said to you, "You're here for the next twelve years"? It takes people who get long sentences a long time before they get out of the shock — at least a month, maybe eight weeks. They are in total shock. There's no light at the end of the tunnel. It takes them that amount of time even to be aware of what's going on around them.

SJC: It's a bit of a rude awakening for the meek middle-class accountant who had one too many the previous night in his local.

CC: Yes. But if we work off the philosophy that we treat everybody the same, why should he be treated any differently? It's important that you don't have a two-tier system.

SJC: Christ was regarded as a criminal, as were Socrates and Thomas Moore and others. Presumably there are some people who are regarded as criminals by the state who others may regard as saints?

CC: You aren't going to convince all of the people that you're an absolute criminal or an absolute saint.

SJC: Some of the sentencing sounds ludicrous.

CC: Yes, but it would be presumptuous of me to pronounce because I don't know the full facts of every case. But life doesn't mean life — it means a very long time. Should we keep a 17-year old here until they're 70 for murdering? What good does that serve?

SJC: So should Myra Hindley be released?

CC: I think her situation has become political now. The judge made a recommendation that she serve at least thirty years. I saw Myra Hindley — she wasn't as I imagined her to be. I thought she was a big woman. She's small. No Home Secretary or Minister of Justice would ever make a decision about releasing someone who's been so evil. The families of those victims haven't had a moment's peace.

SJC: But should she be released or not? Lord Longford says she should.

CC: I've never given it much thought. It's a political football. I was a kid when those crimes were committed. I don't know. I can't see her being released.

SJC: Is there anything you would alter in the prison system or reform in the criminal law?

CC: If you had asked me that question ten years ago, I would have said the facilities and working as a multi-disciplinary team, none of which was there at the time. The 1947 rule-book is there, but we don't stick to the old draconian ways of rules and regulations about whistling or whatever. We throw it out the window. I like the new system we have here in the women's prison. Certainly, a lot of things have to change in the men's prison, which needs to be refurbished.

SJC: Would you hold to the view that when a man murders he has murdered himself morally?

CC: He's taken the heart out of himself.

SJC: Do they recover?

CC: Very slowly, to a point where they can just about live with themselves but not fully. It never goes away. They have a lot of guilt.

SJC: What about those people who premeditate and deliberately set out to kill?

CC: They are in a different category. I'm talking about people who don't set out to harm anybody from the time they get up in the morning. You will only come across very few of them. I have only come across two of them in my whole career.

Sometimes they don't even know why they've done it. They lost it on the day. For example, the other day I was over talking to the women and we were joking and I said, "If you don't do that I'm going to murder you." We all say it. That's the first time I had said it. The girl standing beside me said "Miss, don't say that." It suddenly dawned on me what I had said because she was in for murder, and I said "I'm so sorry. I didn't think." I said to her I didn't mean anything by it and she said, "I know. It's just every time I hear that word . . ." I felt that small. I shouldn't have said it. It was just a figure of speech and I felt lousy. It was the one time I let my guard down.

SJC: Has anybody committed a murder in prison? Presumably they have?

CC: All I can say on that is there's a case pending in the men's prison. It would be wrong of me to speak about it because it hasn't gone to trial.

SJC: Because most of us don't, can't or won't kill, we content ourselves with reading detective novels or going to the cinema to watch murder movies. Would you want to regulate or censor certain movies or films of this genre?

CC: Can I say that I don't think the movies, TV, or the written word are responsible for some of the heinous crimes people commit. I certainly never watch a violent film because I know the hurt it causes everybody. I don't want to pay to have to look at it. I think the world has become a violent place. But who am I to say "You can't watch this"? I don't think it is the cause of crime or contributes to the culture of crime. It all comes back to the family and to abuse there, physical or sexual. The biggest shock I got was when I came down to the men's prison and I had to look after the sex offenders, the rapists and paedophiles who are kept separate. My own vision of these men would be that they were 6'2", 15 stone. The day they first opened the door for me to go in to see one of these guys I got the shock of my life. He was about 5'6" and weighed about eight-and-a-half stone. Every one of them that I met over the seven years I was there were in and around the same. I am thinking "We have it all wrong in terms of stereotypes." They were just like any other normal human being you would meet, except they had done this to children or girls, or teenagers or women.

SJC: Isn't it true that most paedophiles experience and express no remorse?

CC: Yes. None of them believe they have done anything wrong. That's quite clear. That shocked me as well. I remember wives, mothers or girlfriends talking about their sons or boyfriends or husbands who had been convicted of a sexual assault telling me it wasn't his fault. It was her fault. You would then ask what age was the victim and the answer would be 13 or 14. And you're thinking, "What about her?" Everybody is entitled to a quarter remission for good behaviour. I have met one or two cases where I have had serious concerns about him re-offending when he gets out and not even making it to the end of the North Circular Road without committing another crime. Once he serves his time I am obliged to let him go and in the case I'm thinking of he did come back, though not for the same offence. I was so concerned I asked for his victim to be informed when he was being released, and I'm talking ten years later. He was planning to go to his sister in the North and the Garda and RUC were informed. He was put on the train and he didn't make it to the North. He never got out at the station he was supposed to. I don't know where he is. This was a man who said to me, "You locked up my body, you didn't lock up my mind." The hairs stood up at the back of my neck. It was the way he said it. I don't know where he is.

SJC: What are the differences between the rapist and the paedophile?

CC: I never ask a sex offender anything about his crime. I go to the warrant and look. This day I was chatting with a man to see if he needed anything or if I could do anything for him and I said, "What are you in for?" and he said, "Sexual assault." I said, "Did you know your victim?" and when he said yes I asked who it was. I knew I should have shut my mouth, because he said, "It was my daughter." I said, "What age?" and he said, "Two and a half." Then he said, "You know, it wasn't my fault." I wanted to be physically sick. He was trying to blame a two-and-a-half-year-old because of his problems. He just didn't think he had done anything wrong.

SJC: Do you think there is any connection between crime and envy? Envy is a very destructive emotion, as the psychoanalyst Melanie Klein pointed out.

CC: Even today with the Celtic Tiger I think the have-nots want to have what everybody else has. They do resent it because it doesn't trickle down to them. They want a home, a car, a holiday but every day's a struggle to find money for food, clothes and heating. Yes, they are envious and they would give it all up tomorrow morning if they thought they could have what we have.

SJC: What's the worst case you've come across?

CC: I don't think it would be fair on the families to single out one case. I was shocked when I came across a young girl who was expecting twins and I remember saying to her "Is your boyfriend going to be with you?" She said, "I don't have a boyfriend." I said, "You had to have a boyfriend to get pregnant." She said, "No. The father of my children is my father." That shocked me to the core, because I never thought it was possible — I never knew it existed. That has stayed with me for the last 24 years.

SJC: I suppose you try to be unruffled in terms of your facial expressions.

CC: People would say my face never gives me away. I can keep it fairly deadpan.

SJC: How do our crime rates compare with other European countries?

CC: I wouldn't have the figures but we have 3,000 prisoners in custody for a population of three and a half million. That's only in custody, but how many more are out there? A lot of people slipped through the net by not having education — we see that here.

SJC: What do you think of Ireland in the year 2001?

CC: I think we've become a very selfish society. We're certainly more concerned about our own selves. We are involved in our own insular little world and we've excluded everybody else from that. If it doesn't affect me, then it's not my concern. How many of us actually know our neighbours? Are we concerned? If you saw someone in difficulty on the street, would you go up and give them a hand? No, because you'd be thinking, "If I go up I'll be beaten up or killed." That is somebody else's problem.

SJC: I remember reading a report of someone who was being stabbed — on the Ha'penny Bridge I think it was — and he just remembered seeing all these shoes walking by.

CC: Yes.

SJC: What are your interests outside your work?

CC: My work is very demanding and rewarding. My interests outside work are golf, movies, music, reading and walking. I love watching sport. I love looking at art. I like to travel as well.

SJC: Do you have any religious or spiritual beliefs?

CC: Yes, I am a practising Catholic. My faith is very important to me. I try to see good in everything. The way I look at life is this: as far as I am concerned, everybody is good until they prove otherwise. I don't set out to put someone down or to dislike them from the beginning.

SJC: As Christians, aren't we bound by Christ himself to visit those who are sick and in prison? You're part of that divine mission.

CC: I think there are two ways I could have gone as a prison officer. The story I would tell is this. I think I was nearly six months in the job; I must have had a particularly bad day but I remember going home at eight o'clock that evening and I was 20 and living at home and my younger sister (who is ten years younger than me) came into the kitchen and asked me something and I snapped at her. I'm 5'9" and my mother is 5'3" and my mother actually grabbed my shirt and tie and pushed me up against the wall and said to me, "If the job's going to affect you so badly that you can't speak to people in a civilised manner, then it's time for you to hand that shirt and tie back in. I did not bring you up to treat people that way." I thought, "You're right." My mother wasn't anybody special, but she made me sit down and realise things.

SJC: What do you think soul is?

CC: Heart. Concern. Caring. Understanding. Thinking about others, not just oneself.

SJC: Are you happy?

CC: I'm contented. And I think I am happy. I appreciate what I have in life. I don't want anything too extravagant. I think without your health you have nothing. And I have my health, even though I have a cold today! I want to enjoy life and have fun or find humour every day and have enough money to pay my bills and mortgage and go out and enjoy myself.

DESMOND CONNELL
Cardinal

His Eminence, Dr Desmond Connell was formerly Professor of Metaphysics and Dean of the Faculty of Philosophy and Sociology in University College Dublin before being elevated to the See of Dublin as Archbishop and subsequently as Cardinal. He is a dedicated and determined pastor in the traditional mould. He lectured me in the philosophy of being, back when I was a student at UCD, where his dry and droll sense of humour was always apparent. When I spoke with him at Archbishop's House, that idiosyncratic humour came out from beneath the conservative demeanour demanded by his Office. When criticising philosophical and theological positions with which he disagreed, he had a mischievous glint and gleam in his eyes. He taught philosophy for thirty-five years and one gets the distinct impression that he was happier in academic life than in any role since but he has always remained true to the words he chose as his motto: secundum verbum tuum. *This spirit of service is what distinguishes him. He has a piercing mind and exceptional intelligence, which he employed to the full in explicating the scholastic categories of Aristotle and Aquinas. To highlight a philosophical point he used to give "Fido the dog" as an example. When he was made Archbishop of Dublin, his students presented him with a glass figurine of Fido the dog, under which were engraved the words "Metaphysics made clear". He still has it on his shelf as he showed me with pride and a certain nostalgic sadness.*

SJC: You did your doctorate in philosophy on *The Passivity of the Understanding in Malebranche* and included in that thesis a discussion of angels. How did you become involved in that particular piece of research?

DC: I was interested in the scholastic speculation about the separated soul — the separation of the soul from all material things. It no longer has the senses because the body is intrinsic to the senses and the imagination, the pure intellect. How does the human soul have knowledge of material things? I suppose we have memories but every time I opened a book by the scholastics on the separated soul they would refer to the treatises on the angels. That's why I had to go looking up what the angels had to say! That, effectively, is the Cartesian problem. When the scholastics were asking themselves how does the angel know material things — that really is the Cartesian problem. The scholastics had all kinds of tenets on how the angel can know.

These treatises on higher and lower angels were quite fascinating except that St. Thomas had the good sense to draw a line at a certain point and not to proceed any further. Suarez wasn't put off by that at all. He tried to work it all out in detail and he says the most ridiculous things — for example, that the angel can know more lions than horses because lions are more perfect than horses and this kind of nonsense. And I could see the higher angels would know all the winners at the Derby! St. Thomas never went in for that. But where the thing really became important was that the angelic species was modelled on the divine universal species. The divine universal species is the divine essence. This was sometimes put in the form that God was universal being in the sense that God synthesises in Himself the purest of perfections, and Suarez divided up all the ways the angel can know material things and, lo and behold, wasn't it identical to Malebranche's vision in *Recherche de la Verité*.

There I was on to something that enabled me to produce a book that gave a new interpretation of Malebranche's whole vision of God in the light of the scholastic treatment and that's why I had to go into the whole business of angelic knowledge and what Suarez and Scotus and Thomas had to say about it. It was research into the basis of Malebranche's attempt to solve a Cartesian problem of innate ideas. In fact, the experts in France were interested in all this when I published it and they invited me out to give a lecture on it for the third centenary of the *Recherche de la Verité*. So in spite of all Malebranche's anti-scholasticism, he is still drawing heavily upon scholasticism for his whole philosophy. The real interest was that Malebranche had a more metaphysical mind than Descartes ever had. Malebranche was really trying to work out a metaphysics on the basis of the philosophy of Descartes. The human soul contemplates all its ideas within a vision of the divine essence. That was influenced very much by what the scholastics had to say. It is a very difficult plot to solve.

How does the soul know material things? Malebranche was deeply concerned with one issue: what is given in the senses is purely subjective. Now if the innate ideas are created, how do we show that they are not purely subjective, that they are objective? That was the great difficulty for Descartes, who based the whole thing on the proof for the existence of God. Descartes starts with the soul but practically goes immediately to God with the famous proof from the idea of God.

So that's what I was at, and when I was appointed Fintan O'Toole identified me with this esoteric interest in angels and David Norris used it subsequently, when I made some statement about homosexuality, to say that I knew more about angels than fairies but the whole thing was based on solid research, which was recognised, except by Trinity. When Trinity celebrated the third centenary of Berkeley, and Berkeley was heavily influenced by Malebranche, I was informed that I was not invited to give a talk there, though I was invited to give a few quid, but I got great satisfaction from one of the lecturers referring to my work. Trinity insulted me and through me the Catholic people of Dublin because we were celebrating the millennium of the city of Dublin and they invited me to come along to watch Donald Caird receiving an honorary degree. That's their own business if they want to, but to celebrate the centenary of the city of Dublin by awarding the Protestant Archbishop with an honorary degree and leaving me sitting down watching it was a downright insult. They said they had made the arrangements before I was consecrated. That was probably true but there was nothing to stop them altering the arrangements; and when they celebrated the fourth centenary in 1994, they invited Cardinal Daly. When the new Provost was elected I met him at the American Embassy and he asked me would I accept an invitation to lunch and I said I would and I never heard anything afterwards. So if I have a certain view of Trinity I think you will understand why.

SJC: Do our souls pre-exist, because Aquinas said we existed as ideas in the mind of God?

DC: No. It's not simply the soul St. Thomas is talking about but the whole person. There you have an interesting theological history. Origen, in the second or third century, thought that all souls were created in Adam and as people were born souls were put into them. There was a very heavy influence of Platonism on the Church Fathers and the Platonic philosophy would have tended to emphasise the difference between the soul and the body. The body was seen as a kind of burden, a cumbrance, and there was some influence of that on the early Church Fathers, particularly on Augustine because, though Augustine wants to affirm the unity of the human person and does so, he nevertheless has this dualism. Aristotle had the great difficulty about the multiplication of the intellectual soul; how is the intellectual soul multiplied, because form is multiplied through matter, so how can you explain the intellectual soul being multiplied in that case? He never solved the problem but there is a bias in the direction of saying that there is only one soul for the whole of humanity. That was formerly asserted by Avicenna who thought that we all had our own passive intellect but the act of intellect was common to all of humanity and the act of intellect was the separated substance guiding the sphere of the moon. Averroës maintained that there was only one intellect, passive and active, for the whole of humanity. The result of all that was that the human person became simply a higher animal, which has dire consequences for the whole moral life. It was with this that St. Thomas was dealing, in his last years when he returned to the University of Paris, in his *The Unity of the Intellect against Averroës*, in which he worked out his position. It was St. Thomas who in his synthesis of Platonism and Aristotelianism found the way, even beyond Aristotle himself. I did a lecture in UCD on one occasion on that whole issue.

SJC: Aristotle said that soul is the form of the body. Is that the Catholic position?

DC: Oh yes.

SJC: Is there a difference between soul and spirit?

DC: There is in this sense: that not every soul is a spirit. Only the human soul is a spirit. The animal soul is not a spirit.

SJC: So animals have non-spiritual souls?

DC: They have, yes. The human soul is spiritual. Human souls are multiplied through the generation of the human person in the material body. Matter is still the principle of individuation.

SJC: Did Jesus have a human soul?

DC: Oh, of course. He wouldn't be a human being without a soul. This emerges very clearly in the Gospels, where we're told how he advanced in wisdom and knowledge and grace. There's a whole human development in the case of Christ. And you get the whole agony in the Garden and "Let this chalice pass but not mine but thy will be done." This is the human and the divine will. Christ lived a fully human life.

SJC: There's a whole movement in contemporary spirituality, deriving from Meister Eckhart and influencing transpersonal psychology, which says that it's all about reaching the "higher Self" and the divine spark within us. Is that pure Gnosticism?

DC: It depends on what you mean by a divine spark. Certainly we have a divine spark in the sense that the human person is created after the image of God. We are made in God's image and likeness and that is classical Catholic theology. If you like to call that having a divine spark, well and good. But to say that there is something of God Himself in the composition of the human soul would be nonsense, would be pantheism.

SJC: So God isn't in the human soul?

DC: God is present in everything He creates. Without God's presence, nothing could subsist at all but God is present in a wholly supernatural way through divine grace, through forgiveness of sin, through baptism. This raises us to a new level and through this transformation and in virtue of that the whole Trinity dwells in the human soul. "If anyone love me my Father will love him and we will come to him and make our abode with him." I will be talking about the presence of Christ in the pro-Cathedral on Sunday and the first answer I will be giving is that we find Him within ourselves because we are baptised and this is what St. Paul is talking about when he says "may Christ dwell in your heart by faith". This is how Christ dwells in the heart of the Christian. When we are in God's grace, we are temples of the Holy Spirit, as the Pauline epistles make clear. There is the indwelling of God by divine grace but that is not the same as the natural presence of God, which is the presence of the creator to the creature.

SJC: Body and soul form a unity. We are truly one. Soul indicates the innermost aspect of man, his spiritual principle, but aren't we divided against ourselves, split-subjects, as Lacan and other psychoanalysts tell us, due to the existence of the unconscious? How would the concept of an "unconscious" fit in with that whole Catholic philosophy and theology?

DC: It fits in with it in so far as we are embodied. Platonists thought that the soul came into the world with innate ideas, namely knowledge. St. Thomas wouldn't accept that. St. Thomas would say that all our knowledge has its origin in our sense experience: "There is nothing in the intellect that wasn't first of all in the senses." And human development begins from a not knowing to a development of our sense life to the awakening of our intellectual life. But there is a whole area that is unconscious that is provided for in that transition from the first awakening of our consciousness at a sense level. Of course there is conflict within us. There is plenty of emotional conflict. We have all had plenty of experiences of that kind. There are conflicts that arise from experiences we have forgotten. At a very delicate stage, the human being may be subjected to an experience that is preserved in the unconscious and that never fully emerges into full consciousness but which is, nevertheless, of influence in the outcome of his personality.

SJC: Mystics talk about mystical union with the Creator, but is divinisation possible in this earth?

DC: Yes. If you look at the first chapter of the Second Letter of St. Peter where he talks thus: "The divine power has given us everything needed for life and godliness through the knowledge of him who called us by his own glory and goodness. Thus he has given us, through these things, his precious and very great promises so that through them you may escape from the corruption that is in the world and the lust and may become participants of the divine nature." It is a created participation in the early life of God that divinises us as such — the supernatural gifts of faith, hope and charity. Faith and hope come to their end when we die and enter into the vision of God. Nothing remains, as St. Paul says in the thirteenth chapter of First Corinthians, but charity and that charity is a participation in the love of the Holy Trinity, where Father and Son dwell in the unity of the Holy Spirit. The unity of the Holy Spirit is the mutual knowledge of Father and Son. It is knowledge, not in an abstract sense, but knowledge in terms of friendship.

SJC: Knowledge precedes love.

DC: But that knowledge is not the knowledge we have of, for example, Tony Blair or whoever else. That is one kind of knowledge. There is also the knowledge you have of someone with whom you have a close personal friendship. Have you ever found yourself giving out to someone and saying, "You don't really know me"? That is the knowledge I am talking about and that knowledge is the very life of the Holy Trinity, that Father and Son know one another and that mutual knowledge is the Spirit of God. It is love and it is into that life that we are drawn through the saving work of Christ but it does involve a raising of us from our natural condition to an entirely new condition. We are elevated in that sense supernaturally. No creature could have the vision of God — it's only through being raised. This is the supernatural life; through adopted sonship we are made sons in the Son by grace, in a permanent way, and that is the tremendous gift that is lost by mortal sin and that is also why the whole tradition of the Church has had this deep conviction of the evil of sin, the destruction of the divine life to which we are called. Christ overcame that through His Passion and resurrection.

That is the whole problem with modern philosophy, starting with Descartes's identification of the substance of the soul with thought. Thought is an activity, not substance. If you identify the two, you are in trouble. Why? Because activity is always intentional, even if it's only purely material activity. In its activity a thing goes out to the other and the other is included in its activity. It's obviously the case in intellectual activity. And, following Aristotle, Thomas says that by the very fact that a substance is intellectual it is comprehensive of the whole of being. Now if its activity is comprehensive of the whole of being, how can its activity be identical with its substance, because its substance is not comprehensive of the whole of being? It is finite. If you identify substance and activity, there are two ways in which you can go. One is to emphasise the finiteness of the substance and import that into activity, and then you are into subjectivism. The other way is to identify, to import the infinity of the object of knowledge into the substance, and in that case you are into pantheism.

SJC: Does that mean that Eckhart was a pantheist?

DC: Now, I don't know enough about Eckhart. All I can say is this: that I have never been able to grapple with Eckhart. I have never done any work on him. I had a very good friend who was a Dominican, Corny Williams, and who would defend Eckhart to the end. My friend was an expert in mediaeval German and he was able to understand what Eckhart was saying in the light of the German in which Eckhart wrote. Needless to say, Eckhart has led to all kinds of nonsense, including that man who left the Dominicans — what's his name?

SJC: Mathew Fox.

DC: Mathew Fox, yes. He went off the rails on Eckhart. Heidegger had some knowledge of Eckhart. If anything was German, Heidegger was pleased with it, just as Hitler was. And of course Greek, because German is the perfect language of the modern world, just as Greek was the perfect language of the classical world.

SJC: Eckhart says that God became man so that we could become God. Is that not heresy?

DC: No, if it's properly understood. And it's properly understood in the way I have just outlined, divinisation through participation in the divine nature. It's in the Liturgy. "Oh, wonderful exchange of the creator of the human race taking a living body, willed to be born of the Virgin, and going forward as a man without descendants, has given us his divinity." St. Thomas had all the proper metaphysical distinctions, such as between substance and accident, which are essential. They throw all that out as garbage in the present day, with the result that they are metaphysically illiterate. And they go around in a fog talking about these things and there is no real appreciation of what they are talking about. That is a marvellous antiphon.

SJC: The trouble is also that some psychologies, such as the transpersonal and the Jungian, are psychologising all that.

DC: They are psychologising. The trouble is that they are trying to appreciate all that at a purely phenomenological level and the phenomenological level is insufficient. The phenomenological level is the level of experience. But you have to reflect on the deeper conditions of experience at the metaphysical level.

SJC: Would you support, so, Kant's distinction between phenomenal and noumenal being/reality?

DC: Yes, but the trouble with Kant is that he's unable to say anything about the noumenon. I wouldn't see it in terms of phenomenon and noumenon, but in terms of the level of experience and the deeper level, which emerges when one questions this in the light of being.

SCJ: The difference between essence and appearance.

DC: I wouldn't like "appearance". Yes, appearance in the phenomenological sense. Appearance tends to be unreliable but there is appearance in the sense of manifestation.

SJC: Of course, modern philosophy talks about the human subject rather than of substance, as you know.

DC: In modern thought, substance was rubbished because it was seen as a kind of Sartrean *en-soi*. It was an impediment to pure translucent consciousness, impeding our freedom. It's the height of narcissism. There are different ways in which substance has to be understood.

SJC: Angels are pure spirit, pure intellect and exist non-bodily. They are personal and immortal.

DC: If they are intellectual they are personal. By the way, the early Fathers thought they had celestial bodies, but that was an aberration.

SJC: Do we all have Guardian Angels?

DC: Yes.

SJC: And what's the difference between "ordinary" angels, Guardian Angels and Archangels?

DC: Angel means messenger and the Guardian Angels are simply the pure spirits whom God sends to look after us. Every angel, precisely as an angel, is sent by God. The Archangel Gabriel is called an Archangel because he was sent with the most tremendous message. Michael and Rafael are Archangels.

SJC: Every person has a Guardian angel?

DC: That is the tradition of the Church. There is a Feast of the Guardian Angels. They can be very, very helpful. One did a great job for me in October because a fellow came crashing through the window of my room at a quarter past two in the morning. I managed to escape from the room.

SJC: Can angels sin?

DC: They did.

SJC: Lucifer sinned the sin of pride, *hubris?*

DC: That's the tradition. The angel acts with such perfection of knowledge and determination of will that there is no way in which the angel would ever change his mind. So there is no redemption of angels. The same is true at death. If one dies in enmity with God one will never change one's mind.

SJC: So, like the angels, and since the Fall, we men can't repent after death?

DC: No.

SJC: Did Satan, who is a fallen angel, take any other angels with him?

DC: Yes. That is the tradition of the Church once again.

SJC: So there are fallen angels and Satan has a legion of demon angels?

DC: Yes.

SJC: What do they do in contrast to the Guardian Angels who look after us?

DC: There's a marvellous passage in the Apocalypse, which is very difficult to interpret. Have you ever read it?

SJC: Yes.

DC: In chapter twelve it says: "And war broke out in heaven. Michael and his angels fought against the dragon. The dragon and his angels fought back but they were defeated and there was no longer any place for them in heaven. The great dragon was thrown down and then that ancient serpent who is called the Devil and Satan, the deceiver of the whole world." Deception is the work of the Devil. That goes back to the beginning of Genesis. "Did God tell you that you would die if you ate of the fruit? He did. Don't believe a word of what he says." That's deception.

SJC: It's pride as well.

DC: Yes, because it's the desire to be independent. The Pope is very good on this. Something happened at the beginning of the race and this is a representation of it. No one is bound to believe that there was a garden called Eden and a serpent and all the rest of it; this is figurative language. But the temptation is there. John is very good on temptation. If you look up chapter eight of St. John: "If you are Abraham's children you would be doing what Abraham did. Now you are trying to kill me, now that I have told you the truth that I heard from God." Go back to Genesis: they would not die — Satan was seeking to kill them. He was a murderer from the beginning. "That is not what Abraham did; you are indeed doing what your father does. If God were your father you would love me for I came from God and I am here. I didn't come of my own will but he sent me. Why do you not understand what I say? It's because you cannot accept my word. You are from your father the devil and you choose to do your father's desires. He was a murderer from the beginning and does not stand in the truth because there is no truth in him. When he lies he speaks only to his own nature because he is a liar and the father of lies. Because I tell you the truth you do not believe me." It's a tremendous passage.

SJC: Is evil, then, a real force or simply a *privatio boni*, an absence or lack of good, an imperfection in the created order?

DC: No metaphysician would deny the goodness of Satan as he may have been; it's what he has made out of himself through his opposition to God, through his own choice. It's in that sense that he is evil. But everything in so far as it exists is good.

SJC: So Satan is good in so far as he exists?

DC: Oh yes. Satan was created by God. He has all the wonderful gifts of intellect and wisdom, all of which are good, but he has perverted them.

SJC: Satan isn't a personification of evil, is he?

DC: No. He's a creature like the rest of us.

SJC: Is he infinite?

DC: No, he's finite.

SJC: But he's not a person?

DC: Oh he is a person, yes. If he's an intellectual being, he is a person.

SJC: In the Book of Revelation, it says, "Let him who hath understanding reckon the number of the beast, for it is a human number and it's number is six hundred and sixty six."

DC: 666 could be the name of Nero, because when Nero is translated into Hebrew it comes out as 666 or something.

SJC: I'm trying to get my head around the notion that Satan is a person.

DC: Why not?

SJC: Well, if he is a person, where does he reside?

DC: He belongs to the realm of the pure spirits. He hasn't got a residence here on life. He has no address!

SJC: Do you think the Parousia [*Second Coming*] is imminent?

DC: No. I simply don't know. Nobody knows. All we can say is that the Parousia is coming, but we don't know when.

SJC: And it will establish a new heaven and a new earth?

DC: Yes. It will be the end of the present creation.

SJC: And then there are two judgements: my personal one when I die and the Last Judgement, when the body is returned to the soul?

DC: That's right.

SJC: One theologian told me that we judge ourselves.

DC: Well, in a certain sense we do because the judgement of God is simply the manifestation of our condition, and in that sense we judge ourselves. We come to the realisation of who we are.

SJC: And in our post-mortem existence, would it be true to say that we take our place above the angels because we are sons of God and they are not?

DC: No, because they also are the children of God. The angels are a more perfect form of being than us. The idea of trying to walk in before Gabriel . . .! What is true is that Our Blessed Lady is the mother of God and we honour her above all creatures, but as for ranks, ranks don't matter.

SJC: Why did God create angels?

DC: Because God is good and wanted to share the glory of His life with creatures. I mean, there is no answer to that logically. Why does God do anything?

SJC: Well, I can understand why He created us, but not why there are two orders of being, the angelic order and the mortal one.

DC: Wouldn't there be something missing if there weren't pure intellectual beings? We're not the greatest species that are!

SJC: You were saying Genesis is to be interpreted figuratively and symbolically and when I was talking to Archbishop Empey he made a similar hermeneutic point in relation to the stories in the New Testament. For example, when Christ said, "This is my body. Take it and eat it", it seems to me he was talking literally, not figuratively, not least because otherwise he would have said, "This is *like* my body." Of course, the text goes on to say that many left him on hearing that and turning to his apostles he asked them would they also go and they replied in the negative, saying, "Whither would we go? You have the message of eternal life." But how do we know for certain that he wasn't speaking metaphorically?

DC: There are two ways we can take this. You could open the Bible and ask yourself, "What does this mean?" and that's what Protestants do. The other way is to ask, "How has the Bible been understood in the tradition of the life of the Church?" That is the Catholic way. We just don't go on Scripture alone. Scripture itself is a product of the tradition of the Church. The tradition of the Church was there before Scripture. Scripture expresses the tradition of the Church and Scripture is always understood in the light of the tradition of the Church. If you look at all the evidence we have of the Church's understanding of the Eucharist and what it is that the authors of Sacred Scripture expressed, it is to be taken literally. The earliest expressions of the tradition of the Church date from the second century.

SJC: Do you think it's helpful to call that transubstantiation?

DC: Yes. The Council of Trent has said that it is aptly termed transubstantiation, because what transubstantiation is saying is this: that the reality that is here before me now is not the reality of bread. It's the reality of the Body of Christ, and the words of consecration effect that change. This thing that is bread is no longer bread but the Body of Christ. You have what St. Thomas calls the wonderful change, the conversion.

SJC: So theology needs philosophy rather than exclusively relying on the Old and New Testaments like Protestantism does?

DC: A theology that isn't nurtured by philosophy becomes a pure theological positivism. All you do is keep repeating what has been said, but there's no penetration, no deeper understanding. The truths of the faith call for reflection. Archbishop Empey wouldn't have much theological competence anyway. He wouldn't be regarded as one of their high flyers, but Protestants very often go in for a very positivistic theology. Since the Second Vatican Council, we have been tending in that direction, unfortunately. What's interesting about the Second Vatican Council is that all the great figures of the Council were brought up on the Thomistic revival and they had metaphysics, but after the Council and when the whole Biblical movement took over, they threw out metaphysics. It was said that the bishops sang "Should auld Aquinas be forgot"! Ratzinger, of course, is a poacher turned gamekeeper! He was one of the liberals of the Second Vatican Council. Ratzinger was always an excellent theologian. I am not for any moment suggesting that he was heterodox.

SJC: Do you believe in Aquinas's five proofs (so-called) for the existence of God? Do you find them convincing?

DC: I don't believe in them. I am convinced by them.

SJC: Even in the light of Darwinism?

DC: Of course. Surely you must have heard me on this? Have you read Michael Denton's book on Darwinism?

SJC: No.

DC: Because it's not in the public interest that people read books like this. The Liberals wouldn't allow it.

SJC: What's your view of contemporary Ireland and does she still have soul in the context of the Celtic Tiger?

DC: Well, I'll put it to you this way, Stephen. There are so many different issues that arise there that we don't have time to go into. All I would say is this, that one hears it said that we are becoming materialistic. I don't know. But we are becoming worldly and that's what worries me. By becoming worldly, I mean that the Christian horizon, which was never confined to this world, is being eroded and people are living for what they can accumulate and for what they can experience here below. There was a time when people came to this country and were deeply impressed by the awareness of the presence of God. It's no longer the case. I have been trying to combat that. But that awareness of the presence of God has faded and there is a spirit of worldliness, which has been accelerated by prosperity. I have no difficulty whatsoever about Ireland being prosperous, but I have a difficulty in people believing that they can solve all their problems and achieve all their ambitions simply through wealth, and that's worrying. The Church is essentially unworldly. You might say that there is plenty of evidence of the use of wealth in the Church. Of course there is, but the unworldliness of the Church consists in the Church's hope. The Church hopes and its whole life is the expression of hope in eternal life and if the Church was ever to lose its hope, the Church would be worldly.

SJC: Are you happy?

DC: I am, thank God. What I want to convey to the people is the joy of the Christian life. And I go back to the day of Pentecost when the disciples rushed out onto the streets because there was so much joy in their hearts and they wanted to pass it on, which is evangelisation. The joy is not effervescent, but it is the deep joy that is quite compatible with suffering, because when the Lord was going out to his Passion he said, "I have said these things to you so that my joy may be your joy." That is the joy I am talking about and it is compatible with troubles and suffering, and God knows I have had enough of them. It is the immense joy that is ours through the revelation, presence and promise of Christ. It is Easter joy.

BRENDAN DOWLING
Martial Artist

Brendan Dowling is a community activist, a street trader with a stall in Dublin city centre where this interview took place, and a teacher of the Japanese martial art of Aikido. One of Ireland's leading Aikido instructors, he teaches with panache, grace and good humour and I am fortunate to be one of his students in the Whitefriar Aikido Club, which he runs with Brigid Ruane, an equally inspiring instructor. A former Republican activist, he discovered the potentially lethal yet benevolently peaceful Way of Aikido as an alternative to armed struggle. Aikido seeks to use the energy of the aggressor against him without the need to become aggressive oneself. He is a tireless and much respected community worker and dynamic teacher. Intensely disliking and eschewing labels and categories that seek to confine and constrain, he has challenged my most cherished beliefs, ideas and ideals with sustained intellectual rigor and passionate, good-humoured vigour. I am privileged to know him as both teacher and friend.

SJC: Martial arts are growing in Ireland and around the world, with more than 200 martial arts clubs in Dublin alone. How would you explain this explosion of interest?

BD: I suppose Bruce Lee and all his friends have a lot to answer for in terms of the initial explosion of interest in martial arts. There's no doubt that movies keep that interest going. At the moment, I'm not sure there's an explosion of late. There's certainly a change of quality. Martial arts are now presented more as a professionally represented activity, whereas before it was more a guru-based single club unit. What's changed now is that clubs are accountable in terms of insurance and all that.

Even now there is nothing stopping anyone from opening a club saying they are a tenth dan [*a tenth degree black belt*]. Legally they are entitled to. So, hopefully, when recognition comes through from the Irish Martial Arts Commission, a code of ethics will be set up.

SJC: What attracted you to martial arts and to Aikido, in particular, in which you hold a third degree black belt?

BD: I actually was never looking for martial arts. To go back to the source, I am from the North and I was involved in the situation, active in the North, and at around 17 or 18 I realised that the conflict wasn't an end in itself. Not that I turned away from it, but I went looking for something slightly bigger.

SJC: You're saying that you were a Republican?

BD: Yes, I was involved in the Republican movement, an aspect of it, until I was about 18 and I realised that it wasn't, in itself, an answer to the justice I felt needed to be addressed. For a while, I stepped out of all that — I stepped out of politics and of any sense that we should do something. When I first came across Aikido, which was accidental, I saw its potential, in a way a missing part of the jigsaw, a way of standing up to aggression without becoming it, which is what I felt was happening to me through the whole Republican movement. People were becoming what they were fighting against. So I saw this potential and when I see potential my nature is to get in and test it and rock it and see if it works. Nearly twenty years later, I'm still rocking and shaking and seeing if it works! And it's stood up to me, to the test of time. I think there's a missing part of the jigsaw in Aikido, which certainly intrigues me. It's still offering me a source of hope and inspiration and hopefully I will have the guts, if I hit a wall and find it no longer works, to walk away from it.

SJC: Just as you were talking there I was reminded of Heraclitus's statement that there is harmony in conflict.

BD: Yes.

SJC: Etymologically, Aikido comes from *Ai*, meaning to harmonise, with *ki*, which is energy or spirit or soul, and *do* is the way of harmonising with energy. The seat of *ki* is thought to be situated just below the navel but it is an imaginary point. How do you understand the art of Aikido?

BD: In its absolute simplest, it's putting back whatever's missing, I think. So, the yin and yang symbol is a good one to explain that. If the black part is bigger than the white part, then you become a bit of white to level it up or if the white part is bigger than the black part, you become a bit of black. In practice, if you are pushed, you back off and create non-movement. Similarly, if you are pulled you move forward and you create non-movement. The essence, I would imagine, is just putting things back in balance. That's the simplest way of explaining it. Now we can get tied up in technique and all other aspects as you can with any other system and sometimes we can get lost in those, just as in philosophy you can get lost in words, but, at the end of the day, it's just putting things back into balance. The other more practical aspect is in our development of that. In the Aikido opinion, there is enough aggression in the world and by getting good at aggression or at counter-aggression, if that's your logic, you are only adding to the amount of aggression. As a species, we hope that we would be chipping away at that mountain and dissolving it rather than adding to it. The aspiration is to introduce techniques and aspects of conflict resolution that cut down on the overall amount of aggression in the world.

SJC: It is said that you encounter yourself on the mat. What has the art taught you after practising and teaching it for so long?

BD: That we don't know ourselves. There's no doubt that every time you step on the mat it is yourself you meet, and your own ghosts and fears and inhibitions and limitations. It's our nature, in our society, to project all those things onto other people and blame other people for being bad or resisting and not being helpful, but ultimately, we are there everywhere we turn, waiting to meet ourselves. In terms of the dojo [*the place the Way is practised*] and in terms of our club, we would be very aware that everybody who comes to the door of the club is on their journey and most of them are passing diagonally through the room, and going off somewhere else. So, we're not particularly worried about making people into good Aikido practitioners. We are concerned with helping them on that journey. Occasionally, people will be coming in at such an angle that the dojo is part of the long-term journey and they'll stay for years and that's an added bonus, but it's not what we're looking for. And certainly we try to keep the atmosphere in the dojo such that people do know that they're meeting themselves rather than facilitating projections onto other people.

SJC: Were you ever attracted to any other martial arts?

BD: No, probably because I grew up within an aspect of the Republican movement and in those days, in those places, if someone threatened you, you armed yourself and if someone wanted to get you they would shoot you, so . . .

SJC: You're talking about the IRA?

BD: Yes. So there was no illusion about becoming powerful through a martial art or becoming safe. You are neither powerful nor safe in today's society. It's a different game. It wasn't the martial aspect that attracted me. Ironically, it was the opposite — it was the peacekeeping potential of it that attracted me.

SJC: Do you have any criticisms of Aikido?

BD: No. It would almost be a waste of time criticising Aikido because it doesn't exist in itself. It only exists in the people who practise it. I would have criticisms of people who practise tiddlywinks! There are some outrageous bullies in Aikido and some beautiful, beautiful people in Aikido. I'm sure the same can be said for tiddlywinks.

SJC: How would you describe the style of (traditional) Aikido you practise and teach in your dojo?

BD: Individual, in that we would have huge input from lots of different sources so we allow the individual to develop in the direction that they want. We haven't got a core syllabus that everyone has to do or stick to. One of my teachers described it (and I'll borrow that description) as a huge big banquet to which everybody is invited, but when you go to a banquet you don't have to eat everything. You go around and pick and choose and you enjoy what you want to eat and you don't feel guilty about not enjoying the rest.

SJC: Aikido is transferred from person to person; the vibrations pass among those of us who practise it, but it was founded by Morihei Ueshiba, a Japanese martial artist, who is affectionately known as O Sensei (Great Teacher). Do you retain any links with Japan, the home of Aikido? And why do you think so many martial arts come from the Far East?

BD: I suppose it was just their way of doing something. I suppose if they hadn't, we wouldn't be noticing them because they would be so integrated into our way of life, so we notice them because they are not and that is where they happened to come from. Somebody in Japan could be asked the same question about soccer and so a particular society and structure and frame of mind developed martial arts and we just happened to come across them now or be exposed to them. While I acknowledge Japan with a nod of gratitude as the place where Aikido came from, I don't feel any particular loyalty towards Japan. I don't necessarily respect the way it's practised in Japan. It's absolutely a different society. It's very misogynistic and the power structures are just so alien to the way we organise our society. Our society has loads to be criticised over as well, though. So I'm saying I'm not qualified to comment, except to say that it's not my trip. I don't pretend to be Japanese. I'm certainly not trying to emulate the Japanese. In our practice, we do retain some of the clothes and some of the gestures, etiquette and respect, but that would be for the ritual to become transcendental. It helps to change into clothes you don't normally wear and it helps to use a language and an etiquette you don't normally use, because it opens your mind to new possibilities, so in that sense I would be interested in retaining the etiquette. But it's interesting that that element doesn't hold for the Japanese because it's already what they do. Maybe they should do it in jumpers!

SJC: What is your relationship with other martial arts and artists?

BD: Well, as with a lot of Aikido people, initially I was an awful snob! — a martial arts snob, thinking that we were the only ones who had it. My learning process was two-pronged. First, I realised there's some right bastards in Aikido, and then I realised there were some really good people in some of the other, what I would have regarded as crude, martial arts — but they're not crude. Some of the motivations behind the other martial arts are as deep and meaningful as Aikido. Aikido just happens to be the journey I fell on. Over the last ten years I have been very involved in representing other martial arts and that has been a fantastic learning process and certainly I have got closer to some people in some of the karate, kickboxing and tae-kwondo networks than I would be with some of my own colleagues in the Aikido network. It goes back to practitioners at the end of the day; it's not the art itself.

SJC: You are secretary of the Irish Martial Arts Commission. How did this body come to be formed?

BD: That was an effort to address the "cowboy" element in martial arts, to bring in accountability and insurance and quality instruction. Unfortunately, the government has been really slow in bringing us into the national sports policy. Hopefully, that will be resolved quite soon. Overall, there's no personal benefit from being in the IMAC and that's a good thing. It's a group of 100 or so clubs that are genuinely trying to up the standard of martial arts training and the accountability of that training in Ireland. As with a lot of things, when we do get recognition and funding from the government, everybody will want to join and that's when the hard work starts.

SJC: You must have come across some interesting characters in the dojo over the years?

BD: Oh, maybe I should revert to saying that we only meet ourselves in the dojo! Sure. Every character of some form or another comes in. It's been a beautiful experience and Aikido challenges by its nature, because there's a lot of contact and touch, and a lot of areas collapse and get shattered through the process. I can think of one person who came in and by her second class hit a huge crisis because so many doors had been opened so quickly. It can be a really powerful process. People learn to breathe — just that breathing process can open up all sorts of locked up energies and traumas, surprises and gifts. It's a beautiful journey. I haven't seen anything else that would have been the right place for me for all those things to happen. That's the most I could say.

SJC: Are there any people for whom Aikido would not be suitable? And what type of person, in your opinion, is attracted to Aikido?

BD: I don't think there's anybody for whom Aikido wouldn't be suitable. That unfortunately isn't the same question as: is there somewhere where everybody can go to do Aikido? For some people, Aikido may be absolutely suitable but they may need more space. They may need one to one. They may live in the middle of Leitrim and there's no Aikido dojo. They may be in a wheelchair and there may not be a wheelchair-accessible dojo near them. The problem is that there isn't enough Aikido available; there aren't enough qualified instructors available to respond to demand and to adapt it to what people need. It's a very adaptable art. In the whole of Ireland, there are thirty dojos, which is nothing. Tae-kwondo, kickboxing and karate would be in the hundreds. Aikido is in its first generation but the quality is good. Every type of person has arrived at the door. The people who stay seem to be addressing power relations and have chosen not to go the route of domination or trying to be strong and overpowering. In ideal circumstances, more women would be attracted to Aikido. Unfortunately, if a heterosexual couple begin Aikido and there are problems, invariably it's the woman who stops, even if she was making better progress. Our society is still very male-centred. There are a lot of things stacked up against certain groups of people, preventing them from playing their part in Aikido or anything else for that matter.

SJC: What is the essential difference between T'ai Chi and Aikido, as both of them engage with *chi*, which is Chinese for *ki*, though they understand it differently?

BD: I wouldn't talk a lot about *ki* and maybe my whole relationship with spirituality would be similar in that some things are only separate because we haven't dealt with them. I wouldn't attempt to give a definition of *ki* or *chi*. I would prefer to think of working towards being whole and tapping into all our resources and bringing them together and bringing all our potentialities and capabilities into one co-ordinated movement and action. There can be a bit of mystification and I think that can be dangerous, as it's always open to manipulation. I would purposely avoid talking in those terms or encouraging people to think in those terms. There are some common traits, because there are only so many ways we can use our body. With all the martial arts, all we have is the human body and there are very limited things you can do with it, so the longer you're at a martial art, the more you see your martial art in everything else. I'm avoiding the question on purpose because I don't think there is any purpose in comparing. Some people can use T'ai Chi absolutely as creatively as they can use Aikido.

SJC: We sense energy when we are in love or in conflict. Is *ki* non-physical energy or physical energy, which we don't have a metre reading of yet?

BD: I suppose I don't mind saying that I don't know. And not knowing and not being anxious about knowing doesn't seem to have affected my Aikido or my progress in Aikido or my ability to share my Aikido. Just as I would have difficulty in defining the universe.

SJC: Are you saying you believe in *ki* but can't define it?

BD: Maybe it's like the heat from a candle. You can't dissect the candle to find where the heat is, but when the candle is lit, heat comes out of it. I don't know if that stands up to examination, but I think it's the end result of us using ourselves properly and then if that energy is all over the world, we become part of that by tapping into it. My head fills up on hearing the word with more negative than positive associations in terms of how it's presented and all the books being written on it. It's so easy to send people off on a wild goose chase.

SJC: So do you think that *ki* is more about body, breathing and posture than about anything more mystical or metaphysical?

BD: Yes. I would have no doubt that if we use our body effectively, some quite magical things can happen. I'm reluctant to give it a value. I think Bernard Shaw said that the glorification of excellence creates contempt for ordinariness. I'd be really aware of that. I would like to think that, through our Aikido, we're saying to people "You're grand as you are and with what you have." We're not saying there's some Holy Grail you have to find.

SJC: Terry Dobson, who was a well-known Aikidoka [*a practitioner of Aikido*], saw himself as a transmission specialist of Aikido, as a mechanic working on the transmission of *ki*. How do you see yourself as a teacher?

BD: I am a little more selfish. I see myself on my own journey. Ironically, it goes back to my first teacher. On many Sunday afternoons at one o'clock, he and I would be there and no one else and he would cancel the class and I would be thinking, "But I am here and you are here!" At that time I promised myself that if I ever got to that situation, even if I was by myself, I would have the class and I've done that. It hasn't happened in the last ten years, but in the early days when I was teaching there were times when nobody turned up and I would do the full three-hour class by myself and do loads of useful stuff. That got me into a pattern of thinking that I was coming along to my practice and if other people joined in, great. T'ai Chi in China seems to be more on that basis — that the facilitator is out doing their own practice and somebody who wants to learn just stands behind and copies them. As another teacher put it, they are not better, they are just sooner. They started sooner so, time-wise, they are just a little further on the journey.

SJC: Martial arts teach discipline and self-control, etc. Do you think they can lead to profound personality change and transformation even?

BD: Oh absolutely, shockingly sometimes. That's where the dojo you are in and the atmosphere of the dojo can make a big difference. If the place of training has an agenda for you, then you lose a lot of those opportunities and become somebody else. Ideally, you come into a space that is ready to be moulded to whatever your needs are. I think that at every moment of our lives we are working on the next part of the jigsaw, whether we know it or not. Unfortunately, some people get stuck on the same piece for their whole life. Other people have an amazing ability to keep on finding and shaping and developing a piece of their jigsaw and tumbling from reality to reality. I would imagine that the most exciting experience of life is to have these new insights or understandings all the time.

SJC: In a different context, Pascal said that we wouldn't have searched for God unless we had already found Him, so perhaps there's something pre-empting people to enter into the dojo?

BD: Absolutely. In lots of ways, the Aikido techniques are great metaphors for that because, as the attack arrives, if you are open enough, the attack is telling you how to neutralise it. It's hard enough to get your head around that notion, but hard also to get your body to trust and surrender to it! It goes against everything we've learnt and I say "learn" because a baby does it instinctively. We are born with huge potentials in terms of responding to conflict. Our society offers us two: fight or flight. It doesn't explore the third possibility, which is to neutralise and put back in balance, which is neither fight nor flight. That's the territory Aikido is exploring and playing with and checking out.

SJC: Aikido, as you say, is the third way beyond fight and flight. Do you think it has a place in conflict resolution and that its lessons can be brought into everyday life?

BD: In essence, it is conflict resolution. Now, to have the frame of mind to do that is a different kettle of fish. If we learn to find some sense of calmness and fairness when our actual being is under threat, then other such threatening situations, be they physical or psychological, become more manageable.

SJC: And you would recommend martial arts for children?

BD: Oh, absolutely. If someone comes along to our kids class, it's great fun and in some of it we would focus on kids getting out of grips, kids having the confidence to tell adults to "eff off". We have a game we play where the kids line up and they come running up to me, look me in the face and say, "Get lost." We teach them three simple things if someone is hassling them: to shout, run and tell somebody. We teach them very little technique, more confidence building. Even the fact that they know they're coming to martial arts has huge implications on notions of violence and conflict. I think it's great for kids, but that depends on how it's being presented to them.

SJC: Have you ever come across anyone who has abused his knowledge of a martial art?

BD: Yes. The courts are full of cases. In most cases, they would be people who would have abused their physical strength anyway. They just happen to be martial artists.

SJC: Are we talking about students or instructors?

BD: There are numerous cases of instructors abusing their position, both physically and financially.

SJC: And in Aikido?

BD: More subtly, probably, in Aikido. There is at least one internationally known Aikido instructor, very senior, who is just a violent person and who regularly breaks wrists and other parts of people's bodies and has almost built up a reputation on that. I would be very critical of the international Aikido community for not isolating these individuals.

SJC: You mentioned this earlier, that a number of well-known actors and martial artists have popularised the martial arts on TV and in the cinema, people such as Steven Segal, who is a highly ranked practitioner of Aikido, Jean-Claude Van Damme, Bruce Lee, Chuck Norris, Jackie Chan etc. Have they helped or hindered the public perception of martial arts?

BD: It's a double binder. There's no doubt that they have made our job so much more difficult; not so much recently, but after Steven Segal's first few movies I would recognise the young men with little stars in their eyes who would stand at the dojo door for the first time with their pony tails, all ready to go, and I would think "Oh no, here we go again!" In one sense, they have created a whole load of myths and ideas about martial arts that we have to undo. They also brought loads of people to the door and some of those people stay. If you asked most people why they were doing martial arts and asked them is that why they came in the first place, it wouldn't be. The thing that brings them to the door isn't the thing that keeps them there. That's good, I think.

SJC: O Sensei discovered that there's a way in which we can blend with the energy of another and redirect their aggression without becoming aggressive oneself. Do you think this laudable philosophy can really be pursued in the context of a vicious street fight, for example?

BD: Yes, but it's whether you can find the trust and abandonment to the principles you have been teaching at that moment. You might find it one day and not the next. These things are unpredictable. I think, absolutely, it works. The number of situations arising to which you respond instinctively by neutralising it before it happens is the real potential of Aikido. Luckily, I can say in nearly twenty years of doing Aikido, I have never had to physically use my Aikido and that's for somebody who was a right little scrapper! Violence is such a part of our society. It is deep-rooted in our mythology, so people's relationship to it is distorted. On the one hand, we have been at the receiving end of so much violence through our history. On the other hand, through the Republican movement we can attribute so much of our liberty to people who were prepared to use violence, and all this is confused at lots of different psychic levels within our community and we haven't worked it out. We have started to work it out. Maybe the way that the peace process is developing in the North is more encompassing and because everybody is involved with it something may come out of it. It won't be today or tomorrow but we may learn some of the lessons in the next generation and start dealing with the strange role violence does play within us as a people.

SJC: So you are saying that Aikido has altered your sense of politics?

BD: Oh, absolutely, hugely. Different people come out of the Republican movement with different scars and lessons and experiences. I felt that the injustices when I was a kid were real and had to be stood up to and I still think it was a totally understandable way to respond to it. I, as a kid, got all this crap from people who wore uniforms and carried guns, so it is understandable that I would say, "I'll get a gun and show them." I would hope that I grew beyond it and I started to see that this was only adding to the overall problem. Then Aikido offered me that other possibility.

SJC: I am reminded of an Aikido saying that if someone goes to strike you, they have already lost the fight.

BD: Yes. I would certainly agree with that notion. By somebody choosing violence they have already let themselves down. There's a student in our class who wrote a very noteworthy little verse, in which he captured the notion that if a fight happens we are both going to get hurt, no matter who wins the fight. Somebody has chosen aggression as their form of communication and in Aikido it is our considered opinion that it is not a very effective form of communication, so if we can end that choice without anyone paying a price for it, then there is some possibility that we will move on to the next option of communication.

SJC: So you have to look after and care for your aggressor?

BD: Absolutely. Because ultimately we are all the same person and part of the same species and I suppose that's a spiritual notion. We have some collective reality. For me to hit you has to hurt us all, as a whole. Similarly, for me to love and protect you is to love and protect us all, including myself. It's like a positive selfishness — by looking after ourselves properly and holistically, we automatically start including others in that space that we call ourselves and that space becomes safer not only for ourselves but for those around us, including people who want to do us harm. It can sound quite highfalutin', but it's really quite simple and grounded. The biggest obstacle to that is fear — fear that we won't hold our own, fear that we will be damaged. Addressing those fears has to be part of our journey.

SJC: Drawing on O Sensei's philosophy, Terry Dobson taught his students to look between the opponent's brows, instead of into their eyes, lest we become enthralled with the utter beauty of the other person and be rendered impotent in the face of attack. Should we look into the eyes or do they lie?

BD: I do believe that the eyes are windows to the soul and they don't lie. Again, at some level, I believe that people don't want to lie, that at some level we want to be truthful and open and so much hurt forces us into being manipulative and closes off that possibility. There's no doubt that those few opportunities and those few relationships we are involved in where we can be honest are so enjoyable. All of our nature rewards us for it. They are so pleasant and such a relief that everything in us is telling us that that's the way we should operate as human beings, yet all the restrictions and hurts in us from growing up shut those doors and shut down those possibilities.

SJC: Many people put Aikido in with New Age spirituality and Eastern philosophy and religion, quite mistakenly in my view. Has Aikido a spiritual dimension? After all, O Sensei practised the Shinto religion of Japan.

BD: We are a very religious but not spiritual country. We are not encouraged to explore our spirituality, to swim in it and lose it and do all those naughty things we should do with it, so it becomes something separate from us, as something we do rather than as a part of us. We don't live it. In that sense, it is sad that any society finds itself in that position. It doesn't matter what label we put on it, be it Christian or Buddhist or Shinto. Hopefully, we only need to concentrate on it for a while to bring it back into our life, and then I think we should forget it. The most spiritual people I know don't have any label or name for it. They are just living it.

SJC: I know someone who decided not to do T'ai Chi because he didn't want to buy into Taoism, which he believed he would be doing.

BD: Yes. In Aikido we have been refused access to certain premises because people thought we were into or not into particular philosophies or religions. Again, I try to avoid the language because it can be so misunderstood, but I would have a sense that there's a huge part of us that we don't live and anything that encourages us to embrace it has to be good. Unfortunately, such a lot of religions exclude half the population, which are women. Most of the philosophies on offer to us are male hierarchies that are built to perpetuate power structures. That to me is incompatible with spirituality.

SJC: Much of your work is taken up with your involvement in Aikido and the Irish Martial Arts Commission, but you also work as a community activist. What does this work entail and how did you come to be involved in it?

BD: As a kid involved with politics, while I was in the Official IRA, I had to fix people's sinks. It was regarded as community politics but for us it was just what we did. We never lost that. For a while I lived outside a community, in Dublin's flat land, and when I was lucky enough to move back into York Street about twenty years ago, it was such a relief to be back amongst community. I just realised that there were things that I missed about that — kids screaming next door and being known and part of that bigger thing. I regard "community work" as what I do with my neighbours and friends. It's not work. I also dialogue with the powers that be to resource our community — that's politics. My experience allows me to operate quite comfortably in those circles.

SJC: So how would you describe your present political position?

BD: I would have huge hope and trust and faith in the individual. The more concrete and written down and established any philosophy is, the more I'll move away from it! I think we have to be fluid and our ideas have to be fluid. Look at Ireland, look at how much we have changed in ten years. I was talking to a young fella today who fell out of school into a twenty-five-thousand-pound-a-year job, which is now up to thirty thousand — he has no idea. Ten years ago is like yesterday to me. Realising what he needs to survive and thrive today is just so different to ten years ago. I am also involved in the Dublin Community Forum, a huge aspect of which is giving real voice to community. I would openly say that I am sceptical about how much the powers that be want a community voice, but as long as they're saying they want it, they'll have it! And as long as they say they're listening, they will remain accountable.

Maybe there is a genuine move within Western society towards a participatory model of democracy, or maybe there's lip service being paid. On the one hand, I think capitalism is always entrenched as it has been, having an absolute hold on us. At the moment I am leaning against Brown Thomas's window and the conversations I have heard between mature couples about clothes in the windows, and "let's buy that" because it has such and such a label, are just incredible! Where have we got to if these are the things about which we are making decisions? There's as much positive as negative in our new society. I suppose I'm afraid that capitalism has got its boundaries so secure that they managed to push them back a bit. It's like the prison walls are just out of sight. I suspect that there's a good bit of that — MTV and Calvin Klein and Levi's getting stronger holds on our lives so that there is the illusion of freedom.

But then that gets us into the whole matrix debate. If the matrix is the reality, if our life is absolutely unbearable but we think it's not and we're having an absolutely great time, where would you want to be? It's a funny old question and intrigues me because of that. What I should add is that maybe it's OK for us but at the price of the rest of the world. As the white elite men of the Western world, can we afford to regard the whole world as us, because then we're being schizophrenic; we're allowing half of ourselves to live in unbelievable misery so that the other half can have the life we have. We're only beginning to deal with a fraction of that in Irish society, at people coming in and seeing this as somewhere to come to. The fear that is stirred up in us and the greed and possessiveness is something we've never had to admit before because we've always been allowed, as a nation — justifiably — to regard ourselves as victims and we're not anymore and this is suddenly a strange game to play. We're now the rich ones and the masters. We don't like those feelings that are stirred up in us and as always, what do we do with things we don't like? We project them so that it's those Bosnians that are the problem. If we let it, it could be a part of our growth but also part of our demise.

SJC: So your view of contemporary Ireland is ambiguous?

BD: It's a lovely, lovely place to be. I have experienced it as somewhere you can genuinely explore who you are and want to be. As a kid of 16, I was bumming around Paris by myself and Hemingway's *The Moveable Feast* was the only book I had and he opens it with "Any young man who has the pleasure of being in Paris will partake in a moveable feast." I have that sense of Ireland at the moment, that there is such choice, and even if it does crash, we'll cope.

SJC: But look at the house prices, the congestion on the roads (unmoveable!), and look at the murder rate and greed and road rage!

BD: Well, on the housing one, there's a definite clash between expectation and reality. There's only so much space. There's not enough space for us all to have a house, certainly not for us all to have a house in Dublin, five minutes from work. We're going to have to work out these things but they are problems of prosperity.

It's much better to have problems of prosperity than poverty. In those problems, there are more smiles now than in the midst of unemployment. There's no doubt about it. People felt worthless in contrast to the choices facing young people coming out of school now. There are practical problems and we'll find some way of dealing with them. I'm not sure to what degree it has become a more violent place — I'm not sure about the statistics.

SJC: I think the crime rate has decreased but the murder rate has increased.

BD: Well, I think the level of stimulation young people expect from violent movies is just mind-boggling, when you compare it to films of before. When people do cross that line they move into violence and outrageous territory. I would think that, by and large, Dublin isn't less safe than it was twenty years ago. The statistics could prove me wrong.

SJC: Does Ireland still have soul and what is soul?

BD: Oh yes. I think Ireland has loads of soul and I see it in two people standing at a bus stop — one is in a suit with a briefcase and somebody, even a drunkard, standing beside him will, within five minutes, begin to talk. There's a part of us that insists on recognising each other as human and there's much more of that in Ireland than in a lot of places I've been to. There are both places of poverty and prosperity that have lost that — Egypt comes to mind, and Thailand, on the other hand, where there isn't great wealth but people seem more content. The images that flash through my mind when you ask me does Ireland have soul straightaway are based on that awareness that there is a part of us that insists on communicating, which comes through music, etc. Music and art are great exposers of the soul, that people, no matter how comfortable they are inside their suit of armour, want to come out to play! It beckons.

SJC: What does the future hold for Aikido and the other martial arts?

BD: I don't know, and I don't even know if it's important. I think things have their usefulness at periods in time. Alice Miller did psychotherapy in her life journey. That's what she did until she reached a part of her journey where she said, "No. It's stopping me from doing what I want to do." She said it was stopping people from doing what they are or should be doing. I really enjoyed her material — it was very relevant for me, though I'm not a great reader. I'll read for a while and get a great buzz and then I'll drop it. I admired Alice's bravery. At the time, she was one of the leading spokespersons of psychotherapy. When she saw the cracks in it she had the nerve to walk away and this goes back to what I was saying before. At the time I wrote to her and said what I said to you, that if I ever feel that way about Aikido, I'll have the nerve to walk away. It's hard because we mistake these things for us rather than something we do.

SJC: So you might yet walk away from Aikido?

BD: Yes, I might do it tomorrow morning! You might be giving the class yourself tomorrow!

SJC: Are you happy?

BD: Yes, outrageously so! I'm lucky. I do think life is an unpredictable bag of tricks and I got through life long enough so that before I got the first decent kick in the teeth, which was about ten years ago when a very close friend of mine died, I was equipped to deal with it. I've had the opportunity to equip myself for situations before they arrive and arise and that's absolute chance. That's how the chips fell for me. I have absolutely beautiful friends, so life rarely takes over from me. Aikido has also equipped me to take a fall. When I need to take a fall, I do, and then I stand up and see where I am now. That's been a lovely trick or technique or gift — whichever way you look at it — that Aikido has given me.

SJC: Do you believe in a next life?

BD: No. I say that quite clearly. No. This is it. It isn't a rehearsal. This is the shot we have at it. Maybe if I did believe, I would be in danger of losing this chance. I sometimes think, with a bit of sadness, of the people who have invested most of this life in preparation for something else. I think you are missing the party, and I don't mean that flippantly. They're missing the show. I would feel that it has been in some people's interest to convince us otherwise but I'm thinking that the meek aren't going to inherit the earth without doing something about it and in the meantime the people who have the power and the wealth are enjoying it. They're not in misery — they are having quite a nice time, thank you, and they would only have to face up to that if they lose it, but 99 per cent don't. They live and die with it.

RODDY DOYLE
Writer

Roddy Doyle is a well-known author and screenwriter. Films have been made of The Van, The Snapper *and* The Commitments *and a romantic comedy for which he wrote the screenplay* — When Brendan Met Trudy — *was recently released. His acumen lies in being able to depict, with uncanny accuracy, the lives and loves of working-class Dubliners, with whom he clearly empathises. He portrays the stark, sometimes shocking reality of these lives but always with intense humour. He is a hard-working and dedicated professional who has enjoyed immense success.*

SJC: When did you begin to write? Was it always something you planned or wanted to do?

RD: It was a vague ambition for as long as I read. I think it was in my teenage years when I began to read in an organised way and I realised that a book was written by a person who may have written other books, like Flann O'Brien. I thought I'd love to try this and did it to a small degree in University College Dublin. I had friends who had set up a paper called *Student*.

SJC: How original!

RD: Very! They asked me to write for it and I did — satirical things. Then I wrote the odd satirical article for *In Dublin*. When I got into teaching and found myself with a lot of free time and no family to rear, I gradually got into the habit of writing. I went away for three months in the summer of 1982 to London and lived in Wood-green. I forced myself to go to the local library and spent a few hours each day writing in copy books. I remember vividly finishing the first copybook and starting the next one and thinking, "I'm getting there." By the time I came home I was in the habit of writing and I kept at it. I don't think I had a vague ambition — though that's too pointed a word. When I was a kid, and still to some extent today, when I heard a glorious piece of music, I always dreamed I could play it or emulate it. It seemed the writing was an easier ambition or goal than to play an instrument. After 1982, I set out a time to write — the evenings and most weekends.

SJC: What type of family did you grow up in? Was it literary?

RD: It was literary in so far as the house was packed full of books from when I was a kid. I had an uncle in America and once or twice a year, a big brown box would arrive from the States and there was the ceremony of opening it and these glorious books poured out. They were glorious because they were foreign — they were American kid's books, with kids in sneakers and great hair and teeth. Some of them were great, like the *Wizard of Oz*. My parents loved reading and still do. Quite early on, when I was 12 or 13, I picked up the *Godfather* and started reading it and there was an extraordinary sex scene in it very early on, but it was never grabbed off me. There was never any interference in what I read. Maybe there were books hidden away but there was never really any censorship. I hope and think it will be the same with my own kids. I felt quite proud when I was 13 reading books that were probably more suitable for an older readership. I'd look back on that now in gratitude. The house was always packed with books and music. My mother had a cousin called Maeve Brennan who wrote stories for the *New Yorker*. Unfortunately she died under sad circumstances. The legend is that she died homeless. In fact, it's not as grim as that, but she would have been the only writer in the family and she would have been a second cousin and was with us for a few months when I was 14. She was the only person I ever saw writing. There was a typewriter in the house and she was the only person I ever saw using it, in a way that was almost stereotypical, with the cigarette hanging out of her mouth and carbon paper. I can't honestly say I found it inspiring and indeed, even though I liked the woman, I have to say I forgot about her existence until there was an article in the *Irish Times* about her, I think by Fintan O'Toole.

SJC: You taught English and Geography in Greendale Community School in Kilbarrack in North Dublin. Did you enjoy teaching?

RD: I did. There was a retirement do in the school last night which I was at and there were people there whose company I was in for 14 years and, overwhelmingly, the memories are good. I suppose my politics have always been to the Left but up until I started teaching, it would have been in an abstract sense and I think teaching gave flesh to my political opinions. I just enjoyed it; I really loved it. I started teaching in the late seventies, in an era when corporal punishment was made illegal and it was never a policy in this school. It is a cliché but it was more child-centred and it was buzzing with personalities — it was a young school with a young staff. They were wild kids but wild intellectually. There were nine different groups in first year, ranging from kids who are now Dr. this and Prof. that, to kids who can barely cope with tying their shoelaces, and I loved the variety of that. For 12 of the 14 years, I really did love it. I was told I was absent one day in 1989 when I wasn't feeling well, so that gives you an indication.

SJC: The two English teachers I had at school exerted a huge influence on me and inculcated in me a deep interest in and abiding love of literature. Were you aware of being a mentor?

RD: You get through the day but I was always aware of the power of encouragement. If a bright kid in fifth or sixth year was writing an essay, which was showing off and there was no meat in it, I tried to home in on the strengths and to say it would be even stronger if you did this or that. I was always aware of the power of compliments. Of all the teachers I had, and some were good and some were atrociously bad, though memory is fickle and unfair, the one I recall with complete affection and gratitude is a man called Noel Kennedy. The first time we wrote an essay, he told us to rule the margin and then to write a sentence and stop and then to write a paragraph, and he went round reading them and praised my paragraph to the nines. I was about ten and I remember it well. The rest of my story was pretty atrocious — it was about a rainy day. It started well but I lost the plot and it became a science fiction story! That compliment and pat on the back sustained me for years. There was one Christian Brother who in my sixth year never game me a mark of over 43 per cent — I remember this with no bitterness at all — and the previous year my average mark would have been in the 70s. But this man obviously didn't like me or what I wrote and it struck me how unfair the system could be. Though I wanted to do English in college, the message I was getting twice a week was the mark telling me I wasn't up to it. The primary school was great but the secondary school was not so good. Some teachers were terrific, others were sadists and some were plain lazy, living behind the *Irish Independent* for hours at a time. I think a lot of the ground-work was done in primary school.

SJC: How did you find English at UCD?

RD: I loved it. I wasn't, though, a particularly good student. I really didn't know what I was getting into. I was never a good exam candidate. I would have been much happier doing dissertations. I loved the reading and enjoyed doing a third-year paper on Sean O'Casey, comparing the politics of his autobiography to the politics of the *Plough and the Stars*. And once I got into the swing of things, I enjoyed it socially. And I look back on the summers when I went away to work as being important.

SJC: You've written six novels, two plays (*Brownbread* and *War*), a television series (*Family*) and films have been made of *The Van, The Snapper* and *The Commitments*.

RD: And then there's *When Brendan met Trudy*. If you have to put a label on it, it's a romantic comedy.

SJC: You won the Booker Prize for *Paddy Clarke Ha Ha Ha* in 1993, and your most recent book is a children's story, *The Giggler Treatment*. Which is your favourite book?

RD: For reasons that have nothing to do with the book, *The Snapper*. *The Commitments* was actually the second book I wrote — the first was never published. I am reluctant to burn all copies. It's just not good enough to be published. It's almost like a musician's rehearsal. *The Commitments* took me six months and I loved writing it. I remember dashing home from school and getting everything prepared for the next day at work so I could get back into it. I had to decide on the compromises with the Dublin accent on the page to make it comprehensible — it was great fun taking all these soul songs and putting in Dublin lyrics! I was in a bed-sit in Clontarf and I drove this guy mad. There were several knocks on the door from this pretty surly ignorant boor of a student who lived beside me who was getting annoyed with me starting and stopping all these soul songs — you want to hear them from start to finish. I had a great time. I finished it at half-time in the World Cup game in 1986. Then I almost immediately started the second one, *The Snapper*. I wanted to continue the energy of the first book but wanted it to be more intimate and different. It was a lot slower. I was relieved when, three years later, it was finally finished. During those three years I did a lot of living. I hadn't met my wife when I started it and I was married by the time I finished it and I had two plays produced. Twenty-four hours aren't enough in a day but I was really happy with it when it was finished. The first draft was a huge big rambling mess of a thing with all sorts of characters. There was a lot of editing — I trimmed it and trimmed it and trimmed it to this short book. It was less than half the length of the first book. It's a better way to work than the opposite, having to pad. I enjoy getting out the red biro months later and hacking it down to the bare essentials. First, a day's work was filling a page, then it was editing a page. I wrote the third book, *The Van*, very quickly.

SJC: So when you are writing one book, do you have a plan in your mind for another?

RD: Yes, at the back of my mind. At the moment I am working on six different projects at the same time. I can do a page of this and a page of that. I wouldn't like to work on a novel every day, all day. My first love would be to do a novel rather than a screenplay, every time. Up until recently, I always fought the idea of doing other things because I was a "novelist" but then it dawned on me that it was a stupid way of looking at things. There is a good possibility of a play later this year. A couple of weeks ago, I had to make a list of what I was doing, just to remind myself!

SJC: Do you have any plans to write another play or film script, given that you have recently been appointed to the Irish Film Board? Presumably, though, writing a play or film script is very different from writing a novel, as you said, and you would prefer to write a novel?

RD: I think because every word in a paragraph is your own and you're creating. More of you goes into it and it doesn't involve compromise or committees or the market. It's you and you only. It's literary and mechanical in linking things together and it's very engrossing. Just one adjective can bring a character alive. I always found it easy to devote my attention to that. Sometimes when things are going really well I back away from the desk and wander around and fill the washing machine or I go down to the shops for a bottle of milk that I don't need. I am so giddy. Film is very different. It's no longer your work and that to me is an attraction, whereas before it used to be a fear.

SJC: You must be curious to see what other people are going to make of your script?

RD: Exactly. It's a nice contrast to being in your own head, in a room with a bit of music to mask the real world, but basically all on your own. It's nice to get out of all that and to negotiate with people and to choose who is going to act the parts. I enjoy the more public side of it.

SJC: *A Star Called Henry* is the first in a planned trilogy. How is the next one coming on?

RD: Yes, that's going to be my next novel. It's very slow. It wasn't exactly a planned trilogy, but the story was getting so big it became one. The character is walking through this huge history and I couldn't take shortcuts and I thought it would become a bit monotonous. I thought the best way to do it was to break the story into three books.

SJC: It seems to me that your literary style can best be described as "social realism". You are someone who portrays the stark, dark and often disturbing realities of Irish and mostly Dublin working-class life, though always peppered with great humour. Would you class or categorise your works thus?

RD: I suppose if I had died after writing *The Woman who Walked into Doors*, that would be broadly accurate. Labelling is tricky and the older you get, the more you recognise that there is so much grey space between black and white, but I wouldn't disagree with that. In the last book I took liberties with reality — you inevitably do. One criticism in *Hot Press* of *The Commitments* was that one of the characters learnt to play the saxophone too quickly! It was a ludicrous criticism. You tell a nine-month pregnancy, in film form, in an hour and a half. Magic things happen in *A Star Called Henry*.

SJC: Magic realism!

RD: Again, I'm not overly familiar with that. I know it's Latin American and I've read one or two of them, so there may have been something at the back of my mind wanting to have a bash at that but every time I am writing I want to think I am not just repeating myself. I wanted to take liberties and mess around and poke fun. Among these heavy political figures like de Valera and Pearse and Connolly and

Collins, there would be the magic of the underground water and the man with the wooden leg. It's to give a cinematic feel to it.

SJC: What is the function of literature? Should one use words as "loaded pistols", to use Sartre's phrase? The existentialists and Marxists have always maintained that literature has a political role to play and that writers should be socially committed and politically engaged. Would you be sympathetic to that position?

RD: I would see myself as being socially committed and politically engaged — I always have done. At the same time, I would not inflict it on a writer. To me, one of the greatest enemies of writing is political correctness and it's only going to get worse, I suspect. It's the refusal to acknowledge satire. It's important to upset and outrage people. It seems to me it's trickier and trickier to write in a sustained way without upsetting people for all the trite reasons and the real meat of your argument gets ignored. I think a writer's responsibilities are his or her own business. Good writing doesn't necessarily have to be socially engaged. I would like to think that everything I've done is political. I would like to think that the first three books celebrate working-class life. I tried to capture and celebrate crudity, loudness, linguistic flair and slang, which is the property of working-class people. If you try to monitor what you should be doing and what your readership thinks you should be doing, it's a variation on what politicians do these days. They poll and look around for opinions and try to voice them rather than voicing their own opinions and seeing if they can carry people. I wouldn't burden any writer with my own personal opinion and the last thing I want to do when I am reading for leisure is reading people who think the exact way I do. I like being outraged and annoyed. In relation to Sartre's comment, it was the television series of *The Family* that caused the outrage, but half the adult population of the country watched it on a Tuesday night. Everybody reacted in some shape or form. The political engagement was on television. No book would have remotely the same impact anymore. You can be a very successful writer, but only a tiny fraction of literate society reads your book. In many ways, television is a much more powerful force than the page is.

SJC: You open up a world in your books that middle-class and upper-middle-class people such as myself can step into and experience.

RD: It's a world I have sympathy for and empathy and familiarity with. For people of my generation there was a huge grey area between working and middle-class and a lot of us occupied that area. We benefited from free education and the rising standard of living in the sixties and the surplus cash. And though we might have been regarded as middle-class, one leg was firmly on the working-class side of things and it's that grey area that most of my work inhabits. We've two cars at home but they don't mean anything — I couldn't give you the names of cars. They're conveniences and I have never been aware of the potency of an individual brand of a car. There is no reference to furniture or art in my books either, because at the gut it's not there even though I sit on furniture in a comfortable house. The world I describe is a world where commodities are commodities, not statements or fashion accessories.

SJC: Oscar Wilde famously said, in his preface to *The Picture of Dorian Gray*, that books were "well written or badly written — that is all". Would you agree with that?

RD: I would be inclined to go for that. The value of a book is in its ability to entertain in the broad sense and to engross, to clarify the world for you, to make you think and to intimidate you.

SJC: But you don't think that the function of literature is to mirror the ideological forces of social change and transformation at any given moment of historical transition?

RD: No. This new film portrays the new multi-racial society we're living in but it does it humanly and I was keen to acknowledge that and in a new children's book I'll have out later in the year. In it, a young girl's parents are Nigerian but there's no reference to colour, although that will be in the illustrations, I suppose. It's taken for granted. As a writer I can write something that no one else can, not necessarily good, not necessarily bad, but at least unique. In the short stories I am writing now, I bring black and white people together or Irish and Romanian. I get people to meet in the fictional sense and to come away knowing but not necessarily liking each other. The one I just finished is loosely based on *Guess Who's Coming to Dinner?* — called *Guess Who's Coming for the Dinner?* — and it's about a mad working-class man whose daughter brings a Nigerian home and he is very middle-class and arrives in a suit and intimidates the other man who's wearing jeans and runners and who thought the other guy would arrive in a tracksuit. It also forces me out of the house because I had to listen and meet and ask Nigerians how they would say this and that. My Nigerian friends e-mail me with these fascinating answers and are very happy to help. It comes from acknowledging, not necessarily welcoming, the existence of these people and to make sure that visually they are included and that eventually you can reach a point where you can like or dislike a person but the colour of the person won't matter.

SJC: You said earlier that you're quite left-wing. Are you a Socialist? Are you a Republican?

RD: I'm not a Republican as such. I think that borders are becoming less and less relevant. I grew up in a very Fianna Fáil background. My parents' background would have been rock solid Republican. One of my father's uncles was in the Free State army and the other one ended up dying. That feeds my imagination. Brothers on opposite sides was literally true. A lot of the stories I grew up listening to would have been republican. Again, I am reluctant to use labels but I suppose I would call myself a Socialist. I called myself a Communist as a teenager. I remember visiting Poland when I was a student in UCD and desperately trying to like what I was looking at! Gradually, I came around to a form of socialism that I was comfortable with. I joined the SLP, which was a break away from the Labour Party and supposed to be a broad church on the Left. Noel Browne would have been the godhead. I was privileged to have met him once or twice. There was a charisma there. I felt I was in the presence of a star. He was a star but that church fell apart because of the puritanism of some people on the Left and their refusal to laugh. I read a lot of Trotsky and thought he wrote well but when people start brandishing a book like it's the bible and I had turned my back on religion long ago, I wasn't prepared to adopt another one, so gradually I became disenchanted with it all. I haven't been involved in a party since and I don't think I ever would be again. You can do a lot of things with writing.

SJC: You're quite Dickensian, it seems to me. Which writer do you most admire?

RD: Dickens is the one who has been with me all my life. I read Dickens when I was 14 and still do. I love the film adaptations, which are magnificent. The characters are great. As I got older I got impatient with the bland political statements he would make, which seemed to get in the way of the story, and it struck me that the story was making as many statements. I think he is the writer I would most admire. On a completely different track, I like Raymond Carver, the American short story writer. Every word counts. He describes the world of trailers, of the millions of Americans who aren't living the American dream but who have great dignity about them. He was asked why he never wrote a novel and he said, "Because, number one I am an alcoholic, and number two I have kids!" And alcohol runs through all his works as well. He died when he was fifty I think. He gave the disasters of his own personal life a great dignity.

SJC: And within the Irish context?

RD: Currently Dermot Healy, who's a friend, so one is inclined to be gung-ho, but I admire him most of the living authors because I think he goes closer to the edge and surprises and there's dignity and humanity and insanity in his well-disciplined books. Every book he writes contains a surprise and he's going through a terrific prolific phase after years of silence. Reading *Antarctica*, a collection of short stories by Clare Keegan, it struck me that the short story is alive and well.

SJC: Are creative ideas worked at or do they come from the unconscious? Do you fear drying up?

RD: They come from all over the place. If you had asked me the question two years ago I would have said yes, but now I feel there's no end to the ideas. The novels always come to me because I want to do the novels. Virtually everything else I've done has been somebody else's idea, which I am more and more open to.

SJC: How do you think you have been received by the literary establishment?

RD: I don't know what the literary establishment is. An observer would say I have been dismissed completely and utterly. For some, the literary establishment is *The Irish Times* and it would appear that every establishment comes down to *The Irish Times*. I was dismissed for the first half of my career and I haven't been so dismissed since. I have been perfectly content with the quality of most of the reviews of my last few books and the reaction to the books by the, for want of a better word, "literary establishment". Where I have a problem is with people who haven't read me but who have a strong opinion. That gets on my wick. It's like people who have a view of Manchester United without watching them. You either love or hate them — and I'm in that position, which can be amusing but also irritating at times. Twice I was invited to schools last year to talk to transition-year students and the invitations were withdrawn, once because the staff objected and once because the parents objected. And I doubt that most of the parents would have read me and doubt that they would have objected to me if they had read me. I was asking myself: did they not trust me? Did they think I would pollute their children's minds? That was distressing. If you want to upset me, that's the way to get to me, not by asking me about the literary establishment. I will probably never get a favourable word from Eileen Battersby in *The Irish Times*. She's perfectly entitled to her opinion. She writes to provoke people and get on their nerves and long may she do that, but I won't ever try to write something that will get her approval. To me there's an enmity there, but certainly not on my side, but that doesn't drive me.

SJC: Do you write with a pen or on a PC?

RD: A PC. My father was a compositor and his handwriting is beautiful — it's art — and both my sons' handwriting is lovely. Mine is so bad that I can't read it. I have actually lost the ability to write. The only thing I write with any degree of consistency is my name. A graphologist would have a field day with my writing! They'd say this guy is so bland or a neurotic freak or schizoid! I write straight off the PC. I wrote the first two books freehand and then I typed them up. It's much easier on the PC where you can edit, cut and paste, etc. I like to do it slowly and methodically.

SJC: Do you have a plan for the structure of the book first or do you begin to write and see what emerges?

RD: The story emerges. When I am lucky I know how it will end. I don't have it planned.

SJC: But do you have characters' names on pages?

RD: Oh sure. I take some notes but not in any organised way. I write the book, but am always open to new images and ideas.

SJC: Do you have set times you write during the day?

RD: From nine to six. I bring the kids to school and when I get home I start and usually stop at six. When the house is empty I tend to work into the night, when I feel like it. If it were down to nature I would work into the quiet hours. A lot of writers seem to like that, I think because you feel more alone.

SJC: And perhaps because you are subverting the world of nine to five.

RD: Perhaps there's that as well but I was never able to do that too often because I was working as a teacher and when I wasn't working I had two young kids. Assuming I am kicking and keen when the kids are older, I will probably work in a more haphazard way.

SJC: Is it a lonely occupation? It is very solitary? Do you ever get depressed?

RD: I have been depressed in a casual sense but I have never been clinically depressed. There are times I have felt very heavy and dark. I don't know how often it has been related to work. I have felt low. One of the strange things about writing something dark, for example, is that you get a feeling of elation, that you have captured it. You are writing things about which you don't want to know. It's a horrible notion. It could be related to the isolation. The world is at my feet, but there are times when it's very small.

SJC: Which is more important — plot or character?

RD: Character. That's not to underestimate plot, but character brings or develops the plot. Again, I am not going to inflict my rules, but the success (and I mean that creatively rather than in terms of the sales) of the books that I wrote in the first person — *Paddy Clarke*, *The Woman who Walked into Doors* and *A Star Called Henry* — if I was a reader and was asked why they were good books, I would say it was because of the characters. The plot is important and fascinating in a different way but the invention of the character seems to me to be more important than the plot.

SJC: All your novels concern Dublin and its inhabitants, their life and loves, their fights and bitter resentments and high points of transcendence. What's your view of contemporary Ireland and the Celtic Tiger?

RD: There are elements of it I don't like, but twelve years ago I was writing a book about a man in his forties who was an unemployed plasterer and the likelihood was that he would never work again, and now there's no such thing as an unemployed plasterer any more. That's as much as I feel like saying in many ways. I am reading what I regard as lazy and stupid articles in newspapers about how materialistic we have become, and that's all people want in many ways — a few quid in their pockets and less anxiety about filling the fridge and getting shoes for their children's feet. It's not to say there aren't people out there in poverty — there are — but it's less general than it was. There are fewer people hanging around libraries to keep warm these days. There are new problems. I think this economic boom is fantastic to be honest with you. I feel I am living in a big metropolis now — and I always wanted to, but I hung on in Dublin, which I never thought I would. I never wanted to. I fancied living in New York but now I feel I am living in a real city. Twenty years ago as a music lover you could be waiting months before there was anything worth going to see or hear. That's all changed. But there's a smugness out there, which isn't attractive, and there's the *Riverdance* idea that we have become a sexy people. We're not. We're still the pot-bellied ugly bastards that we always were!

SJC: That's why the Irish hate the Spaniards coming over — it's pure envy. They're so young and sexy and good-looking and the majority of Irish are white and not so good-looking.

RD: And pasty. There are negative sides to it but every possibility has negative and positive aspects to it. As an atheist, I am happier living in Ireland in 2001 than I would be if I were 42 in 1981, I suspect. I am more comfortable here. I feel very happy and at home here. Decisions I would have had to take about my children's education I can almost take for granted now. That's not to say that there isn't a negative side. I don't like all the global commodification — if that's the word — of everything. I don't like the blandness of things and I don't like rule by press release. You see it again and again. More and more often the review is a varied version of the press release. It's not a genuine intellectual engagement whatsoever. It's someone just filling space. It's rule by poll and press release. The uniqueness and absurdities and freakishness of a lot of Irish life could disappear along with accents and things like that. But then you hear a bunch of kids screaming at each other and they take a word "cool" — a word I hate — and it's like what happens in *Paths to Freedom*, a brilliant mock documentary about two men coming out of Mountjoy; one is working class and he makes the word "cool" a three-syllable word, "cooul". They take the blandness out of the word and they make it their own.

SJC: So you find pockets of creativity that still give you hope.

RD: Absolutely. Yes. Now I am writing about Nigerians and I am forcing Irish people to come up to Nigerians and to shake hands with them, their first black hand. Life goes on. No matter how wealthy you are, you are still going to feel middle-aged and watch your children growing up. So I wouldn't be at all worried about running out of things to say.

SJC: What is soul and does Ireland still have soul?

RD: I don't know what it is. If you ask me what is soul, I think it's music, a type of music of which I am particularly fond. After that I don't have anything to say about it. As to Ireland having soul, my patch does. Having said that, I don't know what it is. When I walk around my patch, in north-east Dublin, I feel it. I hope it's not too bubble-like. I hope it's open to change and not a closed sealed community. It's interesting what can be done to music when you get cultures rubbing up against each other. Some of it is disastrous and awful, like the Celtic rock from the 70s. We are opening ourselves to different cultures. The possibilities are fantastic and I would like to think that these possibilities aren't just cultural but social too. I find it very invigorating to talk to someone outside the country who's trying to become acquainted with the place, even from a dialogue point of view — listening to the use of language.

SJC: You say you are an atheist, but are you a spiritual person?

RD: I am an atheist but I don't wear blinkers and I think I've got a great respect for religion. Religion now in Ireland doesn't inflict itself on me. The new Cardinal is an irrelevance in my life, whereas he wouldn't have been twenty years ago; my job prospects as a young teacher would have been a lot slimmer, etc. I am wary about the word "spirituality", because it's a word that doesn't have much meaning for me. I don't want to be too disparaging but it's one of these catchall phrases that is almost a political slogan. When my first child was born, I had just finished reading a book by Havel called *Letters to Olga*, which is a series of letters he wrote to his wife, who's now dead, over a four-year period when he was in jail and he wrote them under severe censorship conditions. He could talk about his physical ailments and wanting a new toothbrush, which was fascinating in itself, but then he went off into abstraction because it was the only thing he could get past the censor. He wrote about immortality and the one adjective that was used to describe him was "Catholic". And I was interested because there was nothing overtly Catholic about his abstract opinions, but then he did talk about immortality and what it meant for him. For him, immortality was the impact he would have on other people that he met. That affected me as a young teacher correcting essays, because I felt they would carry that correction with them all their lives. A correction or a compliment could carry that person right through their life. Atheism is always expressed negatively — I do *not* believe. I felt I had to articulate what I felt in a positive sense — that we are on our own, but we are together. We sustain ourselves.

SJC: An atheist isn't someone who doesn't believe. He's someone who *believes* in no God. I am reminded of the Spanish philosopher, Ortega y Gasset, who said that we are radically alone with others.

RD: Yeah. And I do believe in the immortality of humanity. A friend of mine, the writer Catherine Dunne, spoke last night at the school and said she believed that the human spirit yearns for the positive and fights for optimism and I would agree with that wholeheartedly. As to what happens when we die, I don't care. I would love to be proved wrong. I would love to wake up somewhere floating or whatever in a place where nothing happens, as Talking Heads put it. I would like that — a permanent state of being slightly pissed with your friends.

SJC: What are your interests outside writing?

RD: Film, music and life. I really enjoy watching my kids and being with them and my family in general. I've got a great pool of friends whose company I really enjoy as well. I often come away from them buzzing. I would regularly see a film or read a book or hear a piece of music and it still gets to me the same way as it used to when I was a teenager. When I saw the film *Magnolia*, I came home and it was nearly midnight I didn't want to go to bed. I just wanted to write and work, in the same way as, when I watched the FA Cup Final in 1970, I wanted to run out and become Charlie Cooke.

SJC: Are you happy?

RD: At the moment, yes, I am happy. Yesterday I probably wasn't. I don't think happiness can be sustained. I don't think that's reasonable, but being content is as much, I think, as you can manage most of the time. I would say I am quite a content person, although always itchy.

WALTON EMPEY
Archbishop

His Grace Most Reverend Walton Empey is the Church of Ireland Archbishop of Dublin. We spoke in his beautiful house in Temple Road about the state of Anglicanism in Ireland and its relation with Catholicism as well as discussing the doctrinal differences that distinguish Protestantism from Roman Catholicism. This genial, good-humoured and affable churchman is known for his pastoral gifts and involved ecumenism. He is married with three sons and one daughter.

SJC: What attracted you to becoming an Anglican priest in the Church of Ireland?

WE: My father was a priest for whom I had profound respect but, like many people who grow up in such a household, there's no way you are going to end up a priest, and so it was all through my school years — it never crossed my mind. In fact, I was thinking of joining the army but I was too young so my father insisted I go to university for the interim period. So I went to Trinity and during my time there I was asked to help in the mission to seamen, to run the social end of things. And it was from several experiences there that I decided that I wished to be ordained. So it was from my work in the docks in Dublin, even though it only involved me getting sailors to come to dances. Nevertheless, I had lots of experiences down there which made me stop and think, and that eventually led to ordination.

SJC: Traditionally, the Anglican Church has possessed a low, middle and high church — a liberal, evangelical and Catholic wing. Which tradition is now in the ascendancy and how would you describe yourself within that tradition?

WE: I would say, certainly in the North of Ireland, the evangelical wing would be to the forefront. I suspect in the Republic it would be more the liberal tradition and I would be at the Catholic end of that liberal tradition. I hate these labels, but if you can put labels in, that would be a very rough guide. Now some of my friends in the North of Ireland would be shocked to hear that. There's a great mixture, North and South, but increasingly in the North the evangelical wing would be getting stronger and stronger. We don't talk about it very often as a Church. It emerges in conversation and debate. There would be a more relaxed, liberal attitude here, on the whole, but that's a broad generalisation.

SJC: The recent Papal Encyclical, *Dominus Iesus*, questioned the notion of whether the Protestant churches were our sister churches. How do you respond to that document?

WE: It was certainly very controversial and I suppose in a sense the great disappointment was that despite all the movement of the last thirty years, we were going back to pre-Vatican II type language. The Roman Catholic Church has always believed that the true faith subsists within the Roman Catholic Church. There were theological inconsistencies, I thought. Every baptised Christian — baptised in the Holy Trinity — was a full Christian and yet the Church to which you belonged was not. I fail to understand how you can be two-thirds Christian or 99 per cent a Christian! It was a confusing document. I don't know that it's done a lot of harm. It didn't ruffle too many of our feathers, I don't think.

SJC: Well, of course, the vast majority of Catholics tend not to read these documents, or they dismiss them anyway.

WE: This is what I find. I have been invited to annual meeting of the National Council of Priests in Ireland every year for the last five years and I find it a most exciting place to be — there's a huge wealth of talent, experience and a good deal of scholarship right there, and I don't think it ruffled their feathers too much.

SJC: So what do you make of the fact that so many Catholics simply don't toe the papal line on divorce, homosexuality, premarital sex, contraception, etc? They are more Protestant in their thinking.

WE: Yes. That's that liberal wing, but that argument goes on — liberal versus conservative. You find it all over the place. It really is a mirror image of ourselves, in many ways.

SJC: The Catholic tradition has the doctrine of transubstantiation. Do you believe that the bread and wine are actually trans-substantially changed into Christ's actual body or blood, or is it simply symbolic?

WE: No, it's in between. I don't think it's a question of either/or. Transubstantiation was a philosophic approach to that. We approach it as a great mystery in which Christ is truly present and that is both in the ministry of the Word and in the ministry of the Sacrament — Christ is embodied in both. If it were pure symbolism, I would not be an Anglican priest. To me, Christ subsists there. How he subsists there I haven't a clue and the Church does not claim to know. Humans always want to describe something. The Orthodox Church is far better at that — they don't attempt to define. We Westerners love to define, but the Orthodox Church is inclined to say that it is a great mystery. It drives you up the walls when you are trying to talk to them! But I think they have something there. We are confronted with a huge mystery and I simply receive what Christ says: "This is my body. This is my blood." I cannot accept a definition of that. I approach it as a wonderful, wonderful mystery, in which Christ Himself has chosen to share His divine life with us.

SJC: So He's in the bread and wine?

WE: Yes. We have a prayer just before communion — "We don't presume to come to this thy table oh Lord trusting in our own righteousness but in your mercy" — and then we go on to say that we shall eat the body of Christ and drink His blood. We are certainly not saying that Christ is physically present in that bread and wine but that He comes through it and shares His divine life with us in some way that passes our understanding and which we will not define.

SJC: So you are not going to apply the categories of Greek philosophy?

WE: No, I am not. We will not and have never attempted to do that.

SJC: So you are on the side of Jerusalem, not Athens.

WE: Yes, that's correct. Fair enough!

SJC: The orthodox Catholic tradition would be based, to a large extent, on Thomism — the mixture of Aristotle and Aquinas. Would it be right to say that the Anglican tradition would be more fideistic and Augustinian, including St. Augustine, and people like Pascal and Kierkegaard?

WE: I would think so. There was an interesting thing on the radio the night before last. It was late at night and they were talking about *Dominus Iesus* and I just came in on it when Fr Seamus somebody (I didn't get his second name) and Dr Ian Ellis, who's secretary of the Unity Committee of the Church of Ireland, were talking. I heard Ian Ellis say, "I am very surprised to hear Seamus say that the foundation for theology is philosophy. We would believe that the foundation of theology is the New Testament." It was put in a nutshell. That's the difference between the two traditions. You should really have spoken to my predecessor, Donald Caird. He's a philosopher, which I never was and never will be. Himself and Des Connell used to go off into corners to talk philosophy.

SJC: Do you believe that Mary was a Virgin?

WE: Yes I do.

SJC: So Christ didn't have brothers or sisters?

WE: Oh, she was a Virgin when she conceived the Lord. After that, we simply do not know. It does say brothers and sisters in the New Testament, but we do know that can possibly mean cousins, as it does in Africa today. But I do believe in the Virgin Birth.

SJC: Do you believe in the Immaculate Conception?

WE: I wouldn't put it that way. But I do believe in the Virgin Birth.

SJC: Neither, presumably, would you accept the Bodily Assumption, as they go together, in that if she was born without the "stain" of Original Sin, then it makes sense that she was spared death and was assumed bodily into heaven. So in the Anglican tradition, if you don't have a dogma on the Immaculate Conception, you aren't going to have one on the Bodily Assumption?

WE: That would be correct. It doesn't go beyond the Creed.

SJC: What's your view of the alleged Marian apparitions?

WE: No-one would wish for one minute to put God in such a straitjacket that He cannot speak to us in many different ways. It would take an awful lot of convincing for me to believe in them, to be quite frank. This sounds very Anglican now, because I hate to rule out what is indeed possible in God's wisdom and God's way of speaking to people. I cannot see why it should be in that way. It doesn't move me in my heart of hearts; it doesn't fill me with conviction. I just treat it as a possibility and I think that would be true for most Anglicans. We have pilgrimages to Our Lady but that would not be part of the central conviction of Anglicanism. It would be for those who would have a devotion in that particular direction. But we do not have particular devotions to Our Lady, although we hold her in great veneration.

SJC: When Christ said to Peter: "You are Peter and on this rock I will build my Church", wasn't Christ appointing Peter as Pope?

WE: I don't believe so for one minute because subsequently, when the first council was held in Jerusalem, James seemed to be the senior there. It is the rock of faith, the rock of Peter's faith. That's the way we would read it. I think it's a huge step to move from that into primacy and the next step into infallibility. Those are huge strides to make from a text of Scripture. I certainly know that many Roman Catholic priest friends would say that too. I'm not sure they would say it in public but they would say it in conversation. Papal infallibility is very suspect. I mean, the situation has come about where if you look at Christian leadership throughout the world, the Papacy has a very special place and I do not think it would raise the hackles of many an Anglican — but by no means all, certainly not our theologians — to accept that he still could be the first amongst equals but not with all the baggage that has accumulated over the centuries. It would be the realisation of an actual fact, that if you were not a Christian in this world you would know about the Pope and that he was the leader of the majority Church in Christendom. You would not think of one of the Patriarchs of the Orthodox Church and, least of all, the Archbishop of Canterbury. We have got to acknowledge, and it has been actually mooted by theologians, that we would accept the Pope as a first among equals — not with power, infallible power, but as a very fine figurehead for the whole Church.

SJC: You know, Christ said, "Call no man father except your Father in heaven", and yet we call an Archbishop "Your Grace" and a bishop "Your Lordship". We even call the Pope "His Holiness". That's not scripturally based.

WE: No it's not scripturally based but it's pretty firmly embedded in people's minds! From the time I was first made bishop in Limerick nearly twenty years ago, I asked to be called Bishop Walton — that was the case in the ancient Church. But you were fighting an uphill battle. The younger people found no difficulty, but the older people would prefer "My Lord" to even "Bishop" and now "Your Grace" and it's very hard to root that out. And then somebody comes along and says that they all love their titles but it's nigh impossible to get rid of them. Even if the Church passed a law that you were not to be called that, it would be totally ignored.

SJC: I presume the reason why you don't have cardinals is because "cardinal" means a "hinge" — in this case, between bishops and the Pope and you don't have a Pope so you don't need cardinals!

WE: Yes, yes. You don't. You could speak, though, to far more erudite people than I am. I am no scholar. In fact, it's one of the things I find difficult about my position. Whatever gift I may have, I am afraid it's rather pastoral than scholarly and I do find that to be, quite frankly, a drawback.

SJC: Do you believe in angels?

WE: Oh yes, I cannot see why not. Again, if you say no, you are putting a straitjacket on God. But I believe there are many angels in human form, that God uses them in the sense of messenger and healing and what have you. We don't have to believe in wings and harps — it's only the artists who said that, not that type of angel! But I believe in angels as pure spirit.

SJC: Does the Devil exist?

WE: When I read my newspaper I begin to think he does. There is a huge spirit of evil in the world.

SJC: So evil exists and is personified in the figure of the Devil?

WE: I don't think it is personified. I think it is a pure spirit of evil. Mind you, the New Testament would argue with that. Jesus was tempted in the wilderness, but that's to be taken as parable. That is in story form to be told to that generation. Nowhere does he personally speak of a personal appearance of a Devil. He speaks to the Evil One just as we would speak to God in prayer, whom we do not see. He's not a person visible in front of us. I always find this a very difficult area, as I know theologians do because even though I am not a theologian I do read theology.

SJC: Paul Ricoeur, a French Protestant philosopher, said that the question of evil is the philosophical question of all time.

WE: It is. I am certainly conscious of a terrible power of evil.

SJC: Why did Christ become a man?

WE: To my simple mind, it was because God so loved us. In His son Jesus He revealed to us what he himself is like, so that when you see Jesus you know what God is like in his essence — love, compassion, etc. That, to me, is the reason. He came to redeem and save and reveal. He came to love and die for us and to show us by His life and death and through His teaching we perceive what God is really like. Is that very simple?

SJC: No. So if we are made in the image and likeness of God, does that mean the soul is a divine spark? And what's the difference between soul and spirit?

WE: You are a very awkward man! Could you tell me?!

SJC: We have a body and a soul but they are not independent, as that would be dualism. We are one. The soul is the spiritual aspect of the human being. Some people say that the highest part of the soul that is attuned to God is spirit.

WE: Yes.

SJC: What's your relation to the other Protestant churches?

WE: We're in a very interesting relationship with the Methodist Churches. In Ireland, we are progressing in a very warm relationship with the Methodists, which I suppose is unsurprising because they were part of us in Wesley's time and Wesley died saying he was a priest in the Church of England — he did not wish to depart from that tradition. He was forced into it by a very obdurate hierarchy in England. We have entered into quite a deep drive toward unity with the Lutherans of the

Scandinavian countries and that is developing apace. They are episcopally ordained and they can come to celebrate the Eucharist with us and our people can go and receive communion there and vice versa.

SJC: How do you see Roman Catholicism and its relationship with the Church of Ireland?

WE: Everything I see on the ground is a growing respect, co-operation and agreement. This consolidation of mutual respect is getting stronger and stronger. Yesterday, I was at the wedding of the daughter of one of my priests. The only other cleric there was a Roman Catholic priest who was a very close friend of the rector's. I see that happening all over the place. They are firm friends — golf every Wednesday morning. They support each other. He told me they try to do everything they can do together. You must remember, though, that in some places in rural Ireland, like Clare, there are almost no Church of Ireland people present in the communities. So the Roman Catholic priest doesn't know what we are about because he doesn't meet us.

SJC: The President receiving communion in a Protestant Church caused consternation recently amongst a certain group.

WE: All I can say there is that that's a problem for the Roman Catholic Church. The only statement I made was that when people see the churches carrying on like this I feel in my heart that Jesus weeps and the Devil does a tap dance. It's crazy when we are confronted by this wonderful mystery. We have boxed it so neatly. We have bitter pills on our side too who will take the letter of the law for everything rather than what lies behind it. I still have huge hope for the eventual unity of the Church. It won't be monochrome.

SJC: It's a scandal that the Christian Church is so divided.

WE: It is a scandal.

SJC: What theologian has influenced you the most?

WE: I have read so many. The former Archbishop of Canterbury had a huge influence on me. It might shock you, but Pope John XXIII also influenced me in terms of his theology. I think he is by far the most outstanding Christian leader of the twentieth century. He was quite an extraordinary man. I have read what he has written. Michael Ramsey stands out and the present Archbishop of Wales has impressed me. I love reading Enda McDonagh, who is a great friend of mine. I have read almost all he has written. He is recognised internationally now. He spoke to us recently and he was fabulous. I know some Irish people think we are English-oriented. In point of fact, there would be a couple of individual bishops, like Clark and the Archbishops of Armagh and of Cashel also, who would have a lot of contact with England but all of them would be far more at home with the Scottish and Welsh. The English situation is so vastly different from ours. We have more common ground with the smaller churches.

SJC: What about the Episcopalians in America?

WE: I personally have a lot to do with them. I worked in Canada along the American border for six years as a young priest. The Episcopal Bishop of Maine had no clergy that far North, so I had his licence to look after his people. I kept up a lot of friendships and contacts with people there and then six years ago I took a sabbatical and took the place of the Bishop of Bethlehem in Pennsylvania for three months. That was heavenly, because I had no administration. It was purely episcopal.

SJC: Who's your favourite mystic?

WE: I'm trying to think. The author of *The Cloud of Unknowing* — John of the Cross. It's wonderful. There is an orthodox monk who has had a big influence on me as well. I read books and forget the names of the authors!

SJC: You have monastic orders within the Anglican Church.

WE: Oh yes, indeed. Benedictines and Franciscans. We have Anglican nuns here in Dublin, but they are a tiny community. All across the Anglican communion, there are religious orders. Ireland is one of the few exceptions.

SJC: It's said that religion is an interpretation of the experience of God. What's been your experience of God?

WE: God with me, I suppose. That's the first thing that comes to mind, that God is with me. I think I would have to say that first and foremost, because without that consciousness I don't think that I could go on. Does that sound terribly arrogant?

SJC: No.

WE: That's chiefly my experience of God, God as present with me and people generally. I try to see that in others, as far as I can. God is in you. That's the great Benedictine thing in relation to hospitality, that you try to see Christ in everyone.

SJC: Your prayer is the Creed, the Word and the Eucharist. They would be central to your prayer life?

WE: Absolutely. We have two Offices a day for the clergy, in the morning and the evening. They mean a lot to me. In times of utter dryness, the wonderful thing about the Office is that you know that all over the world it is being said. You are carried along by this prayer of the Church and you are sucked into it and I remember how much it meant to me when I was in Canada. I was far removed from the nearest colleague in the Anglican Communion and it was lonely but I remember the huge comfort the Offices provided, that all your friends and priestly colleagues were saying. It was a huge sense of solidarity, being caught up in the entire worship of the Church. After Vatican II, I was in French Canada and the French Catholic clergy took me in and their problems were the same problems I was facing. That coloured my ecumenical outlook. It was an experience of fellowship.

SJC: The Church of Ireland is disestablished from the Church of England, which recently approved the ordination of women to the priesthood, which upset and angered many. A lot went over to Rome. What are the problems, if any, besetting the Church of Ireland?

WE: We only lost one priest. He went off to an ultra-conservative body in the States but he's back teaching in Northern Ireland. I would have a small group of clergy in the diocese who are opposed and would not come if a female were celebrating the Eucharist. They wouldn't be rude with them. They just can't come to consider the female being a priest. In the vast majority of cases, it has been expected. Lay people had problems at first, especially women! They had quite a bit of trouble in accepting this. I have several women clergy in the diocese who have brought an enrichment and different approach to the ministry, more collaborative. We've had if for ten years.

SJC: Has there been a socially significant if not statistically significant shift in the opposite direction, from Catholicism to Anglicanism?

WE: In this diocese alone I have three former Roman Catholic priests who are Anglican priests now and we have several clergy who were former Roman Catholics, but not priests, who were subsequently ordained as Anglican priests. If you talk about this, it sounds like trumpeting and it's not a question of trumpeting. These people felt that they had to make this move. They were disabused in many ways.

SJC: In my view, most Catholics are Protestant in their thinking but they would never make the move over.

WE: Yes.

SJC: What problems do you have though?

WE: If you were to gauge the health of the Church by attendance at Church then, like all the mainline Churches, we would have lost people. Instead of coming every week, they might now come twice a month. There's not the commitment that was there. I am always telling people to stop whining because we are a minority. There is inverse bullying. Oh God help us, we are a minority and we need our schools, etc. You only claim these things if they are a right and some are inclined to whine. I would see one of the difficulties as almost being a member of a tribe as much as a Church and the two things can become bound together. You see this clearly in Northern Ireland, politics and religion becoming intertwined and making a foul and dangerous cocktail on both sides. A club atmosphere in the South can come in and they don't rejoice when the outsider comes in, because he's coming into your club. That's a danger for the Church.

SJC: There is still that perception that "you lot" are more British than Irish but when I used to attend Patrick's Cathedral I was amazed when the priest said "God save Ireland. God save the President", which I thought was wonderfully patriotic.

WE: Really? Yes. We've always had that — "Oh God, defend our rulers."

SJC: The Anglican Communion has always emphasised the relation between man and his God unmediated by priest, tradition or authority. But isn't there a danger in approaching Biblical texts and interpreting them outside the context of tradition and scholarly exegesis?

WE: There is. We would certainly say that there is the authoritative teaching of the Church regarding Scripture. It must always be gauged against that which has been handed down in faith. It's within that teaching tradition, but people everywhere will use their Bibles and take personal messages from it. It's not just everyone for himself. It's about the living tradition of the Church.

SJC: That comes from the General Synod?

WE: Yes, from the General Synod and the Bishops, through the clergy and the prayer book — the thirty-nine articles.

SJC: I remember reading the Book of Common Prayer and there was a lot on Popish heresies!

WE: That's an historical document. Your fundamentalist can fall back and say "It says it here . . .", particularly in Northern Ireland, but those were documents from a period in history and that was the way people talked to each other. Some of the language is now totally out of date. What we need is a new set of Articles. Oh Lord!

SJC: A lot of Catholics have problems with their Church's teaching on contraception, pre-marital sex, divorce and homosexuality. What is the Anglican Church's position on these matters?

WE: In 1958, it was agreed that couples could use contraception and that it wasn't sinful; and abortion only in extraordinary circumstances, like in the case of the life of the mother. Three years ago, we agreed under certain circumstances to remarry divorced persons. I thought I was going to be inundated, but I haven't been. It was with a very heavy heart that we agreed to do that. There would be huge division in the House of Bishops over homosexuality, between the liberals and conservatives. It's a difficult one. We have not pronounced on that yet.

SJC: Does God give birth to His Son in us and is divinisation possible in this life?

WE: I couldn't accept that. The Church wouldn't accept that. That would be Gnostic. There is a divine spark in us all. We are made in the image and likeness of God. Even I have enough theology to know that.

SJC: How do you pray?

WE: I have spoken about the Offices. The Eucharist is the base. The Offices are what I do daily and are my bread and butter because there is intercession, praise and opportunity for meditation. There are days I rush through it, God forbid. I call those days "saying good morning to God"! After that, I love a time of peace and quiet — quiet meditation. I'm fortunate. I have a quiet little chapel here. It's nice to have a place apart.

SJC: Do you think the Second Coming is imminent?

WE: No I don't. How do we know? It's very hard to conceive of.

SJC: What happens after we die, in our post-mortem existence — Judgement, Heaven and Hell and Purgatory?

WE: We would still talk about Heaven and Hell. We don't talk about Purgatory. "Today, you shall be with me in Paradise." We don't develop Purgatory doctrinally. Hell is where there's no consciousness of God and where there is no consciousness of God there is emptiness of soul.

SJC: What do you think of contemporary Ireland and the Celtic Tiger?

WE: I think it's a two-sided coin. On the one hand, it's wonderful, people of my age seeing employment rather than emigration. But a large element gets left behind. There is a *mé-féinism*, for example, in the way we treat the homeless and asylum-seekers. Racism is a bitter harvest in the reaping. Also, change has happened all too sudden and not gradually enough for a lot of people.

SJC: Are you happy?

WE: Very. It has been a wonderful life. I wouldn't swap my life in the ministry for anything.

MARK PATRICK HEDERMAN
Monk

Mark Patrick Hederman is a Benedictine monk and philosopher. He has been a monk of Glenstal Abbey in County Limerick for over thirty years, where he has been headmaster of the school and academic dean. He did a doctorate in the philosophy of education after studying in Paris under the famous philosopher, Emmanuel Levinas. He has lectured in philosophy and literature in Ireland, the US and Nigeria and was founding editor (together with Richard Kearney, a former pupil) of the cultural journal The Crane Bag. *His books include* Kissing the Dark *(1999) and* Manikon Eros *(2000), both published by Veritas. I spoke with him in the Herbert Park Hotel. He was confident, reassuring and quietly strong, because he speaks about the things he knows about. He succeeded in giving me a flavour of the monastic life in Glenstal, where I am a frequent visitor. His mellifluous voice, with that of the other monks singing Gregorian chant, seared through me during my many sojourns there from Matins through to Vespers and Compline. His Benedictine brand of Catholicism is rooted in liturgy. His God is a God wreathed in incense and hymned in lovely Latin cadences. In true Benedictine spirit, he is a seeker after God. He interested and intrigued me and left me hungering for the really real.*

SJC: I remember Fr Celestine [*the then Abbot of Glenstal*] telling me, when I asked him what a monk was, that a monk was a man whose yearning for God could be satisfied only within a monastery. Is that how you see yourself as a monk?

MPH: I certainly agree that the primary interest in my life is finding out what's the relationship between God and the world we're living in, but I don't feel that's necessarily connected to being in a monastery. I am in the monastery because I was in school there and it's the exact kind of environment that suits me for relating to God. As far as I understand it, you could be a monk anywhere, but you need the discipline and I wouldn't be able to be a monk without a certain structure. I would be too distracted and too interested in other things — fanatically interested — in such a way that I wouldn't be able to give the time necessary to actual connection with God and working out what are these basic infrastructures that exist between God and the world we're living in.

SJC: It allows you a complete focus.

MPH: Yes. It's a very luxurious existence because I have from eight o'clock in the morning every day until twelve o'clock completely free. I don't have any complications of family or anything else except to do the work that I am supposed to do, which is to make these connections that other people don't have time to do because of family or whatever; these are enormous responsibilities. So you have that luxurious time which for me would be mostly connected to reading or writing.

SJC: How did your family and friends react when you broke it to them that you were going to become a monk?

MPH: I don't think anyone of them were very surprised. I think I was always a person who was distant from people and other people would have said I was interested in God even from a very early age. My father was very disappointed in the beginning. He thought it was a total waste of my life and his money in terms of the education he had supplied me with, but my mother was very anxious that I would do whatever I wanted to do. They were very liberally minded people, so they weren't going to prevent me. There would have been no problem coming out in a year or two if I wanted to do something else.

SJC: You were at Glenstal School, so presumably the choice to enter the Benedictines was largely due to that factor. You never wanted to enter any other order?

MPH: Not at all. I never thought of any other order. It was a total case of kidnapping from their point of view, in that I was told at the age of fourteen or fifteen by people I admired that the courts of heaven were waiting for me to put on a habit. One part of myself was very flattered; another part of me was afraid of that. I didn't want to do it. I remember saying I'd rather go to Lough Derg than the monastery. I found Lough Derg to be an awful, dreadful place. Everything I repudiate in Christianity I found there at that time. Nowadays, I would be more relaxed and I can see other aspects of it, but the whole thing was unbelievable to me then. The buildings were ugly, all cement, and the people's feet were ugly. When I went to Africa, people's feet were beautiful. But when you come in to Lough Derg on the boat, you get all these feet at eye level. It was an aesthetic and religious repugnance. This business of doing penance and crawling along on your bare feet as if God was some sort of monster who was placated by people's reduction of themselves, their abnegation. So I found all that to be inimical to my own connection to God and Glenstal Abbey is a most beautiful, natural, almost pagan place, so it suited me very well and I never imagine myself being anywhere else. I don't think I would have lasted in any other environment. It's a very tolerant place. There was one monk who died recently and his view was that there are 45 members of our community and 43 of these are certifiably insane and we're all trying to find out who the other two are! That's a humorous way of saying that this is a very interesting group of people who are very individualistic. There's no kind of uniform in terms of a personality chart or observance structure.

SJC: So what's a monastery for?

MPH: For me, a monastery is a connecting link, a powerhouse. The important thing is that there is somewhere that is actually, immediately connected with God, not through structure or second-hand connection but a real connection, and that means you are always looking for something original, in two senses of the word — for the origins of Christianity and also for what's new. It's like art. Artists are animals whose antennae pick up the storm before it arrives, what Heaney calls "the music of what happens". You're picking up that before other people so that there's a preparation made for it. We are free so that the destiny of the universe is in our hands, so we decide. Now that human beings are the dominant species on the planet, we decide the direction we are going to go in. If you believe in God, you believe there is also a prompting which can be recorded and can be suggested to people about what that direction should be. The purpose of the monastery is to be there, like the watchman waiting for the dawn. You are waiting and listening especially. It's like the secret service; you're listening for the instructions for the next part of the salvation plan.

SJC: Listening to the Spirit?

MPH: The Spirit is a difficult word. People imagine that listening to the Spirit means it's other than what's happening in the world. It's listening to the signs of the times. Spirit is manifested in people, in places. There are psychic histories of places. It's incarnate. It's what St Paul says: "The creation groaneth towards redemption."

SJC: How would you describe your relationship with God?

MPH: It is like connecting with a very refined and reticent aristocratic animal. It's very delicate. You don't force it and you don't talk too much and so it's like trying to connect with somebody who has none of the equipment that normal human beings have for connecting with each other. You don't have a voice or a hand or anything. Deep communication between people is also very inarticulate. It's a tactility of silence. That's something that would be very strong at certain points in life and very weak at others. You create a rhythm whereby you know you are in contact. It can be turned off or just go away if you don't cultivate and practise it, if you don't structure your life in such a way that there are places and times when this happens and it should happen on a daily basis if possible. That's what monasteries allow you to do. It's a privilege.

SJC: God is an absent presence.

MPH: Yes, but I think that's true of all relationships. The difficulty is that most people think they know what it means to communicate, to be in love with another human being. The most profound mystery and divergence are between other human beings as much as it is between God as another Person. Our capacities for deep relationships are very limited and I would say in my life that if I've had that connection between ten people, that would be enormous. We imagine we're relating. It's like a film I saw, *Happiness*, which is a marvellous revelation that we haven't a clue what happiness is. People talk about it all the time and imagine that relating to God is very difficult but comparatively easier with other people. Well, I find the difficulty is shared, that both connections are very difficult and very delicate and a lot of work has to go into it if you are going to maintain it or keep it alive for any length of time.

SJC: And is it difficult living in community, in an all-male preserve?

MPH: Not really. There are 45 people in our community and we are in silence for much of the time, so that there are some people with whom you never connect although you are aware of them. It's not being alone, you're not in solitude, but the connection you have with most of the community is very unspoken. It's not a difficult thing, for me anyway. I find it easy and good because it's not demanding. There are 350 acres where you can get away from people. It's not a concentration camp. Other people are very sensitive and they find the tiniest indiscretions and importunities jar on them, which I don't. I think they haven't been in a boarding school. I think a lot of people who have been only children find it difficult to be in community. For me, community is a help rather than a hindrance.

SJC: Why did you decide to remain a brother and not go on to become a priest?

MPH: Because I couldn't subscribe to everything the Roman Catholic Church demands of a priest. If you are going to become a priest, you have to take certain vows and have to follow the party line. For instance, if you are hearing confessions, you have to tell people who are coming to confession that this is what the Curia and the Pope of the present moment believe to be the way you should conduct your life and I couldn't in conscience assume that responsibility. I'm happy that the Second Vatican Council and Paul VI changed the phrase, which was that the whole truth is in the Catholic Church, and he changed that to "*subsists* in the Catholic Church" which is Thomistic terminology, but it means that if you dig deep enough or look around at the dung-heap sufficiently you will find the truth there. That just about allows me to hang on in there.

SJC: What about saying Mass?

MPH: That doesn't worry me one bit. I had a vocation to be a monk and I don't have a vocation to be a priest. That vocation (listening to the Spirit) can come at any time. God can say, "I don't want you to do this job, I want you to do that job." Many people have a vocation to the priesthood and to be monks but I didn't have that and don't have it. It could happen; it could be thrust upon you at any moment. In that situation, I have done all the studies and theology necessary to become a priest if it's required. It would have been normal that a man of my education and situation would have become a priest, but I made a conscious decision not to at the time of *Humanae Vitae* and I couldn't align myself so completely with what was the party line at that time. I am bound by the vows I have made, as the Psalm says, and the vows of the Benedictine brother are stability, obedience and *conversio morum* [a *"conversion of manners"*], which is a wonderful phrase — no-one has actually worked out what it means, which gives people a leeway. I would interpret it as meaning that I am bound to change in my life whatever is preventing me from being what God wants me to be and that doesn't mean I conform to the past or the present of the Roman Catholic Church and what they decide.

SJC: So you could say to yourself, "I can no longer live a celibate life"?

MPH: Yes, that could very easily mean that.

SJC: And still stay a monk?

MPH: Well, in my view, that is absolutely correct, but you would have to be very careful because it's a dangerous area. The prophet Amos was required by God to sleep with three prostitutes in order to show Israel his displeasure and the Virgin Mary was required to have a child. Now if any of the present Congregations of Sisters were required to perform the same service, it would be very difficult to persuade them or the general public that this was the Holy Spirit. It's a very difficult question here of discernment, especially in regard to sexuality. Our own self-will is so fraught with doing what we want to do and calling it something else, but in principle I would agree that every part of you is in the service of God and if, for whatever reason, it was required of you to do anything that God wants you to do, then it is correct.

SJC: Putting conscience before tradition and the teachings of the Magisterium.

MPH: Yes, but conscience is a strange word. What Nietzsche says is important, that it takes great courage to live your life according to conscience, but more courage to go against your own conscience. Sometimes you have this strange conviction from faith or belief that you are required to do something which even appals your self and goes against your own conscience. The obedience of a monk is not like Thomas Moore in *A Man for All Seasons*; that's the lawyer in him saying, "Just argue to the death."

SJC: Etymologically, obedience means "listening to".

MPH: That's right, but to whom are you listening? "Thus conscience doth make cowards of us all." We're all cowardly when we come into that region. Kierkegaard and Gerard Manley Hopkins are the great exponents of the terrific loneliness and expanse of that particular place where such decisions are made.

SJC: Yes. Kierkegaard talks of the "teleological suspension of the ethical" in the cause of a greater good.

MPH: Absolutely. That's very true, very well put.

SJC: Are there any times you wonder what on earth you're doing in the monastery? Have you ever felt like giving it all up? Is there any aspect of your life that does not appeal to you?

MPH: That would have been true in the past but not in the present. I made a vow when I was 19 that I would understand the world I was living in by the age of 40; I would then write that out for other people so they could share the journey and not have to do it themselves; and then I would enjoy the rest of my life, having understood it. Now I'm 56 and it didn't work out as quickly as I had imagined, but I'm writing out three or four books that contain my understanding of the world I was born into. If others find it wrong or odd, I would be delighted to enter into dialogue with anyone who has the time to read and engage, but I'm satisfied that I understand why I was born into the world at this particular moment and I am very happy about that.

SJC: St Benedict says that the monk is a man who is searching for God. You're still searching.

MPH: God is as enormous or more enormous than the universe. Every day we discover that the universe is a vaster mystery than anyone had previously imagined. I'm not fearful by temperament. In fact, I would be reckless. The more discovery I am given access to, the more I am intrigued, but it means more reading. It's a community of searchers because no one person understands it all — and that's what the Internet is about too, all that information at one's fingertips. You meet your brothers or your sisters in the search.

SJC: Couldn't all this information either deepen or dampen your faith?

MPH: Well, I don't think faith is in opposition to reason or knowledge. Faith isn't affected one bit. It's about the heart; about those things I have always loved since being a child of nine. It doesn't change anything for me. I've never had a crisis of faith. I've always known God since I was nine years of age and I don't remember before that. That has never been shaken or disturbed by anything I have found out. I have always felt that God was beyond or behind all that. It's more a case of being introduced to the marvels and mysteries that are not a problem for Him.

SJC: We have been talking about spirit for the last few minutes and I've just noticed that the tape has run out. Is that pure chance or meaningful, is it a synchronistic event?

MPH: I believe entirely in synchronicity. I've been keeping a diary since 1976 of the synchronicities that have happened to me. For me, coincidence is the way in which God is present in the universe anonymously. It's like the unconscious. Nobody knows if things come from God. As far as I'm concerned, a sense of humour is essential in all this. In terms of knowledge, we don't know, but there is another kind of conviction, which is the conviction that people who are aware of synchronicity just know. I know several people who have given up their work to follow that and whether it is true or not, it is the most creative force anyway. I am aware of all that kind of explanation that's given. It's like dancing; you just do it. It's a deed. Then I record it. It's very interesting to find the synchronicity of dates. For example, yesterday was the Feast of Ss Joachim and Anne, which was an important day and date for me, so I sometimes go back five years ago to see what happened on that date. It's amazing how another weave comes into the chronology but other people, including members of my own community, would be vastly amused or highly irritated by that and say, "This is just your old nonsense." I mean there's some truth in *The Celestine Prophecy*. All of those things have a certain kind of truth and as a monk I am committed to finding out about those truths. Other ones are being looked after anyway.

SJC: You sound like a Gnostic!

MPH: John, of John's Gospel, was a Gnostic, as was St Paul. There's a hidden strand of Gnosticism within Christianity.

SJC: And explicitly with the 1946 find of the Gnostic Gospels in Nag Hamadi. Would you put any store by them?

MPH: Not particularly. They haven't interested me. When I say St Paul was a Gnostic, I'm talking about the hidden wisdom of God that was there since the beginning of time that was revealed. It's a secret hidden knowledge that isn't provided in creedal formulae or intellectual discourse. It's liturgical. If all the truths John knew were written down, all the books in the world couldn't contain them. His are beautiful formulae and those formulae in his Gospel are proof to me that the Gospel of John was written with the Holy Spirit, when you compare it to anything that was written within 200 years of it. In terms of style, content and genius, there's nothing that compares at all.

SJC: Prayer has been described, by Plotinus, as the "flight of the alone to the Alone". How do you pray?

MPH: Certainly, it's not a flight. It's a very rooted thing. It's in the centre of my whole being. It's a connection, which means that there is certain warmth and power and attention, a one-pointedness, and I found that my role in prayer is to become one-pointed directed and that's something you do by disciplines of various kinds. It's similar to riding a horse in that you've got to get to the centre of gravity of the horse, especially if you're jumping a fence. That's what I have to do, to get over the centre of gravity of myself so that I can move upwards, but not as flight in the sense of leaving my body behind or of taking off into orbit but of curving my attention towards a particular point. Then that point responds and that's a very sensuous and moving experience and then that subsides and retires and then you recreate it or leave it. That's what I mean by prayer. In the monastery, we sing in Latin at Vespers, so prayer for us is liturgical. It's wonderful. It's like a river, being in some kind of movement. Singing and breathing are very important. It's breath and earth. It's not about mind.

SJC: You're quietening the mind.

MPH: Exactly. I'm interested that James Joyce, when writing *Finnegan's Wake*, drank a particular white wine to the point of intoxication without losing consciousness, so he was releasing another language and quietening or anaesthetising the daily, routine language, both of his mind and of his English or French language and then another system came into play that Jung called a "sympathetic system". This produced *Finnegan's Wake* and it's similar to singing in Latin, which you almost know by heart. You're not asking what it means. It keeps you going in the direction of the point and the Person you are trying to connect to.

SJC: Lacan said that, in the Latin Mass, people comprehended that it was the incomprehensible that was important.

MPH: Very good. That's good.

SJC: And what is the difference between prayer, contemplation and meditation?

MPH: People say there's a difference and I'm sure there is. People describe three degrees, like a rocket taking off. There's the launch pad and then there's these things that fall away as you get higher, then the arrival. There's the purgative path, the illuminative stage and then the unitive. But these categories are very off-putting to people, because they feel you are talking about things they'll never experience. It's like everything else. There's a foreplay to any kind of real connection with somebody and then there's a way in which you have to forget about yourself. Most people, in connecting with another person, are thinking about themselves, which is detrimental to the actual connection. You have to purge that. T.S. Eliot has some wonderful descriptions of this. The chair disappears and you don't notice the room in which you're in. Suddenly space and time disappear and when a third person comes into the room and disturbs you, you land again on the floor. This notion that you have to play films in your head and go back to where Jesus was . . .

SJC: Jesuitical spirituality.

MPH: Not just Jesuitical. It goes back to a whole time in philosophy, with epistemology, with the mind and how it works and how you quieten it and that helps some people. But then there are all kinds of techniques for meditation in other religions, in the Buddhist and Hindu traditions, which are wonderfully practised and they help one to arrive at the place, but nobody can tell you what to do when you arrive at the place because there you are person to Person. It's never happened before. There has never been this combination, ever. Nobody can tell you how to relate to another and if they can, it's a bum relation. You have these books telling you how to confront people, how to relate to people, how to discipline people, and they are all full of these details which actually mean nothing in the end. The real thing is prime energy to prime energy and when you reach that point in yourself, nobody else can tell you how to relate but you know that you're in relationship when it happens because it's like a fusion, like an explosion.

SJC: It's an act of *décreation*, of "unselfing", as Simone Weil says. And Iris Murdoch says that it's being in touch with a source that is Good.

MPH: It's funny you should say that because I have read Iris Murdoch. She's one of the great sources for me for understanding my own life and when she got Alzheimer's, I went to see her specifically to relate to her, because people say that once you have Alzheimer's you are a lump of meat. They have these awful phrases. They were telling John Bayley [*her husband*] that he was chained to a corpse. I went to them and he recorded our meeting in his book. He points out, as I recognise too, that there was a connection between Iris Murdoch and me that was started by her kissing me but there was no connection in terms of talking, because she couldn't articulate. I'm sure she lived most of her life in a monastery. She was actually a monk. And she was working stuff out in her novels and the last one, *Jackson's Dilemma*, was written with incipient Alzheimer's. There is a breath, as Rilke says, which is more than her breath, encaptured in that work. It's not a denial of being. You are not renouncing or annihilating your self. You are defusing everything in you that prevents you from the generosity and the ecstasy that allows you to go and be with another person in a fusion and a flight from the enchanter. It's the discipline of achieved spontaneity that astronauts, acrobats and athletes do. It's outside the domain of normal necessity.

SJC: Are you convinced by Aquinas's five arguments for the existence of God?

MPH: I absolutely never was. I think Aquinas was the greatest mind of the Middle Ages. There are other wonderful minds like Plato. But I think the problem there was that they were trying to make of this a science. It's like transubstantiation, which is a name given to trying to understand how Jesus Christ became flesh and blood. You are making a science of it. There is no proof for the existence of God in that way. If there were, we wouldn't be free. There was another tradition, that of Dun Scotus and St Bonaventure, who was a contemporary of Aquinas. It's like Plato and Aristotle. There have always been those two traditions in philosophy. One has a penchant for relying entirely on the human mind to explain everything, though Aquinas wasn't like that himself. He was a mystic. He was doing this as a teaching exercise for other people and he was condemned three times by the Church.

SJC: He denied the Immaculate Conception.

MPH: The question is why he did, why it is promoted or denounced. In one sense, it is a blasphemy because what you are actually saying is that the human race created by God is so disfigured and had become so evil that it was essential to have a preacher born without any reference to that mess that pertained. If you take an evolutionary view, then you have a different view of the Immaculate Conception. You say everything was an Immaculate Conception. So it depends on what you mean. Those words, the Immaculate Conception, must be the ugliest words ever constructed. They would turn everyone off. It's difficult to know what they mean because it's Latin language that has lost all relation to the real. It becomes a hieroglyphic. The Immaculate Conception is the most unpoetical linkage of syllables that has ever been perpetrated by the human tongue. You have to know what hides and lurks behind those syllables before you can make a pronouncement. These things become banners and slogans whereby we're all burnt at the stake, because we ask do you or do you not believe in the Immaculate Conception and everyone goes to war.

SJC: You studied philosophy both at UCD and in Paris with Levinas, gaining a Master's degree with a thesis on "The Philosophical Integrity of Emmanuel Levinas" and a doctorate on "The Phenomenology of Education" from the NUI. Who has been the most enduring influence on your philosophical and theological thinking?

MPH: Levinas was a very great introducer to two traditions, the Jewish and the Greek. Caputo brought together Aquinas and Meister Eckhart but I would say, without any doubt, that the greatest influences on me have been neither philosophers nor theologians. Number One is Shakespeare. I'm very glad to have been an English speaker by birth and I care nothing for nationality or for loss of integrity, but to be born with the language that Shakespeare spoke . . .! I have never heard an idea or phrase in my life that was not already in Shakespeare.

SJC: Levinas said that all philosophy was contemplation on the plays of Shakespeare and Freud said something similar in relation to psychoanalysis. You have it all, pathological jealousy and murder in *Othello*, psychosis in *King Lear*.

MPH: Yes. He's winning the Oscar awards every year. Recently, you had *Shakespeare in Love* and *Romeo and Juliet*. Rainer Maria Rilke would be another huge influence. Of the philosophers, it would be Heidegger. He's the greatest thinker that I have encountered in the last century and I find it very difficult to hear about the fact that he was a Nazi. I think it's very sad and to do with his human weakness. That doesn't take from the fact that he was one of the people who pushed back the frontiers of metaphysics in a way that hasn't been done before or since. It's wrong not to study him. Levinas, who was a Jew, said he read Heidegger and after reading him he washed his hands. Then he said, "I find myself washing my hands quite regularly." He was with Heidegger and Husserl when Husserl was removed from his professorial Chair. It was part of Heidegger's background and his meanness because of the very restricted and difficult upbringing he had.

SJC: And Hannah Arendt, a Jewess, also supported him.

MPH: Yes, although she was very disappointed. But love is stronger than death and they were lovers. There was a stronger connection between him and her than any ideological possibility.

SJC: So what theologian has influenced you?

MPH: Nobody. I'm not particularly interested in theology. I did theology for my studies but it doesn't relate to anything I feel myself about God. I just find it boring. They tell me the greatest theologian in Catholic circles was Hans Urs Van Balthasar. My great theology has been in Hopkins, in Yeats, in Geoffrey Hill and especially in Seamus Heaney. I get much more theology reading him than these endless books that explain everything. Iris Murdoch is Number One on my list for being a great Spiritual Director for me throughout my life. She wrote novels instead of philosophy because she believed that was the way. Her first novel, *Under the Net*, says it all. The net was a metaphor for catching in categories the fish that was the human reality or truth and she believed that the net was too gross, so that the novel was the only net for catching unrepeatable uniqueness and individuality. That was her great insight. Philosophy can't do that. It is a generalisation that may talk all it likes about particularity but it never dirties its fingers and finds out what these individuals are actually like and her novels were, for me, great philosophy rather than "mere novels", as some philosophers would say about them.

SJC: What branch of philosophy did you teach in Boston and Nigeria and what is your own area of philosophy?

MPH: It would be contemporary philosophy, mostly to do with Levinas and Heidegger and phenomenology and especially Martin Buber at times, but I also teach theology and literature, but nowadays I find I'm just writing myself, which is much more interesting.

SJC: You have lectured, as you say, on literature and written on Seamus Heaney, whom you much admire. What is the function of literature? What is its relationship to society, to morals, to spirituality?

MPH: I think literature is a vast area that can be for entertainment, propaganda or prophecy. It can also be exploration. Literature can rejoin what the monk is trying to do as a particular force. An example is Heaney and a poem in his book, *Seeing Things*: this spaceship is going above Clonmacnoise and the anchor gets caught in the altar and a man has to come down to release it and the Abbot of the monastery says that unless we help this man he will drown here and he goes back up and recognises the marvels such as we had not known them. So I believe Heaney is making that connection between the altar, which is his main image of the forge in *Door into the Dark*; in the forge, the anvil is an altar on which real music and poetry can be beaten out. I believe he is forging in the sense of Joyce and the forge is a place you beat out base metal that is also a "forgery". That is the kind of subtle language that allows you to say, as Joyce says, "two thinks at a time". Heaney is doing it in *The Spirit Level*. All his books are monastic meditations of a monk who is trying to make the connection and there is an ethics to that art which is not saying more or saying less than is required by the actual structures. *Beowulf* is a most amazing restatement of one of the first pieces of English literature in terms of today. I keep shaking Heaney, but it's like having a piggy bank with no money in it. He won't be shook. I keep writing to him saying, "do this, do more". Then another poem comes out.

It's like the Riddle of the Sphinx. If he were to write it out as prose, he would actually be betraying himself. He has been lucky to be allowed to do only his work because he could have had to betray himself in terms of economics or politics, which he hasn't done yet. He hasn't become a perpetrator of drivel for either entertainment purposes or propaganda purposes. I think Geoffrey Hill is a great poet of the English language and Brendan Kennelly has done wonderful service by doing the opposite. He's wonderfully oracular and generous. One tradition is like Louis le Brocquy in art that watches everything; the other is more like Patrick Kavanagh and Dylan Thomas, that flows out. Each person does what he has to do. Jane Austen said she had one tiny piece of enamel to work on. You do the job you have to do. Heaney, as far as I'm concerned, has been one of the great monks in the tradition of the scribes of the *Book of Kells*. It's a Gnostic tradition and it's his work. He's meant to do it.

SJC: For many years you co-edited, with your former pupil Richard Kearney, the cultural journal called *The Crane Bag*. What was that period in your life like? Considering you are a monk and have been one for more than thirty years, you have enjoyed a certain exclaustral existence!

MPH: Yes, absolutely. It was a wonderful experience. What we had thought at that time was what we were saying earlier, that we could get all those people who were supposed to know what truth was together and that, by making a virtual community of experts in their own fields, we would be able to provide the answer, especially in relation to the North of Ireland. We would be able to have a discourse that would defeat all those atavistic forces that were preventing people from overcoming their selfishness and ignorance and to achieve a certain urbanity. Well, it certainly didn't work out like that. It was very interesting, though, while it happened. It never became what we hoped it would become, which was a dialogue. It became very arcane. *The Crane Bag* was put into the category of the Dodo. It was wonderful to have it, but nobody was reading it. It was very hard work going from shop to shop. The most they wanted were five copies. We only used to sell 2,000 copies a go. It was tedious. It became difficult to continue that especially for Richard [*Kearney*] who had his family and his job.

SJC: If you hadn't become a monk, what would you have done instead?

MPH: I wanted to be an actor when I was 20 and I'm glad I didn't pursue that.

SJC: In your book, *Kissing the Dark*, you state: "Our culture has been built on a lie and Christianity has helped to promote and sustain that lie. And the lie is this: that it is possible to work out in our heads a logical system which will give us access to ultimate truth, to being. The name of such a system is philosophy and the particular branch of that 'science' that deals with 'being' and places us within our intellectual grasp is 'metaphysics'. . . . Throughout this century, the artists of the world have been trying to tell us that metaphysics is less like mathematics and more like music. Being is not business. Reality is something we touch rather than something we grasp. Song is existence, it wells up through us from the depths" (pp. 149–50). Strong words.

MPH: Yes but they're saying exactly what we have been saying about Iris Murdoch, about Rilke and Heaney, which is: "If you want to play chess, then do."

SJC: But there's another game going on in town.

MPH: Yes. It's under the net. It's naked combat at a different place. People used to say that you could set your watch by Kant. How could someone like Kant attempt to explain the details of dirty life as it is lived by most people, although we are grateful to him for having produced the prolegomena to all future metaphysics. That's what Martin Buber read when he was 15 and it changed his life. These people are like architects. They provide you with the ground plan necessary. But for day-to-day living and for what it means to be a human being, they are not the best guides. The important thing is saying it as it is, which is done in music or in poetry.

SJC: Plato gave us the Form of the Good but not the form of dirt or blood.

MPH: Yes, exactly. Exactly.

SJC: You have argued for a "theology of presence rather than of power, of paternity rather than of causality, of interpenetration in love rather than of eternal separation into created and uncreated being. Such a perspective translates itself into a theology of beauty in nature, of music in thought, of poetry in word, of liturgy in worship" (p. 138). This, I presume, sums up your own theological position and approach. It sounds very Benedictine!

MPH: Yes it is. It's very Benedictine because the Rule of St Benedict, which was written in 488, carried Christianity through the dark ages because it wasn't a philosophy. It was a day-by-day prescription, like a lattice that allows a framework and structure. It tells you what time to get up in the morning, what to do for meals, how much wine to drink, what to do when you're going to bed. It gives you these practical details about how a community should live and during the time when nobody had the leisure or privilege of being able to read, it carried that message through. It was a doing rather than understanding. And the liturgy is important as well. I agree with the quote of myself you have just read out. I believe in it. The most important part of that is to do with nature. That's what Hopkins has brought from Dun Scotus; in other words, there is a presence of God in the world, that you can find the presence of God in bluebells and dragonflies and "kingfishers catch fire".

SJC: Is it like Mathew Fox's "creation-centred spirituality"?

MPH: Yes, it is a creation-centred spirituality but, at the same time, what it means is that God is in that creation. You're not saying that this is pantheism. It's very Celtic. People have been very cruel and I would say very jealous of John O'Donoghue's books, saying there's no such thing as Celtic spirituality, that it's all poetry. Whether it is or it isn't, it corresponds to a chord in the hearts of millions of people and he has touched a reality. Irish people know that God is as near to them as this door. It's definitely in the flowers, trees and everything. It's the tradition of St Francis and Bonaventure and Dun Scotus as opposed to Thomas Aquinas. Poetry is what makes it visible. The Psalm says: "And no one saw your footprints, O Lord." You can create a poem where the phosphorescence of divinity is made apparent without giving a proof or lecture. Kavanagh says: "Through a chink too wide there comes in no wonder."

SJC: The spirit can be seen in everyday sensuous reality.

MPH: Oh absolutely, and especially in sexuality. God made us in the image of Himself, male and female. It's in the small details of ordinary human life. It doesn't mean it has to be ghastly either. It's also in the miracle and the mystery.

SJC: There is a distinction between soul and spirit. How do you understand these two terms?

MPH: Spirit has to do with the Holy Spirit and soul could be the unconscious, the Celtic unconscious. My book, *Kissing the Dark*, was meant to be an attempt by an Irish Catholic to get in touch with the unconscious that is different for an Irish Protestant or an American Indian. Spirit is something that you create, something new, that is energy. Soul is baggage; it's what you came with, and what your ancestry has hoarded, like the three nets Joyce wanted to escape — family, the church and country. Spirit is Shakespeare's Ariel and Caliban is flesh, "this thing of darkness". Shakespeare personifies these categories and also places. In *Othello*, Venice is structured and Cyprus is wild and dark. Soul and spirit is like discussing two different kinds of drink. It's two aspects of exactly the same reality, from a different point of view.

SJC: What is the relation between sexuality and spirituality? One monk friend of mine in Glenstal told me that I had to find God in the bedroom.

MPH: You've got to find God everywhere, but in another sense what Bonhoeffer said is also true, that when you think about God when you're kissing your wife, that's just bad taste. So, it's not quite as easy as saying everything's in everything. God is everywhere, that is true, but then we can bless things that are wrong by invoking that Presence. When you say that you can find God in the bedroom, that's fine and true, but if you're Othello, that doesn't condone the murder of Desdemona in the bedroom or any of the vile acts that can be perpetrated by terrified human beings when they are naked with each other, so it is a delicate thing to say how and where God is present in the bedroom. It's a very dramatic statement.

SJC: Some critics of the monastic life might say, "Get out there in the world and help the sick and do some work"; or, "Mirror your life on Christ who engaged in an active apostolate." What is your response to that? Do you have any sympathy with that position?

MPH: Yes, of course I do. I think there are different roles that have to be fulfilled and what Martin Buber says is very true, that when everybody on this planet is fed and clothed and has adequate sustenance in a welfare state, that it is only then that the real problems of humanity will emerge and I agree that there is emergency work that has to be done everywhere. But unless there is somebody working out whether or not there is a reality on the top of the mountain and what is the meaning of being alive when all the other things have been met (like Maslow's pyramid), then what next? Plato said, there are the philosophers, there are the soldiers; there are different roads and roles. Some people say there should be free education, that it is a right, but for me education is like love, not food. You can't give it in units to everyone in equal proportion. Education means whatever is necessary for each individual person to reach the age of twenty-one or whatever and be satisfied that they have developed sufficiently, and that is luck in most cases. So monks are a very definite species and they have got their particular job to do. I often think of the yucca moth. It has one job to do at midnight on one particular day of the year: it has to fly to the yucca plant and has to fertilise it. It has no other role and if it doesn't do that, the whole ecological balance on the planet is awry. So some people have big, flamboyant, important jobs to do and other people have tiny, hidden works, but if they don't do them something goes wrong with the whole machinery. Monks are required to concentrate on the space between this world and the other world and that's their job. They are part of the tapestry. And they can do other things as well, but if they fail to make that connection, then there's something missing.

SJC: It's to try to tolerate the tension between the desert and the market place. Basil Hume said that in every Benedictine monk there should be a yearning Carthusian, just as in every Sacred Heart nun there should be a disappointed Carmelite.

MPH: Yes. I think that's true for every human being. Everybody, at some times in his or her life, wants to be alone. It's a difference between being alone and having a vocation to be a monk, because loneliness or being alone is a luxury if it's exhaustion from having too much activity, but most people find that a holiday is the opposite of what you do normally. There is a great difference between yearning for solitude if you're running a war or if you are the Prime Minister of Great Britain, but to do that all your life, the yearning can be in the other direction. I was twenty-five years in the monastery and then I was catapulted into Boston University for a year that was like one 365-day cocktail party. It was an entertainment and enjoyment that no one else on the planet could imagine because they hadn't spent the previous twenty-five years in a monastery, but I wouldn't have done it for more than a year because it was just like champagne; you can't live on that. It depends on the balance in your life. This is what Basil Hume is saying, that in each of us there is the yin and the yang. Every mother of five children would yearn to be a Carmelite nun at least a few times a day.

SJC: The subtitle of your book *Kissing the Dark* is "Connecting with the Unconscious". What is your view of psychoanalysis, of the work of Freud, Jung and Lacan? Have you ever undergone an analysis? Would you?

MPH: Freud, Jung and Lacan are absolutely dedicated to the work of salvation. Lacan's brother was a Benedictine. I'm interested in what the Norwegian Nobel-prize-winning dramatist says, that they were all getting connections to the unconscious through people who were ill, that in Africa, there is a connection to the unconscious through ritual that is a more hygienic way of connecting to ourselves. In a certain way, this was projecting onto the world a view of the unconscious that is essentially neurotic. Eugene O'Neill, Brian Friel and Tom Murphy are our national psychotherapists. They represent Celtic soul. Drama is a purge, of a kind. So for me, art is an equivalent to psychotherapy. Iris Murdoch has been my psychotherapist. Most people only use medicine when they can't go on without it. I have found my life to be full and free and haven't found it necessary. I am very disinclined to read anything or do anything unless it is going to be relevant in the search that is mine.

SJC: You reject natural law (see page 85 of *Kissing the Dark*), are in favour of women becoming priests, pro-divorce, against abortion and compulsory celibacy and in relation to homosexuals you have written: "When we hear of the increase in the homosexual population and the decrease both in the desire for and the number of children in the average family in Europe, we should be rejoicing in nature's capacity to adapt and its versatility in face of restricting circumstances, rather than reiterating anachronistic maxims and condemning variations on the stereotyped profiles of men and women, marriages and partnerships" (page 58). What, then, is your relationship to the teachings of the Magisterium, to conservative Catholicism? You're obviously a liberal Catholic, disagreeing with many of the dogmas and doctrines of the Papacy.

MPH: Of course I disagree with the Pope's view, if he expressed it, that homosexuals are unnatural and evil. If he said that, he's off his head. I think the Church has always distinguished between the person and the act. I do not believe in homosexual marriages. We are in the thrall of marriage as a paradigm that was half perpetrated by the necessity of the species becoming dominant. In order to survive, we needed to promote marriage. I've written a book called *Manikon Eros (Mad Love)* dealing with all this. What I am saying is that there is a great distinction to be made between transferring all that we have learned about marriage and children and partnership to the homosexual situation. You can't demand the right to be married to whomever you want to be married to and to have children. I don't think that follows at all. I object to categorising any form of relationship, homosexual or heterosexual, through the categorisations of philosophy. The real fact is that every time two people meet, no matter whom they are (and the French are great at this), it's a different thing and requires a new category and a new journey for those two people to work out "What do you mean to me and what do I mean to you and how do we best structure that relationship and make it survive". The number of people I know who are so glad they didn't get married! The major problem for people today is that people are condemned to being together for fifty years. Up to very recently, the life span of many people was over after their silver wedding. Now people have to work out how do we live together for, sometimes, sixty years, and that's become a huge problem. I wouldn't pronounce on divorce at all.

SJC: Christ did. He seemed pretty emphatic.

MPH: I have no idea what Christ actually said or did. Joyce was very clear on that. Christ died at the age of thirty-three and as far as he was concerned he avoided most of the problems that come later. It's not for me to say to people you can do this or you can't do that. I believe entirely in the duty of primary relationship, like in the case of my own parents. If you do remain faithful to a relationship with one other person you commit yourself to, then that is a very wonderful and beautiful thing, but I am certainly aware that there are situations where people cannot do that, situations in which they are destroying themselves.

SJC: But you have to decide in order to vote on these matters.

MPH: That's exactly the point. You don't have to vote. That's exactly the reason why I didn't become a priest, for example. The jury is out on so many of those issues. I don't believe there is a single person on the planet today that understands the meaning of sexuality and I've read lots of people and it's all pretty banal and based on presuppositions. None of them is convincing and once you're trained in a certain kind of philosophy, you can judge an argument. What we're all doing is trying to work out the path. The person I find most convincing is Rilke. He's saying the vow that everyone should take on going into a relationship is to protect the other person's solitude. It's not about possession.

SJC: Lacan says love is lack and that in love we give what we don't have to someone who doesn't want it.

MPH: Yes. I find Lacan very incisive but much more pessimistic that I would be. I do believe in love, in the power and the pitfalls of love.

SJC: I'm thinking of Freud's critique of the Christic love commandment. Is Christianity psychologically possible?

MPH: Oh yes. It certainly is possible and wonderful. What it means is living as a resurrected being. It's a new form of life. It's a new energy. The Asiatics have known this for a long time, releasing all the chakras. It's a way of life which allows you to rise from the dead and that's what Christianity is about. Loving your enemy is only a way of saying loving God. "Homo", as in homosexuality, means "same" and "hetero" means "other". Christianity means that you love something other than yourself. When they say, "Love your enemies", what they're saying is that you don't have any enemies. If you and I, as white persons, went into areas where they had never seen a white person, they would scream, thinking you were a monster and the mothers would collect them up and make them touch your face, so I was very relieved that such xenophobia is by birth. It's the same with Northern Ireland. If anybody bothers to meet a Protestant, they say, "They're so nice." It's pathetic what you have to do to realise that what you think is your enemy is not your enemy at all but your own projections. What I do find difficult for people to understand is that Christ came on earth to provide another kind of energy. Energy means the way you move. It includes sexuality and well-being. It's to do with the way you live. Nietzsche said that in order for me to believe in your redeemer, you would have to look that little bit more redeemed. Christianity should mean that people are alive and that they look alive. Attraction is the sexual energy of the body distributed in the right proportions, in the way you move and speak and are and that your life is a life of love. That's easier for some people who have health and a certain amount of well-being, and that's partly to do with having a vertical rather than horizontal energy. It's the kundalini energy that all great religions talk about. And that makes you less grasping; you don't have to be a vampire to exist.

SJC: So it's not, then, being Christologically centred but, rather, relating to the vertical dimension of reality, becoming your self rather than acting like Christ?

MPH: Christ is nothing. Christ came to disappear. He emptied Himself and ascended into heaven. He left us on our own so we could find the Spirit, the source in ourselves. An imitation of Christ is one of the most ambiguous statements that has ever been made because, as Kierkegaard said, "When I get to heaven, I won't be asked why I wasn't more like Christ but why I wasn't more like myself." How do you rise from the dead? Pasternak said that we rose from the dead the minute we were born but that we don't realise it. Most of us are crippled and proud of our crutches and don't want to be alive; it's just too much responsibility. We want an addiction.

SJC: What is resurrected life? What's the difference between the Resurrection and the Ascension?

MPH: The Scriptural account is a story, the Resurrection stories. John doesn't have an account of the Ascension; he has the crucifixion and the Resurrection. Christ rose from the dead and He did it in a way we don't understand. There was no witness to the Resurrection. It wasn't a historical event. There was the tomb and then a few days later some people had an experience of His re-appearance. Sometimes they recognised Him, sometimes they didn't, sometimes He was eating, and sometimes He was walking through doors. The scripture stories are purely attempts by artists to describe an experience. St Paul wasn't there at all. He never knew what the original human being looked like. I always say that's because he was so unbearable, Christ didn't want to be on earth with him. Bertrand Russell said that St Paul did to Christianity what Lenin did to Communism. The Resurrection is meant to be an experience anyone can have. As Kierkegaard said, it's not about days. Once you rise from the dead, you're talking about algebra; you're into eternity. Ascension happens immediately after Christ dies. He goes immediately to the Father. The Trinity are One. The Resurrection and the Ascension are one.

SJC: What happens when we die; what happens in our post-mortem existence? In terms of eschatology, is there purgatory; is there a hell?

MPH: It depends on what you mean by purgatory. There is a purgative stage in prayer, as we said earlier. We are fully paid-up members of the Blessed Trinity. That's what we have become since Christ came on earth. As soon as we can or want to, we become part of the Trinity. That's what happens. Obviously, we may not be able for that. It's like any relationship, any form of love. If you think you're inadequate or can't love or the other person can't love you, there is nothing they can do. Until we know we are equal to God, we cannot have a relationship with Him that is the one that is required.

SJC: So is hell refusing to enter into the Trinity?

MPH: Yes. Hell is being our own "sweating selves", as Hopkins puts it. Hell is the decision to be alone. There's no question of being in hell outside this planet. There are many people who are in hell already. It means being irreversibly encased in your own isolation, in your own incarceration.

SJC: So what's heaven? Do you ever try to picture what it's like?

MPH: I never picture it. I don't care about it. I'm enjoying it at this moment and I trust completely that God, who is my lover, will look after me when I die. I'm convinced of that. I know that, as his lover, He will be anxious to have me with Him for eternity. What that means in terms of whether we are on a bed together or whether we have drinks, I don't know. I have no idea and I have no interest in that at all. I'm enjoying the present moment of existence and finding it very satisfying and when I die, that's up to Him then.

SJC: Some people are really afraid, though.

MPH: Fear is the great enemy of all love. In the Epistles of St John, the opposite of love isn't hate but fear. And the great enemy of Christianity and all religions is fear. Many religions and cults today are based on that fear. Much of Christianity was based on fear. Dostoyevsky, in *The Grand Inquisitor*, said that the Church took over Christianity and made it into a religion of fear because people were much happier with that. That is the antithesis to Christianity, which is about freedom. "That they may be free; that they may have life and more abundantly; that they might love." God is love.

SJC: Do you believe in reincarnation, in transmigration, in the pre-existence of the soul?

MPH: Well, I don't know about that. I don't feel it myself. Our minds are so limited that we do not know the answers to these questions. But I do believe myself that it's to do with personality. Who you are is what relates to God and that's going to be with Him forever. Now whether it entails different historical incarnations I don't believe myself.

SJC: What have you learnt about yourself and God after having spent so long in a monastery and presumably praying?

MPH: The complete conviction that God is love and is my lover. What more can you ask for?

SJC: Finally, are you happy?

MPH: Yes, if you get me at the right moment!

Richard Kearney
Philosopher

Photo: © RTE

Professor Richard Kearney is Ireland's most renowned philosopher. A prodigious writer of philosophy, politics, novels and poetry, he is an engaged intellectual, personally involved and socially committed. His consummate conviction and youthful energy is infectious. Terry Eagleton wrote in a review of one of Richard Kearney's books that he is "equally at home with Gadamer and Lady Gregory, Deirdre and Derrida; and his strength as a critic consists in bringing these twin currents, home-grown Irish and avant-garde European, into illuminating interaction". Richard Kearney's career has been a perpetual search for philosophical pluralism; his themes have been about dualities of tradition, and re-evaluations of received dogma. He lectured me in University College Dublin, before he became my supervisor when I was doing a doctoral dissertation there. He is a friend and mentor. I spoke with him in his office in the philosophy department of UCD where, as usual, there were countless calls on his attention but, though he was busy, as always, he gave generously of his time in a number of meetings with me. It was a pleasure and a privilege to talk with him again and catch up on all the news. When I left his office I felt energised and enthused, as I had done years before when I was his student, though I couldn't help but miss those days.

SJC: What does philosophy mean to you?

RK: Primarily philosophy to me means a questioning rather than an answering. It means inviting students to think for themselves and to question, rather than providing them with solutions. It is not ideology, it is not theology; it is a way of getting students to inquire in a socially committed and personally involved fashion. It is exposing them to a variety of different currents of thought.

SJC: What attracted you to philosophy in the first place? Did you ever want to do anything else, such as medicine, like other members of your family?

RK: No, I never wanted to do medicine because I had a terrible fear of blood and was very squeamish when it came to human pain, inflicted or endured. So I wasn't a good potential doctor or, indeed, sportsman, except sport that did not involve painful physical contact. As a player on the rugby team in Glenstal, I was scrum half, but that consisted of avoiding forwards rushing in at you and getting the ball out to someone else who would get crushed instead of you. Medicine and pain were something I couldn't deal with very well although my brothers and father and uncles and grandfather were all involved in that profession. I would like to think philosophy is another kind of healing, which involves the psyche. Medicine, of course, involves the body and the soul, as my brother Michael has been pointing out in his books on healing and curing. And my brother Timothy has edited a book called *The Prophetic Cry* along similar lines.

But I have always thought of philosophy as a therapy of the soul, beginning with the Greeks. Socrates saw it as that, as you know yourself, as a philosopher — the whole idea of midwifery. My uncles were obstetricians and gynaecologists. In a way, philosophy is another kind of midwifery but this time of questions and answers — allowing the birth of answers by putting questions to somebody. It's a kind of psychic obstetrics. So, maybe medicine and philosophy aren't completely disconnected. Certainly, my family's approach to medicine always involved the person as much as the anatomy. My grandfather, for example, who was a Professor of Medicine in Cork and a doctor, always shook people's hands. They thought he was French initially! There was a recognition that medicine involved the mind as well as the body. But in philosophy, there is also a recognition that the mind involves the body, even though we are focusing on the mind — it's a therapy of the mind, as Wittgenstein put it. Philosophy is a form of therapy and asking questions and discovering which questions can be answered appropriately and which can't. At times, when you reach the mystical, as Wittgenstein says, which is God or Beauty or the Sublime, there is no answer and you have to accept the limits of what knowledge can do. Some questions don't have answers, but it's important to keep questioning. Sometimes there is no definitive answer and if you try to find one and say, "This is the only God, or this is the only government, or this is the only definition of the Good", what you end up with is tyranny or totalitarianism or dogmatism or ideology of the most constraining type.

So what attracted me to philosophy? It was the possibility of finding healing and maybe in time helping to give healing through the profession of philosophy by helping people to ask questions about their lives and to try to answer them and if there are no answers, you go the way of faith or acceptance or letting go or endurance or patience or abandonment. So that was one reason. At a more biographical level, it was through French literature in Glenstal. I had Mark Patrick Hederman as a teacher and Andrew Nugent, both of whom had done doctorates in France and had come back to the monastery. It was through reading Sartre and Camus and Bergson to prepare for French A-levels (as was taught then — we also did the Leaving) that I became particularly hooked on philosophy. The Christian doctrine that was taught there was very enlightened. Andrew Nugent used to come in with the philosophers arguments about why God doesn't exist; so we would have Marx's refutation of religion, Feuerbach's, Nietzsche's, Sartre's and so on and if we survived all the arguments against the existence of God, then maybe our faith was authentic. That was the challenge and it got us thinking and I became very interested in the philosophy of religion, for that reason, being faced with the question of atheism. It was a very brave thing for a Benedictine monk to do — giving us all the reasons for not believing in God and then he put it to us: "You give me a good reason for *believing* in God"!

So it was really through the philosophy of literature and through the philosophy of religion that I came to philosophy and I would say that I am still probably primarily interested in those two areas of philosophy. My most recent book is called *The God who May Be* and that is the philosophy of religion, with readings of *Exodus* 3:15 and the *Song of Songs* and the whole question of desire, but taking it from the perspective of philosophy — Plato and Hegel, Heidegger and Levinas and Ricoeur. And as you know, my work for the past twenty years has largely been in the philosophy of imagination — narrative and myth and symbolism, so that's all the literary influence. I'm on the borderlines of philosophy and that's where I like to be. I wouldn't consider myself a pure philosopher — I'm an impure philosopher! But I believe in the interdisciplinary challenge of putting philosophical queries to literature, to imagination, to desire, to the question of the unconscious (as you know I'm interested in psychoanalysis — Lacan and Freud, in particular), to religion and that interests me more than just the pure problems of epistemology, which I always found a little boring, I have to say. For example, questions like, how can we know, what can we know, etc. Kant formulated four questions: "What can I know?" (the epistemological question); "What can I hope for?" (the religious question); "How should I act?" (the ethical question); and "What does it mean to be?" (the ontological question). You invite students to willingly suspend their disbelief or their belief, their presumptions and their assumptions and you embark on a process of interrogation with the great thinkers — Aristotle, Plato, Aquinas, Augustine, Kant, Descartes, Hegel, Marx, Kierkegaard, Nietzsche, Heidegger, Wittgenstein, Sartre. After this process of radical questioning, you're then in a better position to act. I believe that you must ultimately align yourself philosophically, politically and religiously. Philosophy comes from and culminates in action.

SJC: And presumably that kind of self-questioning can end on an analyst's couch or in a therapist's chair? It might begin with philosophy and end elsewhere.

RK: Well, you know what Julia Kristeva says: we all suffer from the malady of existence, from the pain and pathology of existence and the hurt and confusion of existence; and as Paul Durcan says: "Is there one of us who is not confused?", or as Brian Friel says: "Confusion is not an ignoble condition." Freud calls that neurosis. We're all neurotic animals, to a greater or lesser degree. Hitherto and traditionally, there were answers for questions but nowadays it's not obvious. We're living in a post-dogmatic, post-totalitarian and post-ideological age, we're told, so there are no ready answers for people. But Kristeva, who is a philosophical psychoanalyst, maintains that there are three ways of dealing with the "melancholic imagination", as she calls it, with our sense of separation and pain and want and lack, and they are: *art*, *psychoanalysis* or *religion*. Ultimately, philosophy does not provide the answers. Philosophy gets you to question and then leads you to the limits of what can and cannot be answered; but when you reach that limit, art, psychoanalysis or religion take over, psychoanalysis at the level of the unconscious, art at the level of aesthetic experience and imagination, which goes deeper than philosophical reason and religion and faith. Some choose one of those three, some people a combination of all three, some people none of them — they just remain neurotic. Kristeva might have added friendship, but we're not talking about that; friendship is obviously the cure for all ills, but we're talking about professional areas of help. So I suppose that's where I would see my interest in philosophy — residing in the gap between those three: at the borderlines between the question of *God*, the question of imagination, and the question of the *unconscious*, which is the question of desire.

SJC: Whom have you been most influenced by philosophically and how would you describe your philosophic position?

RK: The contemporary thinkers who influenced me the most would have been two French philosophers, Paul Ricoeur and Emmanuel Levinas. I'm a modern European philosopher (a hermeneutic phenomenologist), who believes that philosophy is a matter of rigorous questioning about our existence in the world, political, personal and metaphysical. Western philosophy originates with the Socratic doctrine of ignorance, that is, it begins with an admission that we do not possess knowledge, that we must doubt what we have hitherto taken for granted.

SJC: Nietzsche ended his life in an asylum for the mentally insane; Camus refers to the absurdity of existence, Sartre says that "hell is other people"; is it not frustrating to be dealing with a subject that questions everything and yet possesses few answers, if any, to the problems posed by existence?

RK: That's the risk you run when you do philosophy. Dostoyevsky said, "True faith comes from the crucible of doubt." It is better to doubt than to believe blindly from birth to death. Everyone in life, whether they do philosophy or not, should question their existence and I don't see that as being incompatible with faith. There must be room for doubting and questioning. If you run the risk of committing suicide, then that's the risk you run. Looking at the statistics of my own students: the suicide rates haven't been particularly high! I believe that the majority of philosophers affirm and enjoy life. Some of them ended up mad and committed suicide but so do other people. I think it's a wager.

SJC: Does the philosopher have a role to play in politics?

RK: I think many philosophers do. Thomas Paine was extraordinarily influential in the American Revolution and Rousseau and Voltaire in the French Revolution. Hegel and Marx influenced the Socialist revolutions of the twentieth century. Even our own 1916 Rising was deeply informed by men of ideas. Pearse, Connolly and Griffith were all intellectuals. They edited journals — Pearse edited *An Claidheamh Soluis*, Connolly *The Workers Republic*, and Griffith *The United Irishman*. They were people of political action and they were thinkers, not mindless Celts, dreamers of dreams, as the English stereotype would have it. Of course, this is not to say that academics should run the country! I believe in local democracy. I believe that everybody is potentially an intellectual.

SJC: How would you describe yourself politically?

RK: I would describe myself as an Irish Republican, understood in the European sense of Republicanism, in the French sense, not in the militant, nationalist sense of the word that has been hijacked by the IRA. I am totally opposed to the division that has occurred in Irish politics, where Republicanism has become identified with the IRA and non-constitutional nationalism, whereas what I would call constitutional republicanism has become identified with nationalism. We should be easing the term "nationalism" out and replacing it with "republicanism" and reclaiming that word from the IRA, because they don't deserve it. I am only for Irish republicanism along the European model in the sense that it is real power to the people. I am for democracy. I am against centralised government — be it from Dublin, London or Brussels.

SJC: Are you a member of any political party?

RK: No.

SJC: Would you describe yourself as a socialist?

RK: Yes.

SJC: In what tradition?

RK: I would describe myself as a Utopian socialist. I am not a Marxist, though I have a lot of time for Marx's critique of capitalism. I am not for collectivist state control. I am not a socialist, therefore, in the conventional sense. I am for Utopian socialism, which is public power to communities in the sense of local, participatory democracy. I am against centralised state socialism. This Utopian socialism is not incompatible, as the Marxists believe, with a religious commitment to social justice. For example, what the Jesuits were doing in Paraguay in the eighteenth century was Utopian socialism and what Sister Stanislaus and her like are doing now in Ireland is the same.

SJC: Is there a political party in Ireland that reflects your views?

RK: I would be closest to the SDLP than I would be to any of the political parties in southern Ireland. If I had to choose one in the south, I would go for Labour, which, in my view, needs a radical review. I think party politics in Ireland is too confused with civil war politics and is ideologically out of date. I am a socialist because I believe in the public — public broadcasting, health and education — at the level of communitary participation. I am for a new socialism, which is not a state socialism.

SJC: You have written over twelve books on philosophy and culture, a volume of poetry (*Angel of Patrick's Hill*), and two novels (*Sam's Fall* and *Walking at Sea Level*). You are a Professor of Philosophy, have been a television presenter, chaired the Film School in UCD, been a member of the Arts Council and the Higher Education Authority and you have made political presentations to both the Forum for a New Ireland (co-presenting the Joint Sovereignty model), the Forum for Peace and Reconciliation and also involved yourself in the Mary Robinson election campaign. Where do you get your energy, passion and consummate conviction from and what keeps you going?

RK: The political contribution that most interested me was a submission I made jointly with Simon Partridge to the Forum for Peace and Reconciliation on the Council of the Isles. That was in 1997. I had been working on that for a number of years and originally it was treated with suspicion, as totally Utopian. We were trying to explore ideas not just of *joint* sovereignty, but of *post*-sovereignty; we were saying we need to belong to a more confederal and regional tradition in the British Isles and in Europe. If I made a small contribution as an academic and thinker to Ireland, it would be to the dissolution of *absolutist* sovereignty, of which Britain was the main offender, not Ireland (we were only a mirror image) and going beyond sovereignty to another kind of relationship where you give power to people regionally. It's very close to John Hume in some respects. It's post-nationalist, which doesn't mean it's anti-nationalist. And it involves a Europe of regions. That's where I feel most passionately in terms of my political commitments and as a critic of British nationalism, which has never been *called* nationalism. The British call it *rationality*! We're labelled as "nationalists", as are the Bretons and Scots — never the British!

SJC: You're juggling a number of balls. But where do the commitment, conviction and enduring energy come from?

RK: I have no real idea where it comes from. Maybe (and I say this cautiously) it's about seeing division and wanting to see healing? Maybe it is something I have inherited from my medical ancestors? It's attempting through ideas, images and metaphors to come up with alternative possibilities, to bring reconciliation where there is conflict, though that sounds banal.

SJC: It's an act of synthesis.

RK: Yes. I remember Colm Toibin, who was in college with me here in UCD, and who reviewed one of my books (I think *Transitions*) saying in one of the newspapers that if Richard Kearney played in a band he would play the synthesiser! I didn't know whether that was a compliment at the time. But I knew what Colm meant. There was something of that, the desire to bring things together. And philosophy has two functions: to analyse and divide, to split things up and make distinctions; and the other is to try to synthesise. As Kant says, there is the analytic dimension of reason and there is a synthetic judgement, and maybe I've been more into the synthetic than the analytic. Ireland is a place of divisions — class divisions, political divisions in the North, economic and religious divisions — and so I suppose there was a passion to do something about that.

SJC: Could all this active and outside involvement be a defence against going inward?

RK: Oh yes, and occasionally I would burn out in terms of all this activity. As a result, I learned through a series of depressions (the Greeks call it *melancholia*) and found myself exhausted and realised that there are just so many things that can't be solved, that things are impossible. Then, ten years later, the Council of the Isles becomes more possible. You run up against so many obstacles and you're called Utopian and idealist, someone who hasn't got his two feet on the ground. I remember Ray McSharry and Charlie Haughey telling me I was totally unrealistic at the New Ireland Forum when we went in to propose joint sovereignty, although in fairness, Haughey was very polite about it. People said, this is impossible, that it could only come from a philosopher, an academic. As Haughey used to say: "Richard Kearney is my favourite philosopher and I don't understand a word he says!"

That can lead to burnout and depression and disillusionment, when your ideas don't translate into reality. Then that reminds one that philosophy is not just a philosophy of action but also of contemplation; the *vita activa* needs to be complemented by, and perhaps even founded upon, the *vita contemplativa*. That's what I learned from Glenstal and growing up; my mother was very religious, not in a dogmatic way — she was never doctrinaire — she was very spiritual. My upbringing taught me that there is a part of the soul or psyche that needs to be catered for, that one needs to slow down. And I did some work at Eckhart House with Míceál O'Regan, which was hugely helpful. The first time I went to see him, I said, "This is my analysis of why I'm not feeling very well", and I quoted Freud and Jung and Lacan and Bettelheim and Kristeva. And he said, "I think what you need to do is not analyse anything but just sit and breathe for thirty minutes every day." So I used to go and breathe and say nothing, which was very difficult at the time. It was to quiet the mind and "go gently", as he used to say, and develop the interior part.

It reminds me of a poem I wrote; we were building a well for our house in West Cork and I was reciting for my neighbours a sequence from this, about going down to the bottom of the well, which I call *Bridget's Well*. It is very much in the Eckhart mode. The last sequence is called *Bridget's Island*, where we now have a little house:

> I will rest, now,
> at the bottom of Bridget's Well.
> I will follow the crow's way
> footprint by footprint
> in the mud down here.
> I won't come up
> until I am calmed down
> and the earth dries beneath me
> and I have paced the caked ground
> until smooth all over
> it can echo a deeper voice,
> mirror a longer shadow.

That's going down like the submarine in the Baltic Sea; going down to the bottom of Bridget's Well. Our driller yesterday dug what he said was one of the deepest wells he had ever drilled in forty years because it was four hundred feet down, beside Bridget's Well. Then the water image in the poem gives way to one of fire.

> Then the fire may come again
> beneath me, this time,
> rising beyond me.
> No narcissus-flinted spark
> behind closed eyes
> but a burning bush.
> A fire that always burns away
> but never is burnt out."

That's when you reach the inner point of nothing, stillness, emptiness, the mud in the dark, then something else fills you with some kind of energy.

You ask, "Where does the energy come from?" I like to think it comes from the burning bush, but there's always an ambiguity as to whether it's coming from the burning bush, therefore from a source deeper and greater than you, like a well that comes up from beneath you; or whether it's coming from your own fantasy. That's something that needs discernment; and for discernment one needs to meditate and contemplate and try and keep things still and quiet, which doesn't come naturally to me at all. It's a big effort.

SJC: That fantasy image could be ego-driven or it could come from the grace or gift of Being, from God?

RK: Exactly. The question is discerning where the fire comes from. Where does the fire come from? It could come from both. It's just knowing the difference. If it's not coming from deep down, from the bottom of the well — and you have to go down there and stay there to ensure you are in contact with that — then the chances are it's what Kierkegaard would have called the "aesthetic eros" of the ego, that's constructing and reconstructing itself endlessly and that leads to *tedium vitae*, that leads to burnout and melancholy. Not that burnout is always a result of egoism; that's not what I'm saying. It's just the body and the psyche reminding you that you can only do so much and you have to acknowledge limits and boundaries and borders.

SJC: And a breakdown can lead to a breakthrough.

RK: Absolutely. And it's not only the Meister Eckhart and John of the Cross image of the dark night of the soul, *das Nichts* (the nothing), which is the very seed of the Godhead, "God beyond God", as Eckhart says. It's also the existentialist notion, which I am very partial to, in Kierkegaard and Heidegger, of the being towards nothingness, of the being towards death, as a breakthrough to authenticity, where you let go of the ego-driven desire to impose power and let things be in their being. We don't do that naturally. We have to be brought down into the mud. Eckhart called it "letting go"; it's the abandonment of the self, which leads to a deeper self. It's not that it leads to you becoming nothing. Nothing is more real than nothing, as Beckett said. That doesn't come naturally to us; it has to be beaten into us by existence. It's a black hand that comes and pulls you under.

SJC: You've mentioned Eckhart House and these moments and moods, in the Heideggerian sense, of anguish and despair. What then is your view of psychoanalysis and psychotherapy?

RK: I use it a lot in my teaching and in my writing and I have undergone it, both in Eckhart House and also for a time in Boston and I found it tremendously helpful. I also have reservations about the potential abuses of it because it's such a deep area and the whole process of transference is so delicate that it can, on occasion — but I think it's rare — flip into a power trip where analysands can become very dependent on analysts. And sometimes it can be very difficult for analysts, as Freud knew with Dora, not to engage in countertransference, particularly if the analysis reverts to some infantile neurosis or repressed or masked memory. I think there can be a danger that it can send people back to their childhood and make them into victims and they blame everybody else for their problems, starting with their parents, then their teachers. That's not to say people aren't hurt when they're young and don't feel huge fear and anxiety. It's very important to revisit that sometimes and come through it and repeat it; but it's the old question of "analysis terminable and interminable". I think that sometimes analysis can become a surrogate religion, where the analyst becomes the God for people and they will just live for their half an hour or their hour a day or a week and it's a huge investment of time, energy and money — and money is a symbol of what you attach importance to. I think that in Ireland, generally, psychotherapy and psychoanalysis avoid these dangers, certainly as practised by the people I've known.

SJC: If you had to choose, though, between Lacanian psychoanalysis and psychosynthesis psychotherapy?

RK: I wouldn't choose. I wouldn't say which I would choose. In Ireland, I did therapy in Eckhart House. In fact, I practised it and learnt hugely from the healers there: Míceál O'Regan, Jo Newman and Joan O'Donovan. I never read Assagioli so I don't even know what psychosynthesis means. I have read Lacan because he's very philosophical and Heideggerian. From the point of view of philosophy, I have been much more influenced by these figures. From the point of view of my therapy, I've been more influenced by the interpersonal and interrelational approach, but I wouldn't want to set myself up as a judge and to say which is better. They both have huge strengths. It also depends on the person; some people need the more Lacanian approach, some the more Eckhartian.

SJC: And on what syndromes and symptoms and structure they present with. If you're very depressed, lying on a couch is going to be quite difficult because you need more ego rather than less.

RK: Exactly. I think the introduction of psychotherapy and psychoanalysis into Ireland has been beneficial to our culture, because we either used religion as a way of solving all our problems (very often not experiencing things personally) or swept them under the carpet or else we drowned them in alcohol or suicide and these things were never named. It's done a huge service in opening up that whole area and I think that's 99 per cent good. The abuses I mentioned of over-dependence and the power/money thing are the shadow-side, which one has to be aware of because people are very vulnerable and fragile; and in a post-religious age, it's tempting for analysts to set themselves up as witch doctors of the soul. It's about the ethics of psychoanalysis.

SJC: Yes, which is the question of desire.

RK: We could spend a couple of hours on that, but we'll have to keep it for another day!

SJC: You have always sought alternative avenues and a wider audience than the rarefied confines of the university campus to communicate your philosophical, political and cultural ideas, but you paid a price. You received some vicious reviews, especially for your post-nationalist position; files were stolen, your car dismantled and threats were issued. You also resigned from the IFC and the HEA and from the UCD Promotions Board and went to Boston on a three-year leave of absence. Was the price worth paying?

RK: Oh I think it was, yes. I wasn't a political fighter. I wasn't tough. When I see some people who survived all that and took it on the chin, I'm full of admiration for them. I used to take aggression much too seriously and I find it very difficult to live in situations of violence and conflict and ongoing mendacity. I saw it as mendacity where others saw it as politics; that's the stock in trade. My vocation, in that sense, is that of an academic, a thinker, a writer, an intellectual, rather than as a cut-and-thrust politician. And some of the cultural politics in Ireland, particularly around the Irish Film Centre and sometimes around the Higher Education Authority, involved hard, dirty politics. I found Irish politics, at that level, very hard to take. I do think that there is something in Irish politics that leads back to what we were saying about psychoanalysis and the need for it here, and that's schizophrenia. I don't mean in just the clinical sense. I mean it in the general sense of a split personality. It's understandable because it's post-colonial — we identified with the coloniser and we were colonised. The English are the people we love to hate and never cease to imitate, as Douglas Hyde put it. We have that master/slave thing and that leads to doubling. If my books have twins in them, as some of the German and French reviews pointed out, it's due to the connection between the Republic and Northern Ireland, Protestant and Catholic, British and Irish. The dualisms go much deeper, though, deeper than religion and language. I think they go to this love/hate level of wanting something you can't have; and if you can't have it, not wanting someone else to have it. Augustine talks about that.

SJC: Envy?

RK: That's one word for it, and covetousness. It's an "infantile imperiousness of imagination", as Sartre calls it, which can't be fulfilled, so there is frustration. Emigration, the famine, and endless defeats led to a culture of scarcity where there wasn't enough. The land was split up and got smaller. A half-acre became more and more sacrosanct. Therefore, there was a huge rivalry around land and that led to internecine war among the Irish themselves. When the coloniser leaves a colonised country, the civil war is amongst the colonised. We inherited something like that, though we didn't kill each other physically in the South as they did in the North. We killed each other psychically. Yeats talked of the "daily spite of this unmannerly town". And Joyce said Dublin was a city of doubling, where we constantly rub up against "inter-misunderstanding minds". It's the porous psyche that identifies with other people and so the boundary between you and them becomes porous. People identify with you and vice versa. I found that a little bit as a teacher and when I did my TV programmes. People would project onto you all sorts of things that had nothing to do with you at all. They would either over-idealise you, which I got when I came back from France (I got too much attention) or the opposite, and I could never understand that.

SJC: It's a process Freud describes: from idealisation to contempt. If they put you so high up on a pedestal, there's only one place to go! And of course, when people project stuff onto you, you can end up unconsciously identifying with their projections. This is projective identification.

RK: Then you feel alienated from your own self because you are carrying all these projections and I felt that. In fact, it was a therapist who pointed it out to me. You have an image to live up to and an image to live down to. And you want to be you;

you don't want to be either of these things. I remember Eoghan Harris saying to me that when you do TV, you have to remember what the Indian says: when somebody has your image they have your soul. It was a warning and a counsel. There's a certain truth in that. Then I had a few experiences of stalkers, which were very frightening. They were students, one in France, when I was teaching there, and one in UCD. These were people who would over-project onto you and when you couldn't give them what they wanted or needed or demanded, which was unconditional love, then it flipped, and I had threats and people following me onto planes to lectures I was giving abroad and turning up out of the blue. I got telephone calls and one even got into my house and into my computer. It was pretty scary.

SJC: Is it simply a case of envy and these people's pathological problems, or is it also culturally due to the fact that no one is really respected here unless they go away, for some unconscious internalised colonial reasons? After all, your work is acclaimed more abroad than here.

RK: Sure. You get over-expectation and over-investment, which doesn't feel as bad as the opposite. It's like manic depression — when you're manic you think the world is wonderful. When you're depressed, there's nothing worse. When *The Irish Mind* came out there was so much publicity, and it was only an edited book. I just wrote the introduction and when I look back on it now, I don't think it's particularly good. There was an expectation that I would really have something to say about the Irish mind and I had very little except to say it's about a "both/and" instead of "either/or" and that we have a double vision. There were certain things there that I hope were interesting and useful, but there was a complete over-inflation of its importance and also around the Forum to some extent. One solution is to try to walk at sea level, which is the title of my second novel. It's about finding the midpoint between over-elevation and under-evaluation. Sea level is the middle space.

SJC: So you're not drowning in despair or taking off into outer orbit.

RK: Exactly. Hyperactivity, over-commitment, no limits, everything is possible. It's a kind of megalomania, though that's too strong a word. You don't know what "no" means. And then, flipping over into its opposite, where there is no hope, no light, no possibility — everything is impossible. So it's finding the midpoint.

SJC: It's having a still mind. A surfer on his surfboard is really still but he can experience both the high wave and the low wave. In fact, in order to experience both, he needs to have a still centre.

RK: That's fascinating. I never thought of that. They're still even though they're going up and down?

SJC: Yes.

RK: "Do not be disturbed", as Teresa of Avila said.

SJC: And the Psalm says: "Ponder on your bed and be still and know that I am God."

RK: Yes, it's all about that. And whether you get there through Buddhism, psychotherapy, art (as Dostoyevsky and Tolstoy tell you) or through religion — Meister Eckhart and the great mystical and spiritual traditions in Christianity, Islam and Judaism or in the American Indian and oriental traditions — it doesn't much matter. I think that every great religion has a certain wisdom about attachment and detachment. It's a very hard thing for us Westerners to learn. When I travel to North Africa or Latin America, I see people sitting on their doorsteps for hours and hours. How can they do that? They have a peace within. I'm not romanticising it — they might not have enough to eat either.

SJC: Something has seriously changed in you, it seems to me. You're writing more fiction and reflecting more on spiritual topics in your academic articles, which I have been keeping up to date on. Are you consciously aware of a different orientation and perspective in your life?

RK: Life and looking for wisdom through philosophy on life is trying to move from the ego to the I or, as Ricoeur put it, from *le moi* to *le soi*, from me to the self. I don't regret any of the cultural and political commitments that I had here in Ireland. The only thing is, if you are not a political animal, which I'm not (I was very ambitious, of course, and I thought nothing was impossible), it can be difficult. There is a prisoner deep down inside discovering that poverty within, and that can become a huge enrichment. For me to do that, I had to let go of the ego, which was over-involved, over-active, although hopefully I was doing some good, but I needed to go on a retreat, and going to America was that. A "leave of absence" says it all. It's important to be absent from the life of involvement for a while.

SJC: A sabbatical of space.

RK: Exactly, a psychic sabbatical. I am working on more spiritual, religious and literary things, and that requires a slower rhythm. I've just come back from West Cork where we're getting a cottage together and I spent the last month digging a well, painting walls and putting down carpets, and it was wonderful. I didn't read or write for one minute in the last month. I don't regret that. There's a house there to live in, which is great, but it requires labour and activity, transforming matter into a house; but now I need time out to read and write, to think and imagine and pray, to meditate and walk. If I had to keep building houses, I would collapse under the rubble. It's an act of balance. Your image of the wave is beautiful, that you can do the work of action and transformation (*praxis*) and also go down into the hollow of the wave and remain steady and still. That's the challenge and I haven't been very successful at it. The old mystic's adage was that you had to drown three times. I had three bouts of depression a number of years ago and I probably needed the three. The monks used to say you had to knock three times on the door before you were let into the monastery. There's something about the three — the Trinity and Hegel. I think I needed those three to do something that wasn't natural for me, which was to go in search of the bottom of Bridget's Well. I had to be brought there and I went screaming and kicking and howling! You and I had a few conversations when I was in that space and when you were in that space. So I know you have been there too. But I didn't choose to go there and I think it's involuntary and unnatural; but you can learn hugely, if you know when you're in that dark, not to try and escape it by going into alcohol or drugs (I'm not against medication — I used medication) but knowing that there's work to be done that can be intellectually and spiritually transforming. Religion and art are forms of therapy but it is a kind of work that I find "unnatural" and that requires a lot of effort.

SJC: You have mentioned that philosophy and faith aren't incompatible. How would you describe your own religious views?

RK: I would describe myself as a seeker for God first, as a Christian second and as an ecumenical Catholic third. I disagree strongly with the present Pope's teaching on women, and sexuality, particularly in the areas of divorce and contraception and on the insistence of a celibate male clergy. I think it's a very patriarchal system with the non-ordination of women to the priesthood. Women are fifty per cent of the

Church, of the real Church, the Church of the people. I am sitting out the present Papacy, hoping that the next Pope will be more like John XXIII. But if not, I'll remain a Catholic, because I don't believe that the Church belongs to the hierarchy. It belongs to the people, to people like Sister Stan and Jean Vanier and to the people who are actively thinking and working through their faith on a day-to-day basis. Catholicism for me is not just a doctrinal issue. The reason I don't call myself a Protestant or a Jew is because Catholicism is my tradition and I still think that there are very valuable things within that tradition, which I am not prepared to abandon. The Catholicism I profess is that commitment to radical ecumenism.

SJC: Philosophically, you have taught on and written about the imagination an awful lot, writing books with titles such as *The Wake of Imagination* and *Poetics of Imagining*. Why are you so preoccupied with imagining? Is it because certain essential things can't be spoken, only imagined; that when words fail and fade away, only images remain?

RK: Well, that's well put. It is for that reason. Imagination takes over where reason falters, stammers and finds its limits. The most important thing with imagination, and the reason I am so fascinated by it, is to know that it *is* imagination and does not mistake itself for reality. If it does, it becomes pathological fantasy. People then can't tell the difference between what's real and what's not; and so they become addicted to movie stars or they become stalkers or alcoholics and live out their fantasies. Healthy imagination is salutary imagination, therapeutic imagination, imagination that knows it's dealing with images and that images are not giving you the real but the surreal — which is necessary for our survival in order to think more, live more and exist more fully. There's a thin line between fantasy as narcissism, where you think you have everything (mania or megalomania), and a more humble imagination, which knows the limits between the real and the imaginary. One of the things that worries me in our culture is the erosion of the distinction between the real and the imaginary, where the real is just a copy of the image in advertising and on the Internet, in popular culture. Andy Warhol got it right, and postmodern artists and philosophers are trying to think this one through. Everything is simulation and simulacrum and endless seriographs, of Marilyn Monroe or Liz Taylor, etc. It's a culture of repetition and fantasy and an inability to know what is real and what is purely imaginary. That is the pathological imagination. It rejoins fundamentalism in camp and kitsch. What's image and what's real? Fundamentalism is about refusing to accept that this is a narrative (if we take the example of the *fatwa* against Rushdie), that what he writes about Mahomet is *not* real. There can be no hermeneutics, there can be no recognition that there is an imaginary world of fantasising. Joyce's lawyer in the *Ulysses* case in New York said that no one was ever raped by a book. It's not a question of underestimating the horrors of pornography on the Internet; but what I'm saying is that there is a difference between that and someone being *really* raped. If we don't acknowledge that, we are saying that real rape is just imaginary. Texts are real for fundamentalists. There is no room for discussion or critical discernment. The fact is the same as the text. That's a kind of tyranny. Postmodernism can have the same kind of tyranny — from the *opposite* end of the spectrum. It reduces the real to the imaginary whereas the fundamentalists reduce the imaginary to the real. They are mirror images of each other. In both cases, you have a one-dimensional model. It's important to sustain a dialogue, *beyond* dualism. *Dia-legein* in Greek means welcoming the difference. But you've got to have a difference to welcome it!

SJC: Are images in the mind enough to stave off the loneliness of memory? In other words, if I am alone in my room with images of my last lover who left me, is that enough? I'm thinking of Sartre's example of Pierre.

RK: I don't think it is and I don't think it should be, because if that were the case, we could replace a real person with an image. Art is about producing surrogate substitute objects for things that can't be thought, felt or experienced, what Lacan called the Real. In stories, writers are saying things that can compensate for loss and lack. It can be therapeutic. The danger is when aesthetic fiction is taken *literally* and we think that the image can replace the *real* person. Then you get people becoming addicted to Madonna, thinking that Madonna is their lost object, their mother or their idol.

SJC: So we should transform the image into something more symbolic?

RK: Yes, into something more symbolic, which also recognises that no image can replace a real person. As Freud said, we must go through the mourning, otherwise it becomes melancholy. Melancholy is the refusal to mourn. If we internalise the lost object as an image, that becomes part of us and we think we haven't lost it. We deny separation, absence, loss, lack. Then that internalised image of the person, that surrogate we have incorporated inside us to fill the gap, cannot do the work of really filling the gap, because the person is dead or gone or has left us or is not there.

Then we turn our desire for that idealised lost object into hatred, as Freud says in "Mourning and Melancholy". We hate ourselves and it leads to depression. So we have to remember the melancholy of memory, even as we play with images that can help us overcome it.

SJC: And not be too quick to go through the mourning.

RK: No, you can't rush it. There's no quick fix. Alcohol will give you a fix for a couple of hours and certain forms of fantasy can help, but ultimately it comes back. It's like a sleeping pill. You get six hours' sleep, but you are more tired when you wake up. Alcohol will give you temporary relief but you feel worse when you wake up.

SJC: Your first novel, *Sam's Fall*, tells a tale of two brothers who grow up in Cork and board at Columbanus Abbey. Sam stays on to become a Cistercian monk and Jack leaves to fall in love and pursue his thesis on Toland. The book warns of the dangers of playing God and living out someone else's desire and dreams. The message I picked up is that we need to break free from the passionate prison of other peoples' desire and find our own place in the sun. When I reviewed it [*Sunday Independent*, 9 July 1995], I wrote: "Certain people will read it as autobiographical, which only in a certain respect it is, translating Columbanus Abbey for Glenstal Abbey and making myriad guesses as to who Jack, Sam and Raphaelle and Anselm really represent. I certainly did. But the simple answer is that Richard Kearney is all these characters and none of them. And so are we. Their sacred struggles, sometimes Sisyphean, are ours. Their black despairs, fathomless depths, secret dreams and fantastic longings are ours too." What were you trying to work out in the book?

RK: I'd forgotten you had written that. I'm flattered. Joyce said that Dublin is a city of doubling, existing between "twotwinsome minds". This cleft mind is something I've been very struck by in Ireland. The almost compulsory and exaggerated politeness of people — "You're so welcome" — the hyperbole. Then there is the phrase by Synge's Christy Mahon: "I was made a man by the power of a lie." We have to invent stories that we killed our father, that we did something we didn't do to prove that we are a man. I think it is using words and images to compensate for something we've never had. You could call it power, in terms of a colonial explanation once again. I think it's deeper than that, too. It's as if we haven't found the Fifth Province. So we reinvent it in words. I think the Irish are a people who fantasise a lot. Everybody does, but there's a view that we are "the music makers, we are the dreamers of dreams". That's a cliché, it's part of the Celtic twilight and folklore; but there's also a grain of truth in all stereotypes and our addiction to fantasy is something I was trying to explore in *Sam's Fall* and that does lead to doubleness and this cleft existence that Irish writing speaks so much about. On the one hand, it can lead to hypocrisy and a mandatory politeness that you also find in a lot of other postcolonial countries like Algeria and Tunisia. That's the ambiguity of being very diplomatic externally, but internally saying, "I wish we could get rid of the coloniser". When the Irish say "Céad míle fáilte" and "Come and stay with me when you're in Ireland", they often don't *really* mean it. Americans and French and Germans think you mean it but you don't. If they turn up, you're horrified.

Not that there isn't a generous spirit, but we overstate and exaggerate our generosity towards strangers. This idea of the Ireland of the welcomes; well, you only have to see when that becomes a reality, when it's not tourists coming to visit and pay money into the economy but people looking for work! We can be as racist as the next, and worse. It can also lead to a compulsion to lie, part of which is humour and irony — Irish people know because there are tribal codes when they're exaggerating and telling stories. Foreigners don't get it very often and they don't know the rules of poetic licence. I often do this myself, but my wife, who is French, though she had an Irish mother, doesn't understand and she corrects my stories, whereas my Irish friends say, "Oh no, let him finish the story"! Of course, they know it's not true!

Joyce said it would be a brave man to invent something that never happened. That's true of my novels. Almost everything in them bears some relation to something I've experienced but it's all retold in a way that bears no exact parallel to reality. This hypocrisy can lead to "Timothy of the two faces", to two-facedness. At worst, that's deceit (we harbour the double within us). At best it can be sublimated and turned into creativity and creative fantasy. There's a thin line between the two. I don't think the Irish are very good about dealing with reality. I think the whole question of paternity is also central to the Irish psyche — the powerful mother and emasculated father. You get it in *Angela's Ashes* and in Joyce. It's in Synge, between Christy Mahon and his father, who are reunited through fiction and fantasy because in reality there is no rapport. I think that crisis of paternity has led to a crisis of authority and of self-identity where Irish people have turned on each other. There is a confusion about primogeniture and who has a right to stand in this or that place. There are signs all over Ireland saying "Do not trespass" and "Private property" and people taking each other to court over rights of way. We think the Americans are litigious, but just go down to Kerry or West Cork where every second farmer is taking a court case against their neighbour and not speaking to them for thirty years. It's nearly always about a right of way or a ditch. *The Field* was John B. Keane's way of expressing that in cinematic form. It's kind of fratricide. Where the father is absent, the sons will fight. It's almost a replay of Freud's primal horde.

SJC: And the *non/nom du père* in Lacan.

RK: There hasn't been enough *nom du père* in Ireland. Religion should carry that role but it hasn't been credible enough. We haven't had enough psychoanalysis, so we've compensated in art. As Joyce said, Irish Catholicism is run through with Mariology. It's a cult of the mother. Let's not put it in terms of symbolic castration, because people misunderstand what that means. But there is no "NO" in the Irish psyche. Hence the temptation to alcoholism and endless fantasy and to doubling — to thinking you can have double existences and multiple personalities. I think one of the reasons I have experienced quite a lot of depression in Ireland — and I don't get depressed in France or America or Canada where I have spent a considerable number of years of my life — is because I have a difficulty in dealing with ambiguity and multiple personality and projections of people and living up to or down to an image. Maybe that's just my problem. I don't know. But I have met many other people who have also gone abroad and felt the same sense of psychic space. Very often such immigrants work harder and are more at peace with themselves living out of Ireland.

SJC: And they feel more Irish.

RK: And they feel more Irish and are very proud to be Irish. Even many people who might reject their religion in Ireland (and I have my battles with the Church in Ireland), when they're abroad they feel very proud to be Christian — I'm not a very good one but I try to practise it. So there is something about that whole nature of doubleness in Ireland, which is our greatest gift and our greatest disease. At its most melodramatic, it's evidenced in the split between Protestant and Catholic, Planter and Gael, Irish and English, etc., and they are all parts of us. That cleft in imagination is central. The fact that Jack and Sam in *Sam's Fall* are the central characters and Raphaelle is trying to suss out this doubling is not an accident. Where the third part of the trilogy goes, I'm not quite sure. I call it "Writing for Nothing" and it might be published or it might not. It's important for me to finish it, whether or not it sees the light of day. Balzac said that you should never talk your novels away! I think a lot of novels are talked away in Ireland because we're talkers and it becomes diluted. We're not good at holding things in and containing things. We tend to let things spill and words are the army of the dispossessed, as Friel says, which compensate for a sense of lack and a crisis of authority and identity. We don't know who we are. That can also be a positive thing. Captain McMorris (who was the first Irishman to speak in English literature) says, "What is my nation?" in Shakespeare's *Henry V*. That's the positive side, to be asking questions. We're a very philosophical nation in that regard, despite the stereotype that the Anglo-Saxons are the philosophers and thinkers and we're the poets and dreamers. I think we're *both*. I think all races are both, but we have tried to disown that heritage. I have tried to write about this in *The Irish Mind* and in *Postnationalist Ireland*. We need to reclaim Berkeley and Toland and other such neglected intellectuals. We're not a very discreet people and I think one of the great strengths of Heaney is his discretion. Whatever you say, say nothing. It's pure gold; he doesn't spill it out.

SJC: My father tells me not to volunteer information!

RK: As a West Cork farmer said to me the other day, "What you don't say, they don't need to know." Just keep your life to yourself, don't give it away, because it will become distorted and they'll use it against you. I think one of the terrible casualties of the "generosity" of talk is indiscretion. It's like the Chinese whisper, that goes around and comes back distorted, where everybody is pottering around in each other's brains. There is an invasion of privacy and a lack of boundaries between where you stop and they begin.

SJC: The private sphere is becoming eroded. Everything is in the public sphere.

RK: We don't need an Oprah Winfrey or a Jerry Springer in Ireland because we're doing it all the time, on the streets, in the pubs, everywhere. I remember a Canadian who came to live in Ireland telling me that he had a pain in the jaw from just answering questions! He couldn't believe people could speak so much. Silence just doesn't exist in our culture! We're terrified of silence. It's not just privacy, but that place of interiority. I think we need to harbour the place within the "well" and spend more time there and that's why the whole meditation practice thing is so helpful, as I learnt through psychosynthesis. We should learn it from our religion; but because religion has abused people for so long, Protestant and Catholic, people have not fully profited from the genuine spirituality that is in Ireland. People like Patrick Hederman and John

O'Donoghue are tapping into it now but it was always there. We've lost touch with that spiritual interiority and some people are regaining it through psychotherapy and through the alternative Church. Sister Stan and Jean Vanier and Peter McVerry and Eckhart House are retrieving this kind of spirituality. The Official Church has lost it. It was so repressed in the unconscious. We have the cases of child abuse. Sexuality was talked about but it was empty speech, to quote Lacan, and full speech was a rarity except in our great poets and writers. Sex-talk hid the truth rather than revealed it, so the truth was repressed and then it came out as a monster, both in the suppression of sexuality and of women. They go hand in hand. The Church has a lot to answer for — it's part of the solution but it's also part of the problem. I think a revolution in the Irish Church is necessary to retrieve what is genuinely spiritual, mystical and healing and to acknowledge the sins that have been committed in the name of God — and there have been a lot of them. Amnesty and renewal cannot be based on amnesia.

SJC: After reading *Sam's Fall*, I felt disquieted and quite uprooted, unsettled, but with the knowledge that all attempts to locate meaning outside myself are doomed to failure. My favourite passage was this one: "By sheer intensity, desire dissolves what it desires. Ravenous thirst, robbing the taste of drink. A drowning man clutching his rescuer so hard he can't be saved. Cries so frantic they deafen the voice they cry for. I pray, but there is no answer." There's a tremendous struggle going on here and a haunting loneliness. You are in there through your characters. Those emotions and existential conflicts and yearnings for the sacred are yours. That's the theme — at least that's what I got out of the book.

RK: I would go along with that. If you asked me I probably wouldn't have said that, but when I hear you saying it, I consent and say, "Yes, that's true." But to go back to the God bit, practising religion for me goes with thinking about religion philosophically; but I'm not sure I could have written a book about God in Ireland, because I have too much of a conflict with the official Church to do that. I would feel I was toeing the line. But when I'm in America, it's a minority religion, because it's basically a secular republic, and even more so in France. You have to fight for the right to believe. I think we should have secular spaces; then religion is something you choose. I am all for the separation between Church and State.

SJC: The Church doesn't need the secular crutches of the State in order to survive.

RK: Exactly. When I say the separation of the Church and State, I'm thinking of the Church too. I think the Church is more damaged by Christ and Caesar getting into bed together than the State is. The separation is to the mutual benefit of both. I don't think there should be a complete antipathy between the two either.

SJC: Talking of religion and spirituality, in one of your poems in *Angel of St Patrick's Hill*, you say: "O angel of the last days where are you?" What I see in the poems is both a spiritual and sensual quest for a vanished face, for the burning bush, for the fire — it's also an odyssey of the imagination and you are again resisting the dichotomy between the spirit and the senses. There is that same drive towards synthesis. The theme echoes again in your poems, novels and philosophical works.

RK: Right. Well, I would agree with that and philosophically, the parallel would be Merleau-Ponty and the phenomenology of the body; in other words, returning to the body-subject. The body and soul both exist — they are not two separate things, as in Platonic and Cartesian dualism. They are like the two sides of a sleeve, or a skin. There is the inside and the outside, the inside is your soul, the outside is your body. We need to retrieve that and it was central to Irish spirituality. If you go back to the Brehon laws, there is a very liberal, celebratory, Rabelaisian attitude towards sexuality. St Brigid used to down two partridges in one bite — she had a huge appetite. There was a celebration of the physical and the body and the terrestrial and then, with Jansenism and ultra-Montane Christianity and the Counter-Reformation, which tried to outdo the Protestants in purism, we ended up with a very dualistic spirituality.

SJC: That's a perversion.

RK: Yes. I'm not saying we want to go back to Celtic spirituality — there's something sentimental about that — but there can be a temptation in the whole movement of Celtic spirituality (whose general spirit I would endorse) to become a new age pseudo-mysticism, and *that's* something I try to warn about in the second book, *Walking at Sea Level* — the Gnostic temptation.

SJC: Well, moving to your second novel, *Walking at Sea Level*, you deal with the themes of duality — corporeality versus spirituality and the search for unity. It's also a type of monastic meditation on life and religion and in it Jack Toland is running from his past and has a profound metamorphosis. The demonic Klaus, at one point says: "Children aren't innocent. They're born with darkness in them. The darkness that's in all of us, Jack. The same lust to possess and be possessed. The same desire to fall. Remember Augustine's *Confessions* — the siblings wrestling at their mother's breast, eyes full of envy?" (p. 189). Klaus tells Jack that salvation is excess, it's either asceticism or libertinism, that either extreme will do. Both Klaus and the Abbot are Gnostics, believing God has a shadow-side, like Jung, that God dwells in thick darkness as much as light. Again, to what extent was writing the book an act of therapy or exorcism? Do hidden Gnostic ghosts haunt Christianity? Have we all a dark double?

RK: Writing was therapeutic, but then all my writing is, philosophical and literary. I think there are two dangers. One is a New Age Gnosticism and a kind of neo-Nietzscheanism too, which says good and evil are just relative, so experiment with everything because everything is the same as everything else, with a dash of Buddhism, with a dash of Christianity and American Indian sun worship. Religion becomes like a supermarket. I am very much for the ecumenical — I would consider myself an ecumenist, as I said earlier, but not an eclecticist. I think there's a difference. And I am suspicious of the patchwork in New Ageism, though I respect the desire in people to look for spirituality. I'm just wary of gurus who set themselves up as having the answers and playing God. Anselm does that in the first book. Anselm is based on St Anselm, who had an argument for God from the idea of perfection — it's this obsession with perfection. If you're not perfect, you are nobody. That's puritanism and dualism, absolute good and everything else is evil. The other danger is that everything is everything else, so good is evil and evil is good, therefore, as the Carpocratian heresy said, you have to experiment with every form of crime, brutality and so on, and, at its extreme, that's Nazism. The Nazis had a mystical spirituality, that cruelty was part of God. There's that in Hegel and in German Idealism and in Jung too, that God has a dark side. I am very cautious and critical about that. In *Sam's Fall*, Klaus is Klaus Stavrogan, which is the Russian for "cross" and he's an Antichrist character in Dostoyevsky's *The Devils*. Dostoyevsky's point is that this guy is seen as a saviour but he's perpetrated child abuse and torture and Dostoyevsky's point is, as you know: how can God exist if there are innocent children who are being tortured? That's the ethical dilemma I am playing with in the book. What I am trying to do is to say that we need an aesthetic imagination and an ethical imagination; and I have said that in all my philosophical works too. I don't mean a moralistic imagination.

SJC: You mean an ethics of the good and not a deontology of duty.

RK: Exactly.

SJC: With all this preoccupation with religion and spirituality, are you a monk *manqué*?

RK: In a way.

SJC: Do you meditate and/or pray?

RK: I do. I am not very good at it. It's a struggle but I do readings from the Old and New Testaments, the daily readings actually, the Psalms, and then I have some kind of meditation reading and some silence. I would like 15 minutes; if I get 15 seconds, I am doing well. I always do the readings and if I don't do them, I really miss them. It's like an alcoholic who misses his whiskey, although I shouldn't say that — it's a bad metaphor! It's been something I have been doing since the depressions. I try to meditate and Joan O'Donovan [*of Eckhart House*] taught me to meditate while walking or swimming if I find it difficult to sit in a chair and do nothing. So I now meditate walking and swimming. I do two walks, first thing in the morning and last thing at night, and I try to swim every day.

SJC: It's meditation in movement. That's one of the reasons that I do Aikido. What are your interests outside philosophy? You mentioned walking and swimming.

RK: I adore going to West Cork every summer, where all seven of the Kearney clan congregate. I love the sea and swimming and fishing. Many of my thoughts and ideas come when I am swimming and going on walks with my wife and children, when I am totally relaxed and off duty. Otherwise, I would become a workaholic. I am an obsessional thinker and worker and so when I start I find it difficult to switch off until the project is completed. I dislike the administrative side of academic life. I much prefer to think, to write, to teach, to be.

SJC: Are you happy?

RK: I have periods of intense happiness, but I also have moments of intense *angst*. It's a mixture. I am a worrier by nature and I have lots of moments of anxiety and then of tremendous celebration; but I am happy at the moment and long may it last!

GRAHAM KNUTTEL
Artist

Graham Knuttel is a prolific painter, a reclusive workaholic, spending up to fifteen hours a day in his studio. He uses colour and form to express the emotion of his figures. He is an instinctive and intuitive rather than conceptual artist, an independent and flamboyant maverick, who has an international clientele from Hollywood (attracting the attention of Sylvester Stallone) to Milan. His expressionistic paintings depict persons who seem to be socially uneasy, solitary, stiff and stilted, but possessing intense souls in gleaming colours of reds, oranges and browns. His pictorial compositions, with their vibrant, brilliant colours, shock and shriek at one. I spoke with him about his art and life over a cup of tea in his home in Dublin city. He was curious and used words economically but to their full value. He was generous with his time and extremely gracious in offering to paint a picture for the front cover of the book, for which he has my heartfelt gratitude.

SJC: Is art anything with a frame around it? What is art?

GK: Art to me is a visual language.

SJC: Do you think that one is born with an artistic gift, is it innate or can it be acquired? I'm thinking of your mother's family, which boasts a number of artists and architects.

GK: No, it can't be acquired. I think it's innate. It's a gift, something you are born with. I think expressing yourself visually or musically is like autism. It means you can't communicate in a normal way.

SJC: Why did you become an artist?

GK: Because it was the only thing I considered being.

SJC: What prompted your move from sculpture to painting? Why do you prefer painting?

GK: I don't prefer painting. I try to work the two at the same time or let one be a step towards the other and try to take the two up at the same time. But originally, when I was a kid, I used to love making things, and when I went to art school I learned how to paint or they tried to teach me how to paint and I enjoyed that and I've always mixed the two. I've been doing sculpture for the last three days.

SJC: Do you approach the two things differently? Do you need a different mind-set?

GK: Yes. You do. Completely. It's a completely different thing. Of course, one is in three dimensions and the other is in two. Sculpture is much more relaxing. It's slower and also I work with wax, so there is nothing between you and what you're making. In painting, you have a brush and paint. With wax, you have just the wax and your fingers. It's more direct. With painting, you're creating an illusion, whereas with sculpture you're creating something real.

SJC: You use oils and acrylics. Is the medium very important?

GK: My main interest in painting is with colour and there are paints that can give you true scientific colour, and whatever the content is, it's just a tool to use colour. Colour is the main focus.

SJC: Is art emotion, is it expression? How would you describe your art?

GK: I think it's expression. You express your life through it. I suppose the images I come up with are the things I see around me. At the same time, when I'm painting, I'm holding in my mind a whole sequence of different colours and the whole thing is like a mathematical exercise in a way.

SJC: Where does it come from, the soul or the unconscious?

GK: It comes from the unconscious, I think. I was talking to a professional gambler the other week and for him it's the exact same thing. He stores different sequences of numbers over a whole lifetime. It's a strange thing.

SJC: You think pictorially, whereas a philosopher thinks conceptually. You think in pictures.

GK: That's right.

SJC: Has art a moral function? What is art's relationship to morals, to religion, to society? Should it reflect and represent reality or stand aloof from socio-political engagement?

GK: No. But I think artists might have a political or religious agenda, no more than anybody else. That's all there is to it.

SJC: But should art reflect reality or should it be art for art's own sake?

GK: It should be art for art's own sake but really it should reflect the time it's created in, so that it can have some relevance for whoever is looking at it. Again, I'm just trying to communicate visually. I think if you try to communicate a message, you won't get anywhere.

SJC: That creates bad art.

GK: I think so.

SJC: Kant says that art exhibits a "purposiveness without purpose", that art is auto-telic, that it has its own inner logic and dynamic.

GK: Yes.

SJC: What is the role of the artist in society?

GK: I think there is a huge need for art in society, for things like design. It's as necessary as music and literature. I think society takes as much art or literature or music as it needs and I think there are probably too many artists. In Ireland, there are eight art schools and ten painters come out at the end of each year. That's eighty a year. In ten years, you have eight hundred artists.

SJC: Is the appellation "artist" bestowed on one?

GK: If you want to be an artist, you have to say you are an artist. Do you know what I mean? And if you have to wash dishes, you must never say, "I'm a dishwasher." You must always say that you are an artist.

SJC: Do you have any political persuasions?

GK: I would be very cynical about politics. I've never voted or anything. I think it's very funny to watch and I follow it avidly but all the political parties have the same policies. I admire them if they are chancers.

SJC: Richard Kearney said that art was too serious to be left to the artists; politics was too serious to be left to the politicians. Beyond both was a place they could meet. What do you think of that?

GK: I think that's rhetoric.

SJC: Many people seem to be under the impression that a strong link exists between artistic creativity and pathology, most commonly depression, even though it would seem that a great deal of solitude is necessary in order to sustain creativity. What do you think? Are artists generally unhappy people?

GK: The most necessary thing is to be able to live comfortably with solitude. If you can do that, you can get on with it. Art is a form of autism. It's an inability to communicate normally and a lot of mental illness would be the same. There's not much romance in schizophrenia.

SJC: You are painting for yourself. It's therapeutic.

GK: Yes.

SJC: Would you say you couldn't *not* paint, that it's a compulsion, an obsession?

GK: Yes, an obsession.

SJC: By what criteria does one distinguish between good and bad art?

GK: If it sells, it's good art! I think good art communicates and can be understood by its audience.

SJC: Is an unmade bed art?

GK: No, that's a product of Saatchi and Saatchi. It's a media invention.

SJC: I saw a canvas of black in the corner of a room in an art gallery and the title was "A big black painting in the corner of the room", something like that. Is that art?

GK: No. That's cocktail party art. You can see that art in any gallery in Europe and similar people looking at it and half of them just want to go to the pub. Nobody is going to buy it. It has no value. Most of that art will end up in the basement, never to be seen again.

SJC: Can you conceive of yourself doing anything else?

GK: No. I always did it. It's my earliest memory. I failed all my exams at school to go to art school. I've never done anything else.

SJC: But what triggered that interest?

GK: I knew I needed to do it to survive. When you are a kid, you have to be good at something and it was something I knew I could be good at. There was nothing else I was going to be good at. Survival.

SJC: You work reclusively and prolifically: from alcoholic to workaholic. What is it that keeps you going, that impels or compels you to work so hard? Has painting become work of a sort?

GK: You always feel when you're working that you're going to arrive somewhere, which you don't, so you have to get up the next day and go again. It's as simple as that.

SJC: You never wake up and say, "Oh, God, I just don't feel like working today. I think I'll go back to bed"?

GK: No. No.

SJC: Do you begin with an idea or is it something unconscious that bursts out or bubbles forth from you?

GK: It's the second one.

SJC: What happens when you stand in front of the canvas?

GK: Maybe in the corner of my mind I'll see a little line and follow that. Gradually, a picture emerges. You never set out to do anything. It becomes apparent to you as you're doing it.

SJC: Downstairs in your studio you have a huge white canvas just sitting there. Does that frighten you?

GK: Yes. It's worrying!

SJC: Do you ever feel that you won't be able to produce anything?

GK: Oh yeah. You have that fear every day and right through the process.

SJC: Presumably, you are your own harshest judge.

GK: I would be because I'm the most intimate with it and I know the mistakes. When I look at a painting all I will see are the mistakes or the things I didn't want to do.

SJC: You are never entirely happy with it.

GK: No. You're always embarrassed by it.

SJC: How does one come to put a price on an artwork?

GK: You get a good agent! I don't even know what price my work sells at. I just don't know. Artists are very bad at that. They would much rather give them away. It's the sense of embarrassment, that I can't ask for money for this.

SJC: But you don't object when an agent says it's worth £50,000, do you? You don't say: "No, it's only worth £500"?

GK: You have to be careful. A good agent values it for what it's worth. In the market, there are set prices.

SJC: Is there snobbery or pretentiousness in the art world, especially in relation to the financial aspect?

GK: There is huge pretentiousness and snobbery but the art world is so small, especially in Ireland. I mean, every art opening you go to will attract the same people. Over twenty years, they won't change, they'll be the same and they never buy anything. It's a social club for a lot of them. It gets them out of the house. The greatest thing I ever did in terms of my career was to completely ignore the Irish art world, because you would just get nowhere with them, and concentrate on my own work. In the beginning, I hung my art in restaurants, which was unheard of. Nobody would speak to me after that. I broke all the art world rules. It's at the stage now that, when I consider doing something, I ask myself would they do it and if they would do it then I wouldn't do it, or vice versa. It's a handy guide. Just do the opposite. I just finished doing a painting for the Rose of Tralee competition. Can you imagine anyone else doing that?

SJC: Is it envy, because so many aren't as commercially successful?

GK: It's indignation.

SJC: Are the artist's stated intentions relevant to interpretations of works of art or is the meaning and message up to each particular viewer?

GK: It's up to the viewer.

SJC: But if they see something which clearly isn't there?

GK: Then the artist has got it wrong.

SJC: Should forgeries be treated as significant works of art in their own right? Has an original painting any greater artistic value, do you think, than a perfect forgery? If so, why?

GK: Oh Yes. Absolutely. I brought a fellow to court over that. The image is the property of the person who painted it in the first place. The forgery may be perfect on the surface but it's lacking the originality of the first image. It's a copy.

SJC: What about the person who painted a moustache on the Mona Lisa? Is that anti-art?

GK: It's graphic art. I think Dadaism was the first anti-art movement, which has been repeated. They should have left it at that, but it's been done to death.

SJC: In a brochure published in 1994 entitled *New Works by Knuttel*, you maintained that the significance of the painting's subject matter resides in its face value and you react sceptically, suspiciously even, to psychoanalytic interpretations of your work. But isn't it conceivable that there are hidden, deeper, more unconscious meanings to any artwork? After all, you yourself have suggested, or at least implied, some connections between your grandmother, whom you describe as "cackling" and as possessing "long white claws" and your drawings of birds, and also between your childhood memories of journeys on trains and ships and your later drawings of railways, etc.

GK: Yes, I think there is, but again, out of embarrassment, you are inclined to say there's nothing more to it than that. I think it's really an autobiography.

SJC: When you look at your paintings, do you know when you painted them and what was going in your life at that time?

GK: Yes. It tells a story and I'd know them down to the month, and I've done an awful lot — more than hundreds. They reckon that Picasso painted more than 54,000. People think if you're painting thousands of thousands of pictures, it's diluted, but that's not the way it works. The professional way is to paint as much as you can.

SJC: Isn't the danger of that approach that you become the Dame Barbara Cartland of the art world?

GK: No, because she wrote the same book five hundred times!

SJC: In the same brochure, you have written: "My earliest memories of my own work are of battle scenes." Did these battles take place within you as well? Are they suggestive of inner conflict and unease?

GK: Yes. I can remember doing those as a kid. Guns and bullets and air raids. It gave you a sense of power, because you felt you could organise the battle and decide who would win or lose and, in a way, it's a form of protection.

SJC: Obviously, to some extent, your work mirrors your private thoughts, your desires, longings and loathings. In the brochure, you wrote: "My own doubts and fears and hopes are expressed on the faces that appear in the bars and bathrooms in my work. Mr Punch is my alter ego. He reflects my moods. We fight the same battles from the same cupboard." I'm struck again by the word "battle" and "punch" and "cupboard" (as in "skeletons in the cupboard"). Are you trying to come to terms, to express rather than repress some difficult, emotionally laden, conflictual memories from childhood, adolescence or adulthood?

GK: I think that's true.

SJC: Birds, fish and cats (as well as female nudes) frequently feature in your pictorial compositions. Are these animals symbolic of something?

GK: That's for the viewer. I'm sure they are.

SJC: You say you paint first and think about it afterwards. What do you think about your paintings?

GK: I judge them not on the content but on the colour, as I said. The content is the colour, the form, and the lines.

SJC: What is your standing with other members of the Irish and international artistic community? What contemporary artist do you most admire?

GK: I don't belong to an art community. If an artist does, then he's diluting his solitude. I wouldn't like to meet too many of the art "community" on a dark night. I don't really admire any contemporary artist. Maybe those who have the same view as me! If they don't admire you, you're not going to admire them.

SJC: What about Carmel Mooney, Ann Madden, Louis le Brocquy?

GK: Not Carmel Mooney, no. I liked le Brocquy's early work, but not all the faces. I think it's a bit dated, very 1960s. Working artists would admire me, but those who are doing other jobs wouldn't. I've been shouted at on the streets.

SJC: As a figurative, expressionistic painter, the people you portray look suspicious, solitary, sinister, almost paranoid, harsh and humourless. No one smiles. Faces are triangular or taut, rather than circular and comforting. The men and women are not at ease, but emotionally and socially alienated, often with their arms across their chests in defensive posturing. They seem altogether alone and seldom in twos or together — their link with others always tenuous. Is this how you see yourself and others in society?

GK: Probably, yes. I generally think that's the way life is.

SJC: You're introverted, not involved in the outside world.

GK: My paintings are very much out there and are my link to external reality. In a way, it's very extravert.

SJC: Do the Irish still have soul? And what is soul?

GK: I've no idea. I don't know what soul is. Maybe it's a feeling that comes from struggle.

SJC: So your art has soul, as do you!

GK: I suppose that's what it is. So I must have soul!

SJC: Do you believe in God? Are you a spiritual person?

GK: No. I don't believe in God. I believe in Good. I don't believe in church. I was brought up without any religion.

SJC: What do you do when you're not working? How do you like to relax?

GK: I read the newspapers for three or four hours a day. I can only switch off by leaving that room downstairs and getting out, travelling to Spain, Marbella and Puerto Banus.

SJC: I know it well. There's a great "pancake house" in Puerto Banus.

GK: There's a great chipper there, which has just opened!

SJC: Finally, are you happy?

GK: Oh yeah. I think I am.

ALICE LEAHY
Director of Trust

Alice Leahy is a nurse and co-founder of Trust, which was set up in 1975 to provide medical and related services for homeless people. Up to thirty men and women call each day on Alice Leahy and her team in the Iveagh Hostel in Dublin's Liberties. They range in years from 18 to 80. I learned so much from my chat with Alice Leahy about homelessness — for example, I was told, to my surprise, that there are no free hostels in Dublin. The philosophy of Trust is based on two principles: the recognition of every person's autonomy and the respect owed to them as unique human beings; and the need to restore the dignity of people whom society has labelled deficient, deviant or undesirable. The success of Trust in supplying not only much-needed services but a hearing ear and helping hand is due, in large measure, to this exceptional and quietly determined lady who works silently with those who are suffering and sidelined by mainstream society.

SJC: You are the Director of Trust, which is a non-political and non-denominational voluntary body that provides medical and social services for homeless people. How did you become involved with Trust? Was it connected to your work as a nurse?

AL: Yes and no. When I came to Dublin to train as a nurse, you had very little time off. I felt that, in the time off I had, I wanted to get to know the city and, particularly when I worked as a midwife in the Rotunda, I came across families living in extreme poverty who were, nonetheless, contented or, at least, appeared to be contented human beings. I then did voluntary work with Voluntary Services International in the city and a group of us were involved in visiting the elderly and mothers and children and setting up a youth group in Benburb Street. I worked as a night sister and I was invited to go to London to set up an intensive care unit (the first of its kind), but I felt I didn't have the time to do the voluntary work I was doing; and while I see the importance and the role of technology in medicine, I also missed the hands-on work, which I think is vital.

I decided to give up being a nursing sister and went to work in Simon. I remember the consultant setting up an appointment for me to see a psychiatrist — and he really meant it, because I had given up a good job! I got to know the founder of Simon, who was a wonderful man. Simon was in existence a few years then but the building was appalling, though there was a tremendous sense of community. I worked there for a number of months and it was very tough. After it, I felt you either never wanted to see a homeless person again or you wanted to do something about it, so I went to England to do some private nursing to make some money, because I had no money and when I was there (and I now look back in hindsight and see a pattern). A number of things happened. One night, a woman who was very battered and bruised and physically unattractive, was ill, and there was a young attractive doctor there in the hospital we brought her to, I think one of the most attractive men I had ever seen in my life. He was beautiful, and he threw his arms around her because he knew her. When I came back to Dublin, he wrote to me and said that, if I were interested in pursuing this, he would be very interested in becoming involved with me. At this time, I had applied for a job in India and the letter went astray — I wasn't meant to be there.

A doctor and I visited the Simon shelter once a week and a job came up in the national Simon office. I applied for it, as Assistant National Director, and I used that time to do a report on the medical problems of homeless people. That was in 1974. The questionnaires went to all the hostels and ideas came back from GPs, voluntary bodies and from people who were homeless themselves. But the main part of our work was visiting the Simon shelter once a week with a doctor and a nurse team. There were people with appalling medical problems, people who had experienced terrible violence; but there was a great sense of hope amid all the hopelessness. There were a lot of professional people who wanted to help as well, but they felt they couldn't cope with the chaos and yet their skills were needed. So I wrote this report and presented it to the Health Board and they employed me as a nurse. I don't agree with wanting to change people unless they want to change. That's up to them.

David Magee was a psychotherapist who, as a medical student, had worked in Simon, and he started to work with me in a voluntary capacity. We had no base and at that time, a young woman, Anne Rush, discovered that she was dying of cancer. She did a soup run for Simon and one of the people she befriended was Kitty, who was well known on the streets of Dublin. She was a very happy woman who walked around the streets of Dublin with loads of plastic bags and used to go in to all the different hospitals where she was known. She did her washing in the toilets and we were all told that those bags belonged to that woman who comes in at night. She would stay in the hallway of one of the hospitals. That was her way of living. She would pass my flat and look in to make sure I was there and all right. So Anne was dying of cancer and she decided that some money was to go to helping people who were homeless. So a group of us got together, from the Vincent de Paul Society, etc., and there was a wonderful solicitor, Eoin Mulholland. We used the facilities in the old Vincent de Paul headquarters and we met there one night a week. We drew up a business plan; we decided to set up a private charitable trust and that together we would provide a service for people who couldn't avail of services. The Health Board gave us the use of the old health centre in Lord Edward Street. It was an appalling building, but was very well known to the people of Dublin and it was a place where the poor went to get free milk and money. Our deeds of trust were drawn up and it was set up as a small-scale medical and social service for people who were homeless.

What to call the agency was a dilemma; Anne herself came up with the name "Trust". I think that's no accident, because if we don't trust ourselves and others, we are going no place in our world. We worked very hard, going around town on bicycles, visiting people who were sleeping rough, and we linked in with all sorts of services. Fred Donohoe, who worked in the Health Board at the time, was very open to accommodating us. We were involving people in their own health care. We didn't see health care as being only about medicine. Professor James McCormick was our Chairman. We decided we would never keep personal records of people's lives, believing that people's privacy is their privacy. We have no right to be extracting information from them. Some people had lives they didn't want to talk about. They wanted to forget about them. Then, after a year, David said he was going off to do psychiatry, so we advertised and employed a doctor for a number of years. We also felt that we needed better premises — we needed showers, for instance. We then got the basement of the Iveagh Hostel and we have been there since 1980.

We strongly feel that homeless people shouldn't be discriminated against, that they should be using the normal services, and that frees us up to work with the more difficult people. So we decided we wouldn't employ a doctor any more. We employed a man who had been in prison for many years. He was wonderful, and great with people who were struggling with their lives. He could also relate to people who were homeless. I remember a young fella coming in one day with the keys of a BMW — he had been robbing cars all over the place — and Paddy said to him: "Come on, cop yourself one, prison is no joy. Do you realise that this isn't going to do you any good?" It worked and he did listen to him because he felt this man knew — he was there.

Now, to where we are now. Over the years, a lot more money has become available and our health services have a lot more personnel. When we started, nobody was going around hostels; in fact it was very hard to gain access, but now you have outreach and re-settlement workers, and so on. Our work got busier, so we cut back and expanded into other areas, to concentrate on our own centre. Paddy retired because of ill health and so we wanted to get somebody who could treat people just as other human beings — we got Patrick. Also at this time our trustees felt that we should be putting our experience to good use and there was a need to get a little involved in education. We looked for another nurse to work with me. We now describe ourselves as a befriending social and health service. We would see befriending people who come in as being much more important than putting on the bandages, because if we get to know people, over time, they will tell you their problems and if there's something you can do to help them. That's very much how we work now. Our day-to-day work hasn't changed. Our philosophy hasn't changed, except that we are doing other things as well. We would constantly be frustrated at the way many services are going and our society is going. There is no place for a different voice. The little people are being pushed aside and silenced. Also, if you work with people who are outsiders, you are likely to be seen as an outsider yourself. I think there is a great poverty of vision out there.

SJC: A poverty of the imagination.

AL: A poverty of the imagination, and there's no sense of how we are all in there together. People are working so hard and compiling statistics and sorting things out and not stopping to ask where we all are in the scheme of things.

SJC: I always think that these endless scores of statistics and sociological research don't translate into practical solutions.

AL: This is very frightening in our area of work. I could spend the whole day in meetings, but I'm not going to meetings unless we're discussing people.

SJC: If people are homeless, one would think that the provision of housing would be the simple solution but, in reality, the solution is more subtle and complex, as many people who are homeless have rejected the community and the conventional values of society and have spent some time in prison or mental hospitals. What brings them to the brink? Why do people become homeless?

AL: I suppose there are no easy answers to that. I think it's all too simple to say that it's a housing problem. If it's a housing problem, why wasn't it solved long ago? I think there's a terrible emptiness in people's lives. I mean, who would want to be locked away in four walls and going to a local community meeting and nothing happening. There's something cruel about locking people away and that's what happening at the minute. There is a major housing problem and people can't afford mortgages, but that's very different from what we're saying. A lot of people end up in prison who shouldn't end up in prison and people end up in psychiatric hospitals who shouldn't be in psychiatric hospitals. I think there's a tremendous danger that we're medicalising and criminalising poverty. Thirty years ago, there would be groups of us huddled in a corner and discussing what Laing said or what Ivor Browne or Noel Browne were saying and doing. There was real debate going on. But now there are people with no training or experience deciding whether someone is mentally ill. Recently, this happened at a meeting when we were discussing a woman who has great difficulty getting her money and surviving. She's had a terrible life. But she won't queue to get her money and somebody said she must be mentally ill. That's frightening and frightening things are happening out there which no one is questioning or challenging. In a way, it's the subtle use of terminology and power and medicine.

SJC: The psychoanalyst Jacques Lacan describes psychiatrists' discourse as being the discourse of the master.

AL: That's right, and we all listen and you can't challenge them. One way of rubbishing people, especially women, is to say they're too emotional. I would say that if more professionals were more emotional, we would have far better services. We are fooling ourselves. If you go to a doctor, he's no good unless he gives you a pill. I don't agree with that at all. This is what's happening to a lot of people who are poor and going around like zombies on massive dosages of medication. People in the professions will privately agree with you but none of them will rock the boat because they feel they won't get promotion. The time has come when they need to ask themselves why they're in those jobs. We forget that people who are poor or whatever keep a lot of people in jobs.

SJC: And Ivor Browne told me that many psychiatrists kow-tow to big pharmacological companies because of the huge profits involved.

AL: That's right.

SJC: Would you say that in some cases they unconsciously want to remain homeless, for whatever reasons, that even as they sit on the street corner exposed to the elements and to other people's contempt, loathing and aggression, they experience, nonetheless, some *jouissance* (i.e. pleasure in pain), that there's something in it for them?

AL: I suppose I would like to say that we never know what's going on in another person's head. We're lucky if we know what's going on in our own heads! We all get recognition some way and maybe the only way somebody can get recognition is by being out there.

SJC: It's almost a protest against society or the "symbolic order", as Lacan would put it.

AL: That's right. We would meet people who will not claim social welfare, even when they're entitled to it. There would be that sense that "I am going to go out there and shame the state". Another thing that comes in is the whole notion of sin, guilt. People would feel that they have to suffer to get to the next life. We meet people who feel a lot of guilt that hasn't been explored so they don't know what they're guilty of. It's all about the human condition and what we see out there is the extreme of that condition that challenges something in us. That's why a lot of people are so afraid to get involved with people who are so broken, because when you do you have to look inside yourself.

SJC: We hear talk of the housing crisis but what is the solution to the homeless crisis?

AL: I think there are some things for which there are no solutions and very often the solution is one we're trying to impose. Sometimes those people are happier than us, that's their way of coping with the world, and it's very hard to understand that in this day and age. I think the housing crisis should be solved. There are massive tracts of land all over the city and country and there is no reason why there shouldn't be a massive public housing programme with all the money we have. We have no free shelters in Dublin. I think people think that homeless people get everything for nothing. In fact, some homeless people won't take a penny for anything. And sometimes people think that all homeless people are beggars. Sometimes the biggest beggars may be the agencies collecting on their behalf.

SJC: Like the government holding out the begging bowl to Europe.

AL: Yes. I have problems with the whole European thing because I think it's impacting on our services here; it's all about performance indicators and endless reports.

SJC: That's the culture now.

AL: Yes. We do a report every month for our trustees but what's in our report is x number of new people sleeping out, the number of people we met, people like yourself, the numbers with showers. The reason we do that is because it costs something for someone to have something as basic as a shower. You can't put a cost on community care, though. Homelessness is a term we can use to . . . what is a home anyway?

SJC: Freud uses a term, "*unheimlich*" (unhomely or uncanny) to describe a sate of being in which we feel that we are alienated from ourselves, that we are not at home in ourselves or our world.

AL: We're not.

SJC: The home is the mother's breast and we're trying to get back to that.

AL: That's right.

SJC: So psychologically, we are all homeless. It's a psychical state.

AL: I would agree with that interesting insight. And I really value this discussion we're having now, which just would not take place in the area of work I am currently involved in. It's important to spend time to reflect on the issues you're raising. There is a space for this type of question. Part of what our essay competition is about is to encourage this type of questioning, questions I try to raise myself.

SJC: The name "Trust" is interesting. Francis Fukuyama wrote a book entitled *Trust*, in which he argued that trust is the central and cardinal ethical virtue.

AL: Well, I think it is too.

SJC: The philosophy of Trust centres not just on important medical, nursing and social services, but also upon the restoration of worth and dignity to those the world would seem to despise or disown. How do you do this?

AL: Everyone is important and nursing helps in a way in that, very often, people are put off by dirt. To be a part of the culture we are living in is to be beautiful and squeaky clean, but we don't realise that others are battered and bruised. What strikes me sometimes is that when someone comes into us and looks in the mirror and smiles, that's so important — someone smiling who normally never smiles. I would see nursing as touching and helping people and healing their wounds. There isn't a value put on this work anymore. We place a value on success and that influences how we see people. But we don't see the wounds, we see the person behind them. People are afraid of difference and we see all types of people in our work, but there's always a gentleness in them, which maybe we don't allow them to have. But part of treating people as equals is to say: "Look, this behaviour isn't acceptable." It's not preaching. It's not saying: "You have been hard done by." We say to them that people might be frightened of your behaviour. We have no fancy courses on anger management.

SJC: You work at the coal face and every morning from 7.30 in the basement of the Iveagh Hostel in the Liberties, you see up to 30 men and women between the ages of 18 and 80 who are sleeping rough on our city streets or who need various kinds of attention. You wash and comb and clothe them and dress their wounds. How do you cope with such difficult and demanding work?

AL: And getting to know them. How do I cope? We make sure that we have time for each other. We have a number of rules for ourselves, like if you make a mistake, just say it and that's the end of it. We don't play one off against the other. If someone is hassled, we discuss it and that's the end of it. So we don't hold any grudges. We are very open with each other. We also work very well together. We all muck in and do what has to be done. It's also important to have time off. We try to have a day, once a month, when we're all out of the place together, a day away. And once every two months, Gerry and I always make sure we have lunch out. We support each other. What keeps us going is realising, not that you can change the world, but that you can make life a bit better. If people want to change, they'll change themselves. We would be very clear that we wouldn't get involved in projects and going to useless meetings just for the sake of it, trying to please the powers that be. We would be very focused on what we're doing and seeing the value in it and you see the value in it by looking at the people coming in. They're the main source of encouragement.

SJC: As you speak, the image that comes into my mind is the image of Christ battered and bruised and Scripture says that he was an object to despise, an object of scorn from which men looked away. It's a failure of vision. Iris Murdoch's whole moral philosophy centres on this. She says that we don't really see people as they are. We see from our personal perspective. It's a projection.

AL: Exactly, we do. When it comes to people who are very noticeably different, people just can't cope.

SJC: Many homeless people come from psychiatric hospitals, from drug and alcohol treatment programmes, from orphanages or the army, from industrial schools or borstals, from hostels or jails. Many end up in crime or drugs or prostitution. Have you any statistics on this?

AL: No, and we resist the pressure to compile statistics. There's a wonderful saying: it's like a drunken man leaning against a lamppost — it's for support rather than illumination! Our services are judged in terms of statistics. If you had a hundred people passing through your door and out the other door, with no eye contact even, that would be seen as a successful service, but if you had a service where ten people came in and spent time and then left feeling happier, that would not be a successful service — but that's how *we* measure success. They're necessary to get money but that raises another issue, because some agencies can't say no to money. Does more and more money mean that services are any better? I don't think so.

SJC: Yes, it's like watching tennis on television. During the Wimbledon season, endless streams of statistics come up on the TV screen about the match and it's a distraction to actually enjoying the game.

AL: That's right. It becomes boring.

SJC: We talked earlier about 18-year-olds coming to you; but what if they're younger, 12 or 13 or 14?

AL: We would strongly feel that if young people came to us, we would link them in to the statutory services. There should be more community care services, especially for children who are at risk. We would see a number of women and men who are in prostitution, but we don't dwell on that. We see the total person. They are primarily human beings. Labels are convenient. They are convenient because you can refer someone on. It's an easy way of dismissing people.

SJC: It's like psychiatric labels, which is just part of the master's discourse.

AL: It's like the word "client". The other day, someone said to me: "We have a client here." And I said: "A man or a woman?"

SJC: A lot of people may not know (I certainly didn't) that there are no free hostels in Dublin, that a hostel bed can cost from a few pounds a night to £50 a week. How do they get that money if they can't avail of social welfare, as they are what's referred to as having "no fixed abode"?

AL: We're lucky to the degree that people can still get money here if they have no fixed abode, generally. The general public thinks that there are masses of free shelters in Dublin. There are no free hostels. Some people book in a week in advance and it's a bit cheaper, but if you like to have a drink or gamble or a smoke, you are going to have very little money left over. The hostels need money to survive but I think it's very important for the general public to know that there are no free shelters. People can end up on the streets for any reason. The general public thinks that these people are scroungers. They're not scroungers. Many of the people we meet would have worked very hard in poorly paid jobs. In order to avail of grants, there is pressure to take on more successful cases. Because of this, many agencies have lost the freedom to speak out on behalf of those who are most needy, and that's dangerous.

SJC: Is there any difference between homeless people and beggars? We briefly touched on this topic earlier.

AL: I don't like the term "beggar". People who are begging are people. There are people who are homeless who do not beg and there are some people who beg who are not homeless. That's discriminating against people who are genuinely homeless. How do you define a beggar? Is it Bertie, going over with his begging bowl to Europe? Is it some of the powerful lobby groups? We can use the term in whatever way suits us. And agencies that make appeals at Christmas time: who's the beggar and who's not?

SJC: Should we give money to people who beg on the streets or not?

AL: I think it's very arrogant for someone in power to say, "Don't give money because they have money themselves." It takes a lot of courage to get out there and beg. I would say to people to find out what services are available. Very often, giving money means that you can avoid eye contact. Sometimes it's an easy way out. It's harder to stop and speak to the person, because you have to exercise your brain. I heard someone say that we should give the money, not to the person, but the agency. But what guarantee is there that if you give the money to the agency that the person will be helped? There's no real debate on these issues.

SJC: I remember a priest in a pulpit saying: "Don't give money to the beggars in the porch. It will only encourage them to come back."

AL: And the Church sometimes takes up two collections during Mass. There are very few public support systems out there for people who want to give up their drug addiction or drink. The question is: why did they get into drugs in the first place? It's very easy to stand up and make a political statement.

SJC: I remember Charles Melman, who is a French Lacanian psychoanalyst, saying to us once about drug addicts: "Why would they want to give up their drugs? What are you going to give them instead of their pleasure: reality?"

AL: We find that with alcoholics too. But these questions aren't being asked.

SJC: One man, Freddie, lived in the hostel, was physically disabled, loved the horses and sport, was very attached to the church on Francis Street where he cleaned the wax off the candlesticks, generous with what little he had. When he heard that the Sligo Rovers football team was in trouble, he sent them a £50 donation. After his death, you found mention of him in a book on Sligo Rovers — his was the only donation received. You must hear hundreds of heart-wrenching stories such as this one?

AL: We do, but then Freddie wouldn't have seen himself as a victim. That was a few years ago, but life doesn't change for people. The other morning we went into work and an elderly man living in the Iveagh (I don't know him at all) had a glass jam jar with £2.60 in pennies he had saved for us. He left us a beautiful note apologising that it was such a small amount. We don't allow people to give. That was better than winning a million in the Lotto.

SJC: There is still a lot of stigma attached to the homeless and some people say that there is plenty of work now available in our thriving economy and that these people are simply lazy. What would you say to that viewpoint?

AL: People who say that have already decided that all these human beings who are homeless are lazy but if they could look at them as people, they would probably find that there is a greater work ethic in that group than in people who are saying it. How do we define work? How do we define what's useful? It's so easy to brand people as lazy.

SJC: I know some people who work nine to five and many of them who appear to be working on their computers are actually writing e-mails to their friends!

AL: Yes. And is their life any less meaningful than people who are compiling statistics and attending meetings? I have frequently gone to meetings and felt that it had been a most useless afternoon. Maybe that person who is labelled homeless might have done a lot more in an afternoon. They would have time to think.

SJC: Sometimes doing one thing is enough. Mark Patrick Hederman told me in his interview that the yucca moth lives to do one thing, and if it is not carried out, the whole ecological system is put awry.

AL: Yes, that's very important.

SJC: Presumably, in terms of our Celtic Tiger, you would be severely critical, seeing both negative and positive sides to our story of monetary success?

AL: I think it has affected everything. Even with phone calls, you get music first, then an answering machine and then you don't get a call back. There are good things about technology — it makes the world smaller, but in our area of work, more money means streamlining services and producing more reports and having more meetings. We have left no space for people who aren't achieving things. It's a rarity to come across somebody who's happy. Everybody is in a hurry. Even bicycles would mow you down. The price of houses has gone way up.

SJC: There's also no cause, no mission in which to believe.

AL: No. There's nothing to protest about anymore. Those of my age are almost seen as cranks if you complain. There's no reflection anymore and no bringing together of ideas and there's no sense of a past. It's as if Ireland only came to light three years ago and nothing happened before that. Plans that are now being put forward for homelessness we were doing twenty-five years ago.

SJC: Are you depressed about Ireland?

AL: Oh yes, I think we are going nowhere. Something needs to happen to bring people to their senses. Our politicians are all the same nowadays. There's no different voice. The voice of reason has been silenced. I think, though, there are still people in the media and people like you writing out there and there must be people all over the place who are feeling the same as I am feeling. Despite the psychobabble and PR taking over, there are a lot of people out there doing great work and getting on with their lives. Somehow these people have to be used, but they're not being used in the political system. You have to be a member of a political party to be in there. Politicians have advisors around them of the same ilk, but they need more vision. We're streamlining everything.

SJC: So do you think Ireland has lost its soul?

AL: I do. Maybe we haven't quite lost it. I think we need to shake it up. It's something to do with our identity. We are an island race and it's inbred in our psyche, but we're not secure in that. Just because we are and should be part of a bigger, global picture doesn't mean we should lose part of our identity. We're struggling to satisfy America and Europe but we are part of a global picture and each place has something to contribute. I'm not talking about bombs and bullets, but feeling we have a voice. We've been sitting here for over two hours and we haven't used one meaningless word such as "partnership" or any of the buzz words. We are using those words to alienate thinking. It's almost like the emperor's clothes. I was at a meeting when they were talking about partnership, and I remember saying that this is like a Christmas cake with icing but no ingredients! People are afraid to laugh and to question and look beneath the surface. There's a terrible sterility.

SJC: Homeless people are citizens of the state and I am reminded of the fine words of the 1916 Proclamation, that all children of the nation are to be equally cared for and cherished. Is there any political party or government that has lived up to that promise?

AL: There are good people in all political parties. I'd prefer to see a politician as a person and politician rather than in terms of the party they represent. But I think that when people join groups, they lose their own identity. In the political parties, the whip tells you what to do. I think that has a terrible effect on human beings — it has to. Look at them — they age by the day because they are losing their own identity and vision. Why do politicians feel they have to be what people want them to be and not themselves? I think we need a National Party. We need to encourage people to vote. They queue for hours in third world countries to vote but they're not going to vote unless things change. But I have great hope myself that, for example, someone like you would feel that what I have to say is worthwhile. The kind of work I am involved in is not seen as valuable. Is it ever going to change? I think it's time to say, "Stop giving out the money and sit and look where it's going."

SJC: At least once or twice, some politicians speak out, like Mary Harney and more recently, Síle de Valera.

AL: Yes. They are saying something and if we could have a reasonable debate rather than saying that it wasn't sanctioned. We've become too narrow.

SJC: There is nobody of ideas left in the political parties, except perhaps John Bruton who seems to be a thinking man.

AL: He does and there's a certain vulnerability and humanity about him. We have the same people everywhere, on the Sunday programmes, on *Questions and Answers*, etc. They shouldn't be afraid of people who have a different point of view. Vision tends to come from people who aren't part of any group, because if you are part of a group the group tends to take over.

SJC: We get what I call The Big Three — the lawyer, the politician and the journalist. We don't get the writers, the philosophers, the psychologists, etc.

AL: You do, that's right. It's terrible. We were a nation of thinkers, of great playwrights, poets and politicians.

SJC: I'm more proud of Ireland's past than its present.

AL: So am I. Present Ireland is awful.

SJC: Where does Trust stand in relation to the Simon Community and to the other charitable organisations, which also work with the homeless. Would you not be better to unite under one single umbrella?

AL: Well, we would never be into comparing one agency with another. We would see ourselves as being one agency out there, constantly asking if we should still be working the way we are and constantly we say that we should, based on what we see in our work. There's a view that we should all come together under the one umbrella and pool the resources, but then you have a controlling influence and the individual voice is not going to be heard. There's no guarantee that any new structure will be any better. Are you any nearer to listening to the person down at the bottom? I don't think you are. Endless conferences and reports give the impression that everything is happening. Very often, they're just talking shops. Now, voluntary bodies are really doing the work that statutory bodies should be doing. Is there any watchdog asking the deeper, philosophical questions?

SJC: Esperanza Productions produced a video, *A Fragile City*, on the work of Trust, and you launched an essay competition in secondary schools on the subject of "The Outsider". How are these projects developing?

AL: The response was very interesting. It was amazing. It was people themselves speaking about themselves. We presented the project to the Department of Justice, because if we went to Health they would see it in terms of illness, and Environment would see it in terms of housing. In Justice, it's seen as matter of equality and discrimination, and *The Irish Times* was used for the media. And Rotary will provide the prizes. We have an e-mail address. Though I'm low-tech, we are using technology to get our message across, a message that won't change. In terms of the essay competition, the "outsider" can be anyone. It can be the philosopher or a wealthy person providing employment.

SJC: Camus wrote a book called *The Outsider* where someone felt such an outsider that he shot a few people. And Julia Kristeva, a philosopher and psychoanalyst, said that society's problem with the outsider is based on the fact that we have failed to face the outsider in ourselves, that we are *étrangers à nous même* ("strangers to ourselves"). Would you share her opinion?

AL: I would and I think that one of the reasons that we can keep working is that there is an outsider in all of us. If you can see the outsider in yourself, you will have no difficulty about that. "The Outsider" is a poem by Micheal O'Siadhail and *A Fragile City* is taken from the name of his volume of poems. His poem said it all. No statistic or sociologist could or would describe that poem. He's Chairman of the adjudicating panel for the essay competition.

SJC: Do you ever relax away from the Centre? Do you have any time for other interests, for yourself? I know you're writing a novel.

AL: Also, I do yoga. I really believe in meditation. I read a lot. I usually am reading three or four books at the same time. I read something light and then read something on psychology or philosophy, poetry and historical novels. And I am also writing a novel, which I have been writing for a long time. I also walk. I believe reading is so important because you realise that other people have gone before you and they're saying the same thing. It's very supportive and encouraging because you realise that you are not alone in your thinking and that's really important.

SJC: What type of philosophy and psychology interests you?

AL: Anything really. I go to the library. I believe in libraries. I read Laing's books. I dip into them. I read government reports and also something light and frivolous. I love John Grisham.

SJC: In the Gospel stories, we are told that the Son of Man had nowhere to lay his head. How do you see your work (if you do) in the light of the Gospel and the Christian message?

AL: I believe in the Christian message, and if Christianity was practised the way it was supposed to be, the world would be a better place. I do believe in the Christian message but I do come into contact with people who claim to be Christian but what they practise in their lives isn't Christianity. I also think Buddhism has a lot to offer, and also being in contact with the power of nature. They're all intertwined. Others would disagree with that.

SJC: In one of the Gospel stories, Mary Magdalene wanted to pour an expensive perfume over Christ and the apostles scolded her, saying that the alabaster jar could be sold and the money given to the poor. But Christ encouraged her to do it and in turn scolded the apostles, saying, "The poor you will have always with you." What do you make of that?

AL: That's right. I suppose you could write volumes on that and read what you like into it but the more you look at what's being said in the Gospels, has anything dated or has anything changed? We use Mary to talk about the sinner but there's a powerful message in her whole role. The purpose of those stories is to get people thinking and do you have to come up with their solution? The Gospels are there to focus and challenge us and make us think.

SJC: Are you a spiritual person? What are your beliefs? I know you meditate every day for at least twenty minutes.

AL: I would consider myself a spiritual person, but the difference between religion and spirituality is extreme. I think we don't often make that distinction but we should. I think we are all spiritual human beings and there's a great poverty in people's lives and a great emptiness. People are searching and we don't place enough emphasis on spirituality. Spirituality is a much deeper thing than religion and I think there's a great hunger out there.

SJC: What does the future hold for Trust specifically and for homeless people generally? What more is to be done?

AL: I think that every day we have to continue to work the way we are working and never lose sight of people. The future of Trust lies in the lap of the gods. I think there's a role and a greater need now for small agencies than ever before. I think the future of Trust will depend on others who come along the way and who value the philosophy of Trust. We owe it to the people who have gone before us to make sure that the philosophy of Trust continues.

SJC: I asked you earlier had Ireland still soul, but what do you think soul is?

AL: I think soul means different things to different people as well. It's almost about a certain vibrancy and difference and vision that makes us unique. The soul of Ireland isn't only about Irish music or dancing but about something that makes us unique. Maybe we're ashamed of our uniqueness. Maybe soul is about energy and spirituality and meaning. We are an island community and soul is that thing that makes us what we are. It's about passion and we did have passion, though it's not politically correct now to be passionate. We have stifled ourselves, stifled our vision and our soul. We are never happy with what we are. We have lost hope.

SJC: Are you happy?

AL: I am. I think life is never about one hundred per cent happiness. I wouldn't work unless I got satisfaction. I would be constantly questioning myself. Like everyone else, I have my good days and my bad days. That's life. It's about balance.

SJC: I want to end by quoting from Micheal O'Siadhail's poem, "The Outsider", taken from the book *A Fragile City*.

> A sheltered arch or where underground
> kitchens of an inn sent
> through grids of pavement grating
> the warmth of the ass's breath —
> where did last night's Christ lie down?

> Every morning for months I watched
> a man I might have been,
> about my age and bearded too,
> his face blotched crimson
> with cheap wine and sleeping rough.

He walked the far side of the street
always hurrying somewhere;
a father who couldn't praise, I wondered,
or what had blurred his star?
For months our eyes never met,

though the street between us was narrow,
until that eve he crossed.
'Some help,' he said, but it must have been
my double's eyes that asked
where would He lie down tomorrow?

An old outsider within me winced,
shook him off and fled;
that street between was so narrow —
I chose the inn and was afraid.
I'm sure I've never seen him since —

but tomorrow when carafes go round
a lone presence will pass
tremors through our frail togetherness;
again those eyes will ask
where did last night's Christ lie down?

Jo Newman
Psychotherapist

Formerly a Dominican sister and lecturer in philosophy at University College Dublin, Dr Josephine Newman works as a psychosynthesis psychotherapist in Eckhart House Institute of Psychosynthesis and Transpersonal Theory. Jo Newman taught me moral philosophy when I was a student in UCD and I remember her classes on Iris Murdoch in particular, as she was personally involved in those lectures — they weren't just exercises in detached philosophical speculation. She was personally implicated in her teaching. I had an absorbing conversation with her in Eckhart House about soul, self and society. She had asked me for a copy of the questions in advance and worked on them beforehand. All her conceptual conclusions and quiet confidence are the product of an experiential exploration.

SJC: What is your understanding of psychosynthesis?

JN: I would describe it as a psychology of the Self, the centre and organising principle of the human psyche. Let me talk here about a few of the important characteristics. That Self or centre of the person is inclusive of body, feelings, mind, soul and spirit, conscious and unconscious. We aren't just talking about my conscious self, or self-identity, but of possibilities and potentials of the whole person. This centre of the person is a unifying dynamic, throughout the many phases and stages and levels of a person's experience or becoming, of being and becoming whole. When that unifying dynamic within the person is ineffective, dormant or blocked, then fragmentation, dissociation, denial and repression take hold. In that sense, psychosynthesis reflects the old, foundational, philosophical principle of the One and the Many, of the parts in relation to the whole. The whole is in each part and the whole is greater than the sum of its parts. Psychosynthesis, then, builds on the psychological experience of the parts in relation to the whole. It construes each part in relation to that whole — body, feelings, mind, soul and spirit. Within the individual, this inner movement towards wholeness takes root in the question: who am I? How am I one and yet many different parts?

In saying this, I want also to emphasise that psychosynthesis, in my view, has significance not so much for its specific theoretical components, many of which are drawn from different strands of psychological, religious and philosophical traditions, but as a map of the territory of the psyche as the Self forms and shapes its own unique development and expression in life.

SJC: What attracted you to the philosophy and psychology of psychosynthesis in the first place?

JN: It's now almost twenty years since I first encountered psychosynthesis in the form of a week's course. At the time I found it quite powerful and I had a strong sense of it as a key to something I was missing, which was very central to my sense of inward direction in the concrete context of my life. With hindsight I can now say that I was, at the time, searching for clues in answer to that basic question: who am I? Psychosynthesis gave me a way of recognising and owning the many desires and divergent parts of my life, which at the time, left me with a sense of fragmentation and polarisation of parts and a lot of anxious struggling with that. So maybe I could say that, at a psychological level, what attracted me was precisely the map it provided, which set out the geography or territory of the psyche, the different levels of experience and the connection and interrelationship between each of these levels and the place of the Self as a central, organising principle in the psyche. This perspective was very empowering for me at the time. It didn't, I might say, address the philosophical aspect of my work at the time but it certainly helped to amplify my own understanding of some philosophical concepts relating to moral philosophy in particular, which I was teaching at the time. I think, in particular, of Iris Murdoch's book of the seventies, *The Sovereignty of Good*. She was deeply critical of the philosophical views that ignored or explained away the inner dimension of our moral consciousness. She drew attention to the centrality of moral being and moral knowing. This to me was very important and it opened up a whole new way of approaching the study of moral philosophy.

SJC: You are involved in Eckhart House, which is an Institute of Psychosynthesis and Transpersonal Theory. What is the transpersonal theory that is taught in Eckhart House?

JN: For obvious reasons, I'll have to be limited in my response to this question. Let me give you a few core ideas. Our starting point in Eckhart House is that the reality of transpersonal experience has always been recognised and accepted as part of who we are as human beings. Such experiences are perhaps more familiarly called "soul experiences" but they are normal — we all have them some time or other, though we don't always recognise them as soul experiences or, indeed, remember them. In fact, we more often deny or repress them or explain them away. So what are the characteristics of these experiences? They are moments of insight or higher intuition that touch us or give us an intimation of deep spiritual qualities of being. I would mention qualities such as integrity, peace or gratitude, justice, love, compassion, goodness and many others. We call these experiences transpersonal in that they are beyond, in the sense of being more than or deeper than, our usual mode of experience; that is, what our usual thought patterns, feeling patterns or behaviour patterns are and set out to achieve, namely the happiness, esteem or survival of our personal egos. They are not organised by the ego, which consciously or unconsciously maintains its own system and life energy. In that sense, they come to us gratuitously.

SJC: They are a gift of Being.

JN: They are a gift of Being. So for example, you could imagine a person working to achieve a sense of peace or gratitude or justice as part of his/her self-identity yet one might, at the same time, lack an inner sense or embodiment of peace or gratitude or justice as a quality of one's being. These qualities of being are transpersonal and point to a spiritual level of being. We cannot achieve them. We discover that they are part of us beyond what we set out to achieve. These kind of transpersonal experiences are well known and well documented in the annals, so to speak, of the race. They are often expressed in poetry, art or music or in the simple communion with nature. They can also, however, come through pain or suffering or through a sense of meaninglessness and despair, when we experience, perhaps, a breakthrough moment to a different dimension of our being. An example of that would be in Brian Keenan's book, *An Evil Cradling*, where he talks about a moment when he experienced compassion for his torturer in the midst of his pain and suffering. We must also point to the many records of authentic, mystical and spiritual experiences associated with the different religious traditions throughout our history.

Let me now say how Assagioli approached the questions and issues relating to these kinds of experiences. First of all, he attributed them to a level of our psyche that is unconscious and beyond our ordinary level of consciousness as personal selves. As such, they are expressions of an in-pouring of a higher or deeper unconscious centre within us, which he calls the Higher Self and which I prefer to call the Deeper Self. These experiences are fleeting; they are breakthrough moments in consciousness of the higher and transpersonal unconscious dimension. They are not, in themselves, reducible to the lower unconscious of Freudian theory. Assagioli differed from Freud in that he construed the person from the perspective of wellbeing, rather than from the perspective of pathology. His aim in psychosynthesis was to develop and highlight both the possibility and the difficulties and distortions in integrating the more spiritual level or dimension of our psyche. Essentially, this required a person to develop and practise a meditative capacity to open, to receive gratuitously, to embody and express these spiritual qualities of the Self as soul and spirit. Ultimately, meditative practice can be transformative in and through a surrender of the personal self-centre to the transpersonal or deeper centre of one's being. However, Assagioli is clear that this level of synthesis and integration presupposes and requires, on an ongoing basis, a process of synthesis at the personal-self level. He did not dispense with Freud's insistence on the analysis of the lower unconscious or with its necessity in principle and in some form of practice in order to achieve an adequate level of personal integration or synthesis. Assagioli was well aware that the acquisitive capacity of the ego-self will all too readily pursue and use transpersonal experiences for its own aggrandisement or as compensatory consolation in relation to its own need fulfilment. Real need deficiencies at the level of the ego (personal self) are to be worked through in the context of the dynamics of the personal, lower unconscious. The possibility of synthesis at the level of soul presupposes a sufficiently well integrated ego or personal self. (This is not to say, however, that "synthesis" is mandatory for salvation! Synthesis is a psychological thrust in the psyche that fosters wellbeing and wholeness and can heal the sense of fragmentation that so often besets us in our lives).

Let me now try to indicate to you what we mean by transpersonal theory as we teach it in Eckhart House. Míceál O'Regan, OP, who was the founder and director of Eckhart House, was clear from the beginning that psychosynthesis provided a much-needed psychological perspective on the path that leads towards recognition, acceptance and integration of a spiritual dimension of human experience. He was equally clear that this psychological perspective needed to be grounded by drawing on the insights into the vision and practice of the spiritual path embodied in the wisdom traditions of both East and West. Practice in these traditions is not a technique in our contemporary sense of the word. It implies, rather, a vision, a theory of an Absolute and an existential path or direction towards the Absolute. (Within the Judaeo-Christian tradition, which is the tradition we specifically connect with, the Absolute includes, of course, the reality of Person.) The practice we teach in Eckhart House is one of presence to body, feelings, mind, soul and spirit. It is a practice of inner, embodied self-awareness. Let me remind you that in the West we've had terrible difficulties about inward awareness or knowing. Suzuki, the Zen teacher, warns us: "The eye that looks outward leads to knowledge, the eye that looks inward leads to wisdom. But if we look inward with the eye that looks outward, we confuse the inner with the outer." In the West we have lost the tradition of inner knowing and so we keep looking inward with the eye that looks outward and we try to grasp what this is as if it were an object. This causes confusion in our understanding of the idea of presence to self as a way of spiritual practice.

SJC: Eckhart House is named after the fourteenth-century German Dominican mystic, Meister Eckhart. In what way does his thinking influence the work carried out in Eckhart House?

JN: Eckhart's mysticism sets out for us the way of inward awareness. Again, we must see this in the context of vision and practice, or theory and method, which the great spiritual traditions embody. Eckhart's vision of the Absolute and the existential path towards it emphasises the person's capacity for self-reflective awareness and its ground in participation of the divine nature. The practice or method he set out was the way of detachment or the letting go of all the desires we experience and become attached to. For Eckhart, it was the clinging to our desires that gave us a false and limited sense of who we are in God. This notion of detachment has very negative connotations for our modern ears and indeed it has been the source of great misunderstanding and distortion of the true nature of the religious way. It suggests a letting go of desire as getting rid of or forcefully overcoming our desires. It has often been practised that way, unfortunately. This kind of attitude to our desires surely diminishes us as human persons and this is not what Eckhart meant by his use of the word "detachment". He was pointing to the search of the human spirit for its true ground and fullness of life.

Contemporary developmental psychology can help us revise our faulty notions of detachment through its concept of identification and disidentification. Briefly, I develop my sense of self by identifying with or becoming the shape, form or content of my experiences through the different phases and stages of my development, physical, emotional, intellectual and spiritual. This identification process has three dynamic moments or phases within it: I identify with my experience. I become, therefore, an athlete. I disidentify from or let go of that identification in order to open to a new identification; for example, becoming a parent. Letting go one identification and beginning to engage another identification is not getting rid of the former in favour of the latter. It is, rather, a letting go of the exclusive identification with it in order to include more experience of who I am and who I may become. However, the experience of the disidentification phase is always psychologically difficult because it feels like we're losing a part of our self until we find our feet, so to speak, in the new identification. Only then can I truly say, "I am an athlete and I am also a parent and I am more than that." It's always about being more than any identification. Detachment, in Eckhart's sense, may be interpreted as a way of disidentification. Each disidentification gives a particular form and content to my experience of myself. To disidentify or detach myself from it is to include it rather than exclude it, by integrating it as part of who I am. I do not let go of life; I go into more life. For Eckhart, this letting go into more life is experienced as an ongoing emptying process, whereby we practise letting go of all that limits and blocks us from sinking down into the ground of our Being, to find who we truly are in God. When you ask, "What is Eckhart's influence on Eckhart House?", it is really about his teaching on the practice of letting go, or detachment, but we teach and evoke this through the dynamic of identification/disidentification.

SJC: Psychosynthesis is a transpersonal psychology. How does it relate to other transpersonal psychologies, such as Jungian psychology, for example?

JN: There's a growing volume of research and study in the area of transpersonal psychology today. The best guide and certainly the most comprehensive analysis and critique of this is provided by Ken Wilber, who is a transpersonal theorist in the USA. I would also like to point out that in Eckhart House we do not talk about transpersonal psychology but about transpersonal theory, because we relate to insights from philosophical and religious traditions as well as to those of psychology. As I have already said, it was a conviction of Míceál O'Regan's from the start of Eckhart House that psychosynthesis, as a psychology, needed something more and at the same time that something more needed the psychosynthesis perspective. He was referring to the tradition of meditative practice, which we call meditative presence — presence to body, feelings, mind, soul and spirit. To facilitate this meditative practice we use the psychosynthesis map as it points to and differentiates the levels of soul and spirit, as deep centres unifying the complexity of phases and stages of our experience. The real work in this area is in facilitating the awareness of whatever blocks us from enacting and connecting with soul level experience in our personal lives. Since you asked about Jungian transpersonal psychology, in particular, let me add a few brief points. In psychosynthesis, the territory of the higher unconscious has its ground and centre in a transpersonal Self, usually called the Higher Self. This is not to be confused with the archaic archetypes of the collective unconscious of Jungian psychology. Assagioli wanted to distinguish between the prepersonal and the transpersonal contents of the collective unconscious and also between the transpersonal higher unconscious and the Higher Self as soul and spirit. Spirit level in Assagioli's map is beyond the images and symbols, which express the higher unconscious. It is the level of Absolute or Universal Spirit or God. I suppose in the Christian tradition we know of that from the writings of the great mystics, which point to the level of spirit as beyond image and symbol. It is a knowing by not knowing. Ultimately, it is described by some mystical writers as the way of the heart.

SJC: Lacanians would say that we are subjects of the signifier and that if Spirit exists it can only be accessed via the signifier.

JN: I am not sufficiently aware of the implications of Lacanian analysis to make any useful comments on this. But I refer you to Ken Wilber's work, especially his book *Sex, Ecology and Spirituality*, which explores this topic in the context of transpersonal theory.

SJC: We have had four thousand years of the codification of human experiences of the Divine, so that all these women and men are either mad or mystics.

JN: We cannot say they are all mad, nor can we say they're all mystics! But we *do* know that a great deal of time and energy throughout the ages has been spent in drawing up criteria of validity, which distinguish genuine mystical experience from illusory experience. Authentic religious traditions set great store on such criteria of validity and their emphasis on the way of religious practice rather than on pursuit of spiritual experiences for their own sakes as the hallmark of their authenticity.

SJC: What's your view of psychoanalysis?

JN: Let me say that we have always had great respect for the principles of psycho-analysis in Eckhart House. As Ken Wilber reminds us, Assagioli was one of the first to call for an integration of depth psychology with what Assagioli called "height" psy-chology and to combine psychoanalysis with psychosynthesis. Indeed, the names themselves point to the basis for such a combination: namely the "analysis" of parts in relation to the ego-self followed by "synthesis" of parts in terms of the whole. Assagioli, of course, was a contemporary and friend of Freud's and the scientific studies of medicine and psychology were firmly in place before he developed his theory of psychosynthesis. He wrote his doctoral thesis on psychoanalysis. How-ever, Assagioli was unwilling to ignore, because unscientific in the accepted sense, the many testimonies of the reality of spiritual experiences embodied in spiritual tra-ditions of both East and West. His own Italian and Jewish background, his classical education and study of several languages, including Russian and Sanskrit, nourished and refined his religious sensibilities and influenced him as much as his scientific studies. So he construed the self of human consciousness as body, feelings, mind, soul and spirit and addressed the issues, difficulties and possible distortions in the self's efforts to unify the multiplicity and complexity of different levels of experience.

There is a story told about Freud and Assagioli, which points to this. One day, Freud called on Assagioli in Italy and asked him to consider introducing psychoanaly-sis to the Italian medical community. Assagioli replied: "Well, Doctor Freud, I would be delighted to, but you must know that I will have to make some adjustments in your theories if I am to teach them. You see, you teach that we are a house with a basement and a first floor, whereas in my theoretical house there is a basement, a first floor, a second floor, a third floor, a sun-roof and an elevator!" So far as our work in psychosynthesis is concerned, the elevator spends a great deal of time moving between the basement and the first floor of the house!

The point I want to make is that any attempt to deal with the ground level of the psyche must necessarily rely on Freud's foundational insights. However, that is not to say that psychoanalysis, as such, is an essential part of psychosynthesis. What is essential is the development of a capacity for a non-judgemental awareness of one's reactive patterns of behaviour, feelings and thoughts, which block one's capacity for inner freedom and a willingness to direct and express one's inner freedom in the choices that one makes. However, let me stress that this is a process one practises, not a technique that achieves it as a goal. It is never an end product we achieve.

SJC: When you were talking a minute ago of the basement and the various storeys of the house I was reminded of Freud's letter to Binswanger in 1936 where he wrote: "But of course I don't believe a word of it. You claim that there is a fine building with upper storeys in which there are high-born guests such as religion, art and philosophy. I have spent all my life down in the cellar and on the first floor of the building, and I found a place in my cellar for religion when I categorised it as an obsessional neurosis of mankind, and I've no doubt that if I had another lifetime I could find a place in my cellar for all those other high-born guests. You and other culture-specimens of *homo natura* think as you do. But you are the conservative and I am the revolutionary."

JN: Well, it's a question of different perspectives really!

SJC: Lacan, for one, is extremely critical of the whole idea of "synthesis" and "integration" and "wholeness", these humanistic ideals he puts in the Imaginary order, arguing that the reality of man is that he is divided against himself, that he is a "split subject". Is there such a thing as synthesis and is it the same thing as integration?

JN: Well, Lacan's work has, of course, recently become academically acceptable and as a consequence it carries weight in some academic circles. But there are other viewpoints, which construe the human person's experience from different perspectives, ones that may or may not be of interest in academia. This, however, does not negate their right to claims of validity and authenticity. Other criteria than those recognised in current academic practice may be pertinent. (Wilber's viewpoint is interesting in this context.) With this in mind, I would like to take up the last part of your statement only and say that synthesis is the same as integration. Assagioli called it synthesis because he lived in a time when psychoanalysis was being developed. He went with the dynamic of synthesis, of relating all the parts within the whole psyche because he construed the person from the perspective of wholeness and wellbeing rather than of his/her pathology. Martin Buber also talked about synthesis in relation to the core self, as the healing dynamic in the psyche. He said that the more dissociated the person is, the less able she/he is to connect with the healing centre within his or her self. Buber knew Assagioli and it is thought that Buber may have been the first to use the term "synthesis" in this context.

SJC: Some say Assagioli coined the term "transpersonal" and others say it was Jung.

JN: Yes, but the transpersonal for Assagioli is not the same as the archaic, collective unconscious. He was clear about this. Wilber deals at length with the significance of the distinction between them.

SJC: Wilber says that Freud reduces the transpersonal to the prepersonal and Jung elevates the prepersonal to the transpersonal and confuses the collective unconscious with the transpersonal. Both commit the "pre/trans fallacy", as Wilber puts it.

JN: Yes.

SJC: What makes you so sure that there is this drive towards synthesis and that we are not just split-subjects and eternally divided against our selves?

JN: We are all that too, but I do think that there's a movement of synthesis within us. The sense of one's own personal identity has to include its unity. Ultimately, I think it goes back to the profound and original philosophical insight of the One and the Many: somehow reality is multiple and somehow it is one. So too in the psychological sphere the perennial human question is: "How am I one and many at the same time? I have many parts and levels and yet I am one."

SJC: But the aim really, as far as you are concerned, is to recollect and unite the disparate parts of the personality?

JN: Well, not just the personality. The point is that there is more to the person than the personality as socially constructed and shaped. There is a further *level* that we call transpersonal and it includes but is more than the personality as such. It is the level of soul and the soul is the deep centre and organising principle of the psyche as a whole. But let me also add, by way of reflection, that a distortion of the whole thing would be to claim that you cannot reach the spiritual level or that you cannot be deeply spiritual unless you get synthesised at the personality level. Rather, it means simply that there is a natural thrust in the psyche that can make us more open to our spiritual potential. We stress the unifying core of the self, rather than the contents of consciousness.

SJC: So why should anyone have an analysis?

JN: Well, it is a well tried and proven method, which facilitates people in coming to terms with the unconscious roots of their personal motivation and desire.

SJC: But they're only living in the basement, as you see it! You would see a top floor to which they could go!

JN: It's not about getting higher and higher. This would lead one to think that some people are higher in being than others.

SJC: But there is that height metaphor, so it is tempting to see it like that.

JN: It is of course and that's one of the difficulties with psychosynthesis, and that's why I prefer the metaphor of depth than height.

SJC: But with that model in mind, it would seem that psychoanalysis is only working in one area of the psyche and that they are missing out in the transpersonal dimensions.

JN: Nobody is missing out on having a transpersonal dimension. Some people simply don't want to recognise or integrate it in the way psychosynthesis does this. For others, there is the classical Freudian assumption that every spiritual experience is reducible to the lower unconscious.

SJC: Assagioli is famous for his egg-shaped diagram, which distinguishes between the lower, middle, collective and higher unconscious and between the self and the Higher Self or soul. Can you go through these for me?

JN: Let me say first that Assagioli portrays it in this egg diagram and you could be forgiven for thinking that he reifies it. It looks static but it is not so in reality. In psychosynthesis, what we address is the story of the self. One has to be clear about the underlying assumptions held about the Self because this affects how we tell the story. For example, the Christian and Buddhist starting points in the story would be different because the western Christian tradition construes the Self as body, feelings, mind, soul and spirit. In the Buddhist tradition, on the other hand, the starting point is the no-self. In Eckhart House, we make the following assumptions, which reflect our rootedness in the Western Judaeo-Christian tradition: the Self is complex, dynamic, relational and embodied.

If you look at the map in that context, it focuses on the different levels of that story. The lower unconscious is the territory of life's fundamental energies, shaped and sculpted by genes and early learning experiences; the middle unconscious represents psychological processes and events accessible to conscious awareness by a small trigger (it is Freud's ante-room of consciousness or what Assagioli calls the "middle unconscious"). It's what I can record easily. It's not deeply unconscious. The higher unconscious or the superconscious is the territory of a person's aspirations or thrust to express love, creativity, justice, beauty, goodness and so on. According to Assagioli, it is the region from which we receive our higher intuitions and inspirations, artistic, scientific or philosophical, ethical imperatives and urges to humanitarian or heroic action.

Assagioli describes the field of consciousness as the part of our personality of which we are directly aware, that is to say, the incessant flow of sensations, images, thoughts, feelings, desires and impulses, which we can observe, analyse and judge. We receive such awareness in our bodies, feelings and mind. The conscious self or "I" represents the distinction between the contents of awareness and the one who is aware. It points to our capacity not to identify with the contents of our awareness and to open to the reality that no experience exhausts all our possibility in relation to experience. The Higher Self is the deeper subject or source of inner processes and outer actions. It is beyond and is the conscious self, as ground and figure. In Greek philosophy it was referred to as "soul" (the organising principle of life).

The collective unconscious is the outer line of the diagram that delineates but doesn't divide. For Assagioli, it is analogous to the membrane delineating a cell and permitting an active and constant interchange with the whole body to which the cell belongs.

Assagioli says that, properly understood, it is extremely useful as a crude and elementary picture that can give only a structurally static, almost anatomical representation of our inner constitutions; but it is especially useful in distinguishing the different levels of a person, which are distinct though not separate.

SJC: So is a psychosynthesis practitioner a Freudian in that he will accept the pre-personal realm of the psyche; a Jungian in that he will accept the collective unconscious; and a Wilberian (or whatever) in postulating a transpersonal realm?

JN: I would prefer to say that psychosynthesis includes these levels you refer to. Perhaps it uniquely portrays the way in which each level relates to the other levels.

This is very important if we are to avoid confusion and distortion of levels in our psychological experience.

SJC: Jungian psychology is psychologism. Jung psychologises the spiritual. For him, God is an archetype.

JN: Well, Jung has certainly been accused of psychologising the spiritual. But, perhaps, Jung wouldn't be too bothered about that. In psychosynthesis, we claim that the spiritual cannot be reduced to the psychological. So, in Eckhart House, we stress Assagioli's claim that psychology brings one to the door of spiritual transformation but not beyond that.

SJC: Can one be a transpersonalist and not a theist?

JN: Yes, in a manner of speaking. If you see theism as primarily concerned with belief structures, dogmatic and doctrinal statements, then one might not claim to be a theist and yet be very connected with the transpersonal dimension of life. But faith in the deep sense is not only about correct doctrine but also about opening to the perception of the Divine. Such perception is the hallmark of our spiritual nature as human beings.

SJC: According to the psychosynthesis model, we are biopsychospiritual beings, possessing a body, feelings, mind, soul and spirit. These five reveal the whole person. Is the idea that all five must be properly balanced in order to enjoy mental health and "happiness"?

JN: I don't see mental health and happiness as the primary goal of psychosynthesis. It is much more a question of self-realisation and wholeness through living an embodied, relational existence in the real world, subject to the difficulties and contingencies of all human life. To say that it is primarily about happiness and mental health is to sell it short, I believe, and to settle for an egoistic view of life as about "me-fulfilment". That said, however, it is very easy to succumb to the temptation of becoming self-absorbed in engaging one's psychological processes in any psychotherapy. We need to be aware of Hillman's critique of psychotherapy in his book of the 1990s: *We've had 100 Years of Psychotherapy and the World is Getting Worse.* What he is referring to, of course, is that psychotherapy in the past tended to make people more self-absorbed and less willing to engage in public life and in the active life of community service. He is making the point that psychotherapy needs to decisively turn away from any tendency it may have had in the past to avoid active engagement in any and all aspects of life. Psychosynthesis, in particular, needs to be careful, also, to avoid any tendency it may have had to pursue spiritual experiences as compensation for lack of ego-fulfilment, thereby cultivating, however inadvertently, avoidance patterns in relation to ordinary life demands on the person.

SJC: For Iris Murdoch, love is grasping and selfish, as it is for Lacan, though Iris Murdoch holds out hope in that she has a purified notion of love, which she labels the Good (following Plato); but in the Freudian tradition, love is narcissistic. For the Lacanians, love is lack. So is there a love beyond the love I have just talked about?

JN: For Iris Murdoch, love at the ego level is grasping and selfish. But that is a distortion of love, she would claim, arising from the quasi-mechanical energy of the unregenerate psyche. But love is capable of infinite refinement, according to Murdoch, in that we are necessarily attracted by the Good. This reality, for her, is the hallmark of the spiritual being. In psychosynthesis terms, then, we would say that, at the ego-level, love is always experienced in relation to the lack in one's ego and the desire to fill that lack. At the transpersonal level, however, one can practise living out of a sense of abundance rather than lack. In that way one can experience love as an in-flowing of the deep Self centre and the desire to express love in one's life. Such love is a gift of Being and is not achieved as an ego desire.

SJC: So you wouldn't deny the notion that human love is selfish and that we see the other as an enlargement or expansion or extension of our selves?

JN: No, not at the ego level. But there is another level in which we receive love as a gift and express it in life. It comes to us through a practice of meditative presence, being receptive to the whole self.

SJC: That implies God, doesn't it? Which I have no problem with!

JN: It implies the Higher Self. Obviously, God or the Universal Being is the overall context. If you are talking about the theory of psychosynthesis, love involves an in-pouring of the Higher Self but, in turn, the Higher Self is open to the in-pouring of Spirit, the Absolute Source of Life.

SJC: God?

JN: Well yes, provided you realise we are here in the order of gift and grace, not of ego purposes.

SJC: It seems to me that you can't be an atheist and at the same time buy into all this?

JN: I'm sure an atheist wouldn't buy into this, as you say. But that might be more a question of the language we use with its overlay of history and historical disputes about such matters. What we're talking about in psychosynthesis is the domain of human experience, and in particular the experience of spiritual qualities of being. Within that context, I'm saying that human persons are capable of spiritual experience. In Aquinas's terms, man is *capax Dei*. At the level of soul, the language that expresses experience is that of image, symbol and ritual. At the level of spirit, the language of knowing is beyond image and symbol. It's a knowing by not knowing. If you look at the wisdom sayings of the Buddha, for example, they are all expressions of paradox. The principle of contradiction is transcended. Yet these sayings are meaningful in a deeper spiritual sense.

SJC: Let's say I have all these images in me; what do I do with them? A Lacanian would say it's all very well having these images but they have to be translated into words (signifiers). So there's no point in having these endless images floating around the psyche.

JN: It's not about having images flying around your psyche. The image and symbol-making faculty is needed. It's about the *act* of imaging. In the psychosynthesis context, it's about asking: "Who am I? And what is emerging for me?" I can relate to such questions at a deep level only in an *act of imaging*. The contents and interpretation of the images are of secondary importance. In imaging here, I am engaging my faculty of creative imagination. It's a soul-making faculty, which I need to evoke as I engage a sense of my inner direction in life.

SJC: You work with sub-personalities, with the many split-off selves within us. How do we go about integrating these?

JN: Assagioli drew his map topographically, so when we look at the sub-personalities on the map we see them as subparts of the ego. They are instinctually organised centres of energy adapted to achieve some perceived want of the ego in the life context of the person. We're all very familiar with these in ourselves and we commonly talk about them when we say, for example, that "X is a control freak or a high achiever or all in the head". We also comment on the negatives of the personality, for example, X is jealous, envious, selfish and so on. The point about these sub-personalities is that we experience no choice in activating them. We are driven by them. The stimulus in activating them comes from the environment, so I meet someone I deeply resent and I find myself acting in a hostile way towards her or him. So these sub-personalities are split-off parts of ourselves that I am identified with in the moment. I am acting out. I am not free in relation to these parts. I might try to hide them but I am unable to disidentify with them. Synthesis at this basic level of the self's development is about aligning these intrapsychic splits within ourselves and not about repressing or controlling them. Why? So that I can experience the reality of inwardly authoring how I see and respond to life. This process is never-ending. It's not something I do or achieve and then forget about. It has three phases we can point to: recognition, acceptance, and integration. The process of recognition and acceptance may be long and difficult since it may bring to mind painful memories and associations long since repressed and forgotten. When we come to recognise, accept and respect them as coping and defensive mechanisms, which we instinctually developed in order to survive and get our needs met, we will then find ourselves less driven and more free from being absorbed in maintaining them. This, in turn, will open up our capacity to engage and relate with reality in a truer and more real sense of ourselves. Needless to say, psychosynthesis psychotherapy here must draw on the very significant body of research into early developmental psychology and psychodynamic theory in general. Assagioli's topographical map needs to be seen within a developmental perspective.

SJC: The notion of the "will" is central in psychosynthesis. Metaphysics speaks of the will as a power of the soul, together with memory and understanding. And Aquinas sees the will as rational desire. Is this how you conceive of it too?

JN: The "will" is very difficult to understand. I suppose I would again point to Iris Murdoch who has some very insightful things to say about the "will". She says that the philosophical idea of the will needs to be attached to the metaphor of vision rather than that of movement or action. The idea of the empty choosing will, as she calls it, hovering over our rational deliberations, over who we want to be and what we want to do and of freely choosing our course, seems unrealistic at best and a dangerous illusion at worst. The reality is, she says, that we are attached to reality, attached to the environment. Our decisions flow from how we see and relate to the environment. I think Murdoch's critique of the idea of free will in current philosophical thought should be studied not only by every educationalist but also by every psychotherapist! I suppose the older pre-dualistic ideas of the will, which you mention in your question, are healthier in terms of the psyche if we could understand them properly. Will is rooted in desire and intentionally directs desire towards its fulfilment. Assagioli talks about the will at different levels of self. The will manifests itself as a drive at the level of the lower unconscious. It is the natural energy of the psyche. At the ego level the appropriate energy of the psyche is to survive, develop and maintain itself in relation to the environment of life. When it comes to the spiritual level, he calls it willingness rather than a wilfulness; a willingness to open to receive rather than achieve and that's quite a different energy. We can't achieve the spiritual; we receive it. An act of will at this level is an act of receiving and expressing who I am as body, feelings, mind, soul and spirit.

SJC: Is that doing the will of God?

JN: Yes, in the older traditional sense but that has so many distortions and negative connotations for us. We need a theory of the will that honours each level of will in our human experience. Assagioli's idea of the will as the expression of self is close to this.

SJC: Wilber says that the higher includes the lower and transcends it.

JN: Yes. And Assagioli's theory of will does that.

SJC: What are the other major concepts or important ideas in psychosynthesis?

JN: I would want to say the practise of presence is central in psychosynthesis as we teach it in Eckhart House. It is not a technique but a practice and a path of being and becoming whole. In Eckhart House we also take Martin Buber's ideas about dialogical psychotherapy, as developed by Maurice Friedman, as centrally important. That has to do with the whole nature of the self as relational and the nature of dialogue. We ourselves take seriously the writings of the great spiritual traditions, especially some of the mystical writers of the Christian tradition, such as Meister Eckhart, and some of the writings of the early Fathers.

SJC: Is the transpersonal simply the spiritual? It's not past lives, UFOs, clairvoyance and parapsychological phenomena in general?

JN: No, it's not any of these. The term transpersonal refers to a level of our human experience that is beyond what our personal efforts can achieve.

SJC: Yeats said, "Things fall apart, the centre cannot hold. Mere anarchy is loosed upon the world"; and Iris Murdoch said: "The centre must hold."

JN: The centre must hold. That's what psychosynthesis is all about. We have no interest at all in things like clairvoyance, the pre-existence of the soul or reincarnation, etc. We're interested in a more traditional sense of spirituality. I would say that a lot of our work in this regard is about clearing the distortions of preconceived ideas and of the culture in relation to the spiritual dimension of being.

SJC: Wasn't it controversial to call your house after Meister Eckhart, considering that Pope John XXII promulgated the Bull, *In Agro Dominico*, in which twenty-six of his statements were listed, with fifteen of them declared heretical and eleven "ill-sounding and suspect". Some regard him as a heretic while others regard him as the forerunner of mystical atheism.

JN: Not so nowadays. All sorts of people refer to Eckhart, such as Heidegger, Suzuki and, of course, contemporary writers on spiritual topics. He seems to have a way of communicating about spirituality as a living thing for today. Of course, a lot of people find John of the Cross more appealing and so on. There is no blueprint that works for everybody. Each must find what resonates with their own spirit.

SJC: And, of course, Aquinas and Eckhart were Dominicans!

JN: Yes. The whole notion of desire in Aquinas is important: desire as self-stretching to become fully who I am. I also find the writings of Thomas Merton very interesting, especially the writings of his later life. Merton's whole teaching is about the silence and solitude within that opens one to the centre of one's being. Silence, he reminds us, is not about stopping and stilling the voices of life and movement around us but about stilling the voices and movement within us that keeps us from the experience of our own inner core and its depth.

SJC: And there is such a centre!

JN: Your mind won't tell you there is. That's what you're practising when you are disidentifying — you are letting go of being absorbed by your thoughts or feelings. The stillness of emptiness, which is a fullness of life, is what it's all about.

SJC: That emptiness permits an inflow of spirit. You can't pour water into a full glass — it has to be empty.

JN: But it's not being empty of everything; it's about being empty of attachment to things. It's a journey into receiving the fullness of life.

SJC: What did Christ say on that point?

JN: "He who loses his life will find it." It's the whole message. "I am the Way, the Truth and the Life." What happened to Him? He was crucified and rose from the dead. He let go of His attachment to life in order to enter the fullness of His life in God.

SJC: Ken Wilber is the great scholarly theorist of the transpersonal. How important is his work and what is the nature of his influence, if any, on the theory and practice of psychosynthesis?

JN: Well, I wouldn't say he has any direct influence on it. For one thing, psychosynthesis was there before he started his work. He does say that Assagioli had an accurate understanding of the distinction between the prepersonal and the transpersonal. He also sees that psychosynthesis can be misinterpreted and misconstrued as it was in one of the Institutes that he was familiar with in California. Mícéal always emphasised that psychosynthesis needs grounding in more than its own context.

SJC: The "more than" is the dialogue with the spiritual traditions?

JN: Yes. It's a way of grounding psychological insights in the insights of the great spiritual traditions. This is not the way of other Institutes of Psychosynthesis, and that's fine.

SJC: Wilber says about psychosynthesis that because of its emphasis on disidentification, it attracts a lot of dissociated types and that, in some cases, the patients took over the hospital. Does it attract dissociated types?

JN: It could. But as in any good psychotherapy, it deals very directly with the sources and symptoms of dissociation in a person's process.

SJC: So you work up from the prepersonal through the personal to the transpersonal, from aggression and sexuality to spirit?

JN: Yes. You cannot skip any one. If you do you distort. I cannot love anyone properly if I don't know how to bond or self-delineate. These are the processes of the ego. They have to be dealt with. We are wounded at this level. Most of the time in this sense love is about merging and filling up my lack but that's not what real love is — real love is love of other, relating to the other as real and not as one who fills my lack.

SJC: Who are the best guides in transpersonal psychology?

JN: As a theorist, I would say Ken Wilber. Stan Grof is one of the significant figures in transpersonal psychology but he goes a different way: he focuses on the rebirthing processes. And there are others like Charles Tart in the US school. I would say that, as a philosophical expression of what transpersonal psychology is, Iris Murdoch has a lot of very grounded things to say. I think that Karlfried Graf Dürckheim and Jacob Needleman have a great deal to teach us. And, of course, Martin Buber: his whole emphasis on dialogue is important. Levinas is also important in pointing to the transcendence of the other, other than our own ego-system. In our own time, there are also many authors, poets and writers who illuminate the sphere of the transpersonal and it is important to keep remembering that.

SJC: Psychoanalysts would be critical of psychosynthesis, saying that the psychosynthesis people emphasise the superconscious too much and almost shy away from the "lower unconscious" and that spirituality can be a defence against sexuality. Do you think that there are any dangers in this regard?

JN: Yes, of course there are. Ignoring one or other of all the dimensions leads to repression or collapsing the higher into the lower or interpreting the lower in terms of the higher. Synthesis seeks to correct that. Of course spirituality can be a defence against sexuality; it can be a defence against anything. All through history we are aware of the distortions of spirituality, aren't we? I think any system can distort. You can repress the superconscious and the spiritual as well as repressing or denying the lower unconscious. Assagioli talked a lot about the repression of the sublime.

SJC: Do psychoanalysts repress the sublime?

JN: I don't think they necessarily do. You have lots of people who are psychoanalysts and who are profoundly spiritual, but the method they work with doesn't allow recognition of the spiritual as transcendent in the way I have been talking about it here.

SJC: Sam Keen felt that the shadow-side of psychosynthesis was its eclectic tendency. Do you have any criticisms of psychosynthesis as a therapy and methodology?

JN: I think one needs to remember that it can promise more than it can deliver as a theory. I become more and more convinced that psychosynthesis needs to develop its notion of meditative practice. Otherwise, it can fall into the trap of just trying to produce spiritual experiences. It needs to be very careful about the levels. It is destructive to collapse everything into the spiritual. Psychosynthesis is eclectic in that its vision is drawn from many other spiritual disciplines including psychology, philosophy and the spiritual traditions. It could become an eclectic mishmash if the levels are not rigidly adhered to. It depends on how you use the map.

SJC: One of the aims of Eckhart House is to guide personal change through reflection and meditation, as a basis for change in society. Do you think that you have been successful in this? And how has Irish society responded to the work of Eckhart House?

JN: I would say over the past twenty years individuals have received help in living their lives and connecting with their potential to become whole. I am talking about a very wide range of people from every level in society. We try to facilitate people to become agents of change in society. This can't be measured or quantified but we get enough feedback to know that it has made a difference.

SJC: Fr Míceál O'Regan OP, founded Eckhart House, as you said earlier. How did the Dominicans come to be involved in such an enterprise?

JN: Through Míceál O'Regan, who was a Dominican. The Dominicans gave him the support and validation he needed in setting up this Institute.

SJC: The present Director is a Dominican too.

JN: Yes, a Dominican sister. The ethos of the House is grounded in the Dominican tradition.

SJC: What is your view of the human person and what have you learned about him/her after practising psychotherapy for so long?

JN: I think the search for the spiritual is very strong in people today. But I think they come to it from a different perspective than before. Because society has changed so much the demands on people are quite different from what they were even twenty to thirty years ago. The "fallout" from this, I think, is that people feel lost and un-grounded. And when that happens there is fragmentation within the person — the centre cannot hold. This results in a great sense of anxiety, restlessness and distur-bance within people, a sense of losing touch with the thread of life. One of the things that attracts people to Eckhart House is the fact that we work with a clearly defined map of the territory of the psyche. This can give people a renewed sense of inner direction and of their own human journey.

SJC: Do you find that your training in philosophy has helped or hindered your work in psychosynthesis?

JN: My own approach to psychosynthesis is very influenced by my philosophical training and former career in philosophy. Philosophically, I will always ask the philo-sophical question and I take my own stance and sense of direction in psychosynthesis from that.

SJC: Is there a difference between prayer and meditation?

JN: Well, I would say that prayer is a more comprehensive category than medita-tion. In fact, real meditation is a form of prayer whereas prayer is not necessarily meditation. It could be a desperate cry of petition, or a joyful prayer of thanksgiving and so on. To meditate in a formal sense, we need to practise stillness and silence within and in that stillness and silence within we may come to receive ourselves as we are in the Vision of God. The great mystical writers have pointed to this level of the human journey. The practice that opens us to meditation and prayer in this sense is that of meditative presence, the practice of being present in and to each moment.

SJC: So if I drink a cup of tea, am I praying?

JN: It depends on how you drink it. Are you present to your act of drinking the tea? One of the most inspiring writers on this practice of presence to self in our everyday lives is the Tibetan Buddhist monk Thich Nhat Hanh. His writings are utterly simple yet utterly profound.

SJC: What happens to us when we die? Do we return to the One from whom we came?

JN: I hope we will rest in peace when we die! We return to God. We return to the Source. As a Christian I believe in the Resurrection. But beyond this faith and hope, we simply do not have the faculties to say what it is about. It's a mystery, as our life in God is a mystery.

SJC: Is God One?

JN: Yes, God is One. So the great philosophers of old tell us. But as a Christian, I also believe that God is three persons in One. Now don't ask me to explain that! I relate to it as part of the mystery of who God is and who we are in God.

DAVID NORRIS
Senator

David Norris is a Senator in Seanad Eireann, Joycean scholar and formerly a lecturer in English literature in Trinity College Dublin. He is trustee of the International James Joyce Foundation. He is perhaps best known for his successful action in the Irish courts and the European Court of Human Rights to have the laws forbidding homosexual acts between consenting adults declared unconstitutional and in breach of the Convention of Human Rights. He is an openly gay, caustically witty, passionate, polemical and mischievous man. Always dressed in sartorial elegance, he brings a conservative grace, outspoken humour and unpredictability to his every public appearance. One could not say that the Senator is shy of the limelight. I never laughed so much, both talking to him in his office and listening later to his voice on the dictaphone. He is a colourful and caring character.

SJC: Where do you get all your energy from? You're involved in the preservation of Georgian buildings, you've lectured in English literature, you give talks and put on a one-man show on Joyce, you've fought tirelessly for the rights of homosexuals and you're involved in politics in your capacity as Senator!

DN: Some of it is genetic, you inherit it, but it is also mental in that if you are interested in things, then that gives you the energy to go on, because I am fascinated by life. I'm fascinated by certain problems; I am motivated and what people imagine is physical energy is motivation. The reason people seem so drained is because they are still buried in meaningless jobs like doing computer keyboarding or whatever it is. You know, repetition, repetition, repetition, so of course, they are as limp as a dishrag; but if they had something they were motivated by . . . I mean, politics is wonderful because you can affect things marginally sometimes, not always immediately, but you know you have caused change. Three or four years ago, I managed to get whole new sections added to the Child Care Bill, which has already saved several children's lives. That is a wonderful feeling. Nobody took any interest in it because it was technical, but it was absorbing. And on the last day of the Senate I got a more progressive motion passed on East Timor than the establishment civil servants had catered for. It outrages and infuriates me, but at the same time gives me energy.

SJC: Which hat do you most enjoy wearing?

DN: The one I have on at any given moment. I loved teaching in Trinity but I did not care for the academic politics one bit, which is nastier and sharper than national politics, and I didn't enjoy marking exam papers. Universities have lost their self-confidence and they were insisting on double-marking all over the place, which is absolute nonsense. What you need to double-mark are the borderline cases, the problematic ones. They combined that with forcing people to mark papers on subjects they hadn't actually taught, so it was idiotic, because on the one hand they were going to these absurd extremes to try and regularise and harmonise marking and on the other hand they had people who were less than competent marking the bloody papers, so all this nonsense is a sure sign of a lack of confidence. It got me down.

SJC: And the insistence on publishing.

DN: Rubbish. It means a lot of drivel is published. It's nonsense. Absolute nonsense.

SJC: You are such a public figure. How do you juggle between the private and public personae?

DN: My private life is lived in Jerusalem. My public life is lived here. I don't have time for very much private life. I do have some and I have started to try to keep weekends free and I do go to Church. I go to the Cathedral and I won't give up that. They are always pushing at me to try to do radio programmes on Sunday morning but I say I won't.

SJC: So you're strict about Sundays.

DN: As much as I can be because I think it is important and good to have a day off for reflection. I like the Cathedral and think it's good to keep that tradition going but the rest of the week is usually very busy.

SJC: What lies behind your disarming jocularity and how do you keep your sense of humour?

DN: I don't know. I'm not aware of it. I enjoy life and I also find humour all over the place including in my own behaviour. I'm quite happy to laugh at myself. But I find a great deal to laugh about in life and to enjoy and celebrate. I think it would be very dull if we didn't.

SJC: But you seem to see humour in adversity and in some pretty awful events, including the hate mail you get.

DN: I enjoy them. Look at what I got a little while ago. It's a copy of a letter, which was written to Pat Kenny: "You were extremely rude to Mr Norris on your show last night. . . . Norris is brilliant, intellectual, scholarly, sophisticated, and witty. He has a great charismatic presence, a wonderful accent and superb vocal delivery and He Is A Protestant". Now isn't that lovely? And then I got this one: "Dear David, Kevin Myers got it spot on. You are a publicity-loving prima donna. Try a little humility for a change." Neither of them signed their names.

SJC: That's typical. Is your active involvement in the life of this nation a defence against lack, against depression?

DN: I don't know. I never really thought of it like that, but it certainly has operated that way. There is no doubt about it. I just don't have time. I do miss people. Ezra was over for a week and I missed him terribly when he went and I've just had two lovely friends from Los Angeles over and I had to leave the day before they did so I had to leave them in charge of the house and I had to take off for Turkey and I really missed them terribly. It's having people live with you for a while. Because when you live alone, which I do in Ireland (I live with Ezra in Jerusalem), it's when people come and stay for a short while and then they're gone again that you feel the emptiness. Otherwise I don't. I have the wireless on all the time. I listen to Lyric FM and then I switch over for Val Joyce because I love the way he puts the CDs in and something funny happens and he says: "Oh, that's interesting. Didn't know it did that. We'll try again." He has a lovely relaxed way and a nice voice.

I read a lot and that, I think, keeps you in touch with other minds, even when they're dead! I'm not a lonely person, I never have been, but I will be agonisingly lonely for particular people. I suppose I would describe Scottie as an old flame because he entered my life when Ezra had just evaporated with somebody else about fifteen years ago and I really care deeply about him. It was lovely to have him and his partner over from Los Angeles. He's a lovely, lovely fellow and they were the first people in my new guest-room and, yes, I missed them when they were gone. When I came back, there were still the flowers they had put by my bed. It's lovely to keep in touch with people and I have friends in different parts of the world and I don't lose friends. For example, with Scott, he's classic American. He moved from small town in Pennsylvania out to Lancaster, to university, then he came over here, then he went to San Francisco and now he's in Los Angeles. He would have had friends in all these different places and lost touch with them. That is the disposable element of American society. [*In an American accent*]: "You have your friends but you move on. Gee. That was my Philadelphia period." Gone. Goodbye. What happened? But I couldn't do that. For instance, Scott had a friend in New York called Rich Plastic. I mean, how could you lose track of somebody with a name like that? I mean a good New York Jew. I think he died of AIDS, actually, but he's gone pretty definitely now, which is rather sad, but he was such a nice person. I have happy memories of him. I only met him the one time and I remember him. But he's obliterated. Ezra's the same. I am the oldest and strongest friend he's had because he goes through periods. He says it himself.

SJC: I can understand that. Sometimes you need to put up a barrier, to forget.

DN: I don't. I keep them all!

SJC: I'm struck by the fact that the public David Norris is witty, caustic, clever, ebullient, effusive, but the private David Norris, at least the one that comes across in *The Cities of David* [*his biography*], is a man who is often troubled, haunted, prey to loss, to loneliness, whose relationship with an Israeli, Ezra Yazhir, is a very difficult and problematic one. You have been hurt quite a lot.

DN: Yes, but I suppose everyone has insecurities and mine . . . well, my father died and made no impression on me at all that I was aware of. I was six years old and he had been in the Congo most of the time and I would see him every so often for a leave of a month and then he was gone again. It wasn't as if he was around and I was aware he was dying. There was no funeral. There was nothing. There he was one day and the next he was gone. Then I was shattered when my grandmother died. Because I was close to her and I did go to the funeral and then I was sent to boarding school. It can give you terrible insecurities, I think.

SJC: I was at boarding school — Castleknock.

DN: Were you? Well, it's rather nice I think.

SJC: Yes it was.

DN: St. Andrews was appalling. Dreadful. Too much of a shock for a small child. You feel the people you love are going to abandon you and that creates a sort of a panic. I'll never see them again. I certainly went through that with Ezra when he went off with Isaac, who is an Israeli disc and javelin champion, and I had this awful feeling of being abandoned. But you never quite lose people anyway and now Ezra and I are back, as close as ever, and Isaac put himself out of the picture. Finally! In the last week or so. It's such a saga I won't go into it. It's hilarious in one sense.

SJC: Do you think you are patronised or taken seriously?

DN: No one is ever taken completely seriously by everybody. But I think people enjoy the sense of humour. I think you can make a political point quite strongly but also humorously.

SJC: How do you think Official Ireland and the man on the street see you? Are they threatened? Is your involved presence a menace, a novelty, a no-longer-questioned simple reality?

DN: I don't think very many people express it that way. At one stage, I got a lot of hate mail, which I don't get as much now, except the occasional one, but I did get a lot of phone calls and there were people who were disturbed by difference. There were people who wanted a very neat, ordered world into which everything fitted nicely. And my bouncing out . . . I didn't fit into the nice neat idea of getting married and doing this, that and the other, and on the other hand, I had been to Trinity, so I obviously wasn't some kind of criminal lunatic. It wasn't so easy to dismiss me.

SJC: And you dress so sartorially!

DN: I don't always. I mean, today, I'm opening the Joyce Summer School but you could just as easily have come across me in a pair of worn denim shorts and a string vest and I do come in on my bicycle dressed like that here. I observe the decorum of the House when it's sitting, but otherwise this is just an office and I don't see why I should dress up just to come into this little rat-hole.

SJC: What do you think soul is, because whatever it is, you seem to have it?

DN: Well, thank you very much. I don't know what it is. It's an unquantifiable property. I think the rap people use it a lot. Soul music.

SJC: Yes, Ricky Martin and Latin soul.

DN: Exactly.

SJC: So what is it?

DN: I think it's the will to live and to live really. It's what's been called the "flame of life". I think that's what it is and I think it's also the distinctive qualities of your personality. I was pleased to be told by some friends of Ezra's that I had Jewish soul. I think that's rather nice because they are Jewish and what they mean by that is that you have a soul which understands us even though you aren't Jewish yourself. I found that very pleasing and flattering. Everybody has their own soul, their own individuality, but an awful lot of people are afraid to express it because they are afraid of being seen as eccentric. I don't give a damn if I'm seen as eccentric. It doesn't worry me in the slightest because if you are not eccentric in some way, you are just a carbon copy of everybody else, which means your life is dull, uninteresting and flat. And I think that's a shame. With regard to anything more metaphysical, soul is . . . the problem is, we'll only know when we pop. Is there anything afterwards? Is there a soul beyond the natural, beyond the physical, beyond the material? I think there could be. They are able to decode the messages of the brain and it's all electrical circuitry and all the rest of it and I'm sure that will eventually be replicated in a machine, in a computer that can give the appearance of thinking; but there remains the mystery of consciousness. I don't believe you'll ever have a machine that's aware of its own processes and the human and other animals are aware of that. I think that is a wonderful mystery and it doesn't seem to me to be axiomatic that consciousness is dependent on the physical. In the meantime, it's a wonderful privilege to be alive and to be able to register these impressions and just feel.

SJC: But you have obviously experienced the sense of the noumenon or else you wouldn't keep returning to St Patrick's Cathedral week after week.

DN: Oh yeah. Absolutely. In a way, it's a kind of discipline, but I can thank my aunt for that because I was her chauffeur to go to St Patrick's. That's why I kept going and so it was accidental. But I always loved it. I loved the music and the ritual but both are quite variable. Either the music can be superb or else it can be absolutely bloody awful. It is not consistent and in terms of the ritual, I like a certain elegance. I like the wearing of the copes and all that sort of stuff. They have gone. The new Dean has locked them in the cupboard and instead of the wafers, which he regarded as too Roman, we are now reduced to wholemeal brown sliced bread, which I don't like at all. You get crumbs, which I think is awful. I battled to save the vote on candles in the side aisle and this awful new liturgy, the product of illiterate minds, both theo-logically and aesthetically. And this "Peace of the Lord be with you. And also with you. We will now exchange the sign of peace." We will in our fanny. I won't. I put my hands behind my back and I just say Happy Christmas, Jingle Bells, Merry Easter and all that stuff and whatever you are having yourself, but I do not touch strangers.

SJC: Is it not the Christian thing to do, though?!

DN: Not as far as I'm concerned! You never know where they have been. They could have been scratching their balls or picking their noses. There was a quartet of these people in front of me about three Sundays ago and they were kissing — the sound out of them [*imitates kissing*]! I thought they were going to start on me!

SJC: You took the Irish government to the European courts in order to have the ban on homosexual acts between consenting adults lifted. Isn't there more to do? Like the recognition in law of same-sex relationships akin to marriage? That seems to me to be the next step. Is anything happening around that?

DN: A little bit. I got correspondence from a couple in West Cork who were going out with each other for fifty years. One of them was 80 and the other was 75 and the older of the two thought it would be a good idea to put the house in the other person's name, which he did. But then the younger man got cancer and died. The older man had to pay £250,000 debt duties for the privilege of living in his own house because the relationship wasn't recognised. That was savage and disgusting and inhuman, although no doubt the Pope and [*Cardinal*] Ratzinger would think it's a good idea; but I raised that and then started to get more letters, not just from people in gay relationships, and eventually I got universal support in the Senate. At first they thought, "There's old Norris up to his old tricks." But they then took it seriously and I did manage to persuade Charlie McCreevy to make alterations in the last Budget for the recognition of inheritance tax for these people. I was very pleased about that. That's where it really counts. Dressing up in white suits and going up the altar of the Pro-Cathedral is not what's really important and that will take a very long time. Although, according to Boswell, there were, in the Middle Ages, clear liturgical rituals within the Roman Catholic Church for same-sex marriages, which has been buried out of sight. What I was doing was dismantling the idea of marriage to look at the component parts, which were of a practical nature, such as the tax situation, and it's much less threatening for the average person on the street to go for it piecemeal rather than for the idea of gay marriages. And gay relationships are not necessarily the same as heterosexual ones anyway. There is a difference. I suppose I'm a fairly conservative person anyway. Ezra always said that it was a very good idea that I was gay because if I wasn't I would be the squarest person on the face of the planet!

SJC: He called you "a straight gay"!

DN: Yes! But even I have to recognise that gay relationships are not exactly the same and lazily creating a model based on the heterosexual one is foolish. Because gay people are outside the structures of society, it's a wonderful opportunity to create more manageable relationships. As far as I'm concerned, I would have been quite happy living with both Ezra and Isaac. I always said to them that my idea of heaven was Ezra doing the cooking, me doing the tidying and Isaac doing the sex. Hell would be me doing the sex, Ezra doing the tidying and Isaac doing the cooking!

SJC: Do you have any theories on the aetiology of homosexuality? As you know, the Freudian position states that it's something about attachment to the mother.

DN: Ah, not at all. I think that's all balls. No, I just think that's rubbish. It couldn't be, because if you look at the number of siblings in exactly the same condition, including identical twins, one of them may turn out gay and the other not. Personally, I think a lot of it is social conditioning, but I think it's a spectrum. I think there are people with a greater inclination towards their own sex. I have had friends, for example, who are heterosexual and who tell me that the male body is more beautiful, but they can't have children, so there's the practical, functional thing and society is engineering you all the time towards this goal of marriage for the purposes of reproduction — but God, we've certainly overdone that little item!

SJC: You knew you were gay before you were nine. So is it innate, genetic?

DN: Yes, I'm sure it is. It's a complex mixture. You find that you are instinctively attracted to something and maybe it is something about the bigger, protective man who provides shelter and reassurance. That's part of it. There's an aesthetic thing as well. People are drawn to different things. Some people like the sea, some people like the mountains, some people like both. Bisexuality exists. I think it's a small number of people. I recently met a couple who have been living together for a very long time, about thirty years, and obviously the sexual novelty has worn off and they have a string of partners who are married. I'm not going to criticise them, but it shows you that there are a significant number of married people who engage in it from time to time because it is fun and there is no responsibility and it's a different kind of experience and I don't think that it's particularly destructive.

SJC: Do you think there is a shadow-side to the increased liberalisation of homosexuality?

DN: There is, because there is a trivialisation of sex. Personally, I think there is a place for a degree of reticence. I do not wish to see every person passing down the street in a sexual light. I want to draw a veil over it and I imagine they want to draw a veil over me as a sexual item too! It's wonderful when you do come across a situation in which someone is immensely sexually alluring. As a duty, I went to the theatre recently because I was a patron to the group involved, and sitting in front of me was one of the most beautiful men I had ever seen in my life. I got talking to him and it was quite fun because he had done law in UCD and he said that if he ever met me he would tell me what a misery I had made out of his life, because every second case he had to learn seemed to involve me, about buggery or getting thrown out of the Senate or whatever. He said there I was and they were always bloody long. I spent part of the performance admiring the back of his neck and his lovely little ears and his huge wide shoulders. Then it turned out that he was the boyfriend of one of the women in the show.

SJC: Is there a part of you which still says, "Yes, I'd like the support that society gives to the heterosexual life", in terms of marriage, public recognition, and so on?

DN: Not really, because it wasn't what I drew by my lot; but yes, on the other hand, I think to have children which are the fruit of yourself physically and the person you love is a beautiful thing. But I don't believe in having children just for the sake of having children. I think they are a bloody nuisance most of the time. At least you can hand back your nephew and niece.

SJC: What's your relationship with the gay community?

DN: Practically non-existent now, because I've got too old. I was always interested in a broad spectrum of things and I was heavily involved during the period of the Gay Rights Movement and the Hirshfield Centre. I moved heaven and earth to keep that place going but it proved absolutely impossible, partly because of Temple Bar Properties, who promised us they would be developing the square in a particular way that would leave us the side-wall free for the fire-escape. But without consultation, they built another building slap right up against it. When we started off trying to defend people in the courts, Garrett Sheehan was among a small number of people who would go in *pro bono*. He was a terrific man. But for ten years, I was in running the Centre every bloody weekend and I didn't go to the theatre once in about ten years. Then there was the fire. Then a group approached me with a view to continuing on a FÁS scheme and I was happy for that to happen, so I turned a blind eye to it; they were supposed to make some contribution by doing running repairs, but they did absolutely nothing. The company had to have an Annual General Meeting and make returns and there had to be an architectural report. The structural engineers said it was dangerous and had to be closed down and that members of the Board were individually and collectively liable if anyone was injured. We had to clear the place completely. So the second time we wrote to them, they told us it was their building, which meant we were exposed to huge danger liability and I actually offered them all my shares on one condition: that they absolve me, because I was the guarantor for the debts, which at that stage were about £30,000. My house was mortgaged for it and what would have happened if they ran up more debts? I would be stuck. Lose my home for them? You have got to be fucking joking. That led to a very unpleasant court case. The costs were over £100,000, which was outrageous, and then there were all the accumulated debts, and then we gave £50,000 to Out-House. That gave them a good start, better than anything we ever had. The most we had in the Hirshfield was £10,000 that I put in out of my own resources. But I don't like the loud music in the discos with everyone shouting at you and you can't hear them properly and then you get hoarse screaming back at them. It's not at all relaxing.

SJC: Do you ever experience any conflict between sexuality and spirituality? I'm thinking of the official, hierarchical Catholic Church's view that homosexuals are intrinsically disordered.

DN: Well, the Roman Catholic Church is intrinsically disordered. I mean, look at it. The fundamental and squalid dishonesty of Rome on sexual matters is what's caused them so much trouble. For example, Eamon Casey. What could be more natural than for a man having a child with a woman? The awful thing was the abuse of his position with regard to that woman, because he was *in loco parentis*, and of course in the way he lied, and his awful hypocrisy in preaching against contraception, which was a pity because in many ways he was a good man. But he was forced into this lying situation. Then, of course, you have the Cardinals who have boyfriends, which is well known all over Rome. A lot of people who are against gay people live the most sordid lives themselves.

As for the Anglican Church, well they just dither along. The Pope, to my mind, is a figure of considerable political importance and I have no doubt he regards himself as a good man and in some ways he is. But he's also an instrument for evil as far as I'm concerned, because these constant, unremitting, ignorant, ill-informed attacks on the gay community have led to violence against gay people. [*A few days prior to this interview, the Pope had described homosexuals as "unnatural and evil".*] It's wicked, calculated and a deliberate wickedness, what the Church used to call "invincible ignorance", because he does not want to know the situation. He closes down scholarly enquiry and of course behind him is Ratzinger, who is, in his mind-set, a Nazi, and they have marginalised all the wonderful people like Oscar Romero, Leonardo Boff, Hans Kung, Charles Curran, all these marvellous people who are the future and the hope of the Church and instead put into place these mindless bureaucrats, which is intensely sad. Now the Church of England is a disaster.

SJC: But you'll stay an Anglican?

DN: Yes.

SJC: How do you pray?

DN: Like a grocery-list. My prayers aren't terribly spiritual. They're just a means of remembering people who are in difficulty and need help and I do believe that prayers and intercessions like that are good and trigger something. I think it's just that this image of the people is in your brain and that's why I light candles. I don't worship the candles. I light them and say, "This is Ezra, this is Isaac, this is my brother, this is my sister-in-law." It reminds me to phone them or do something. That's my prayer.

SJC: It's a ritual of remembrance. Your prayer, then, is practical.

DN: Well there's damn all point in praying for a lot of other things.

SJC: Do you like living here?

DN: I love it. I think we're extraordinarily lucky in our political set-up, which has its scabs, God knows, but it is a democracy. It works. It works haltingly, but it works. The people aren't too much squashed down, except economically, and I hope that with the Celtic Tiger things will change. We have an opportunity to intervene, for example, in places like the inner cities and really inject money in there because that's what it really needs. People worry about the drugs, which is a lot of rubbish. People are prepared to risk death, the most savage death. The only way to stop it is to destroy the financial incentive and then if people want to get zonked, let them get zonked. It's their choice. That's my attitude.

I love Dublin. It's the source of all my conscious memory and it is a city I love and I think it's getting better, architecturally for instance. But I was never imprisoned here, even though it used to be very claustrophobic. I always travelled. I always got out and now I spend part of the year in Jerusalem and I love that. I could end up there. It depends. The climate is wonderful. When you're older, you need something like that because if I get really old I won't be able to cope with the house I've got in North Great George's Street unless I put in a lift, which would be very difficult — unless I put up a glass bubble on the outside wall and go up the chimney, which I'm exploring!

SJC: So Ireland has still got soul or do you think, with the increased greed that has come with the Celtic Tiger, that we have lost something sacred, something special?

DN: Oh absolutely, but that is the danger of it, that we move from being an un-thinking Catholic country to being an unthinking materialist country with no stop in between. I think it would be a great shame. There has been a vast change in my life-time from the time the place was literally crawling with priests and nuns. They were all over the place. I mean you couldn't take a walk to Sandymount without meeting half a dozen of them and all these wonderful nuns with the great big coifs and wim-ples. There were French nuns and the Little Sisters of the Poor and the Franciscans with their ropes. You don't see them now. They're gone, evaporated, vanished. I think that we're the poorer for it. I know there were abuses, but that's inevitable when you have the neurosis that the Church was involved in. If only we got an hon-est Pope who would not be afraid to tell the truth. The awful thing about that Polish person and the Nazi is that they are afraid to tell the truth. They won't even let themselves be in the presence of the truth because it would shatter their very styl-ised view of things. You would have known that Pope John XXIII believed in God. I really don't think this one does.

SJC: I know you don't particularly like Lacan, but . . .

DN: No I don't.

SJC: But he says that the only atheists he knows are those in the Vatican!

DN: He goes up in my estimation. You have managed to do something I didn't think was possible: you have made me have a grudging respect for Lacan! Did he really say that?

SJC: Yes, and he also said that theologians can get by without God more than the average person. Anyway, you have a love of literature and especially of Joyce. What is it in Joyce's works that has you so enthralled, as distinct from, let's say, Wilde or Beckett or any of the other Irish writers?

DN: It's the richness. I mean, Wilde is a magnificent surface and underneath it, if you can decode it, is a very complex social criticism, but it's a brilliant, glittering surface, principally. As for Beckett, well, the whole process of Beckett's life is towards con-striction where until the end almost nothing is happening, a breath on stage, a mouth. That's it. That's the play. Joyce becomes enriched all the time, it's further and further elaborated, it's wonderful and it's absolutely saying "yes" to life and it's asking the most important questions, including, "What is the human consciousness, does it survive in any way?" These are the questions in *Finnegans Wake*. There is the beauty of his language. Joyce is to language what Bach, Mozart or Beethoven were to music. He's a supreme master of language and there's also the humanity, there's the decency. Joyce could be difficult as a man. I recognise the warts. I accept Joyce, warts and all. There's something wonderfully human about him and the fact that he could accept and celebrate the father who caused the destruction of the family. He said, when his father died, that "he was the silliest man I ever knew and yet strangely wise" and that "I loved him in spite of or even because of his faults, many of which I have inherited." That's a remarkably mature thing to be able to say, to weave his father in with gusto to *Ulysses* and *Finnegans Wake*. It's terrific. Thank God, though, he wasn't my father. Georgio was a frightful alcoholic, although he had a beautiful baritone voice. Lucia spent the majority of her life in mental institutions. I used to have a correspondence with her. I never went to see her because I thought there were too many people going over for a gawk. What put her over the edge was that nobody recognised her as an individual; she was a function of the personality of the great James Joyce, the writer. That's what tipped her over the edge, and also Georgio. She used to refer to her father as "The James Joyce", as if he were The Tower or The Pillar.

SJC: Jung called Joyce a prophet and Lacan said that his writing saved him from becoming psychotic.

DN: Yes, I knew that because I was friendly with Patricia Hutchinson and it was she who went to Jung in the forties or fifties and he gave her the psychological profile he had written of Joyce and Lucia. There was a wonderful phrase in it, where he said that they were like two people going to the bottom of a river, but whereas Joyce was diving, Lucia was drowning; and he referred to *Finnegans Wake* as a "controlled schizophrenia".

SJC: What do you think of that judgement?

DN: Oh, I think there is some truth in it. For me, Joyce was one hundred per cent right to refuse to attend Jung (Edith Rockefeller McCormack tried to make him) because he might have been cured of being the creative genius he was.

SJC: Kafka said he feared psychoanalysis, because if it took away his demons, it might just take away his angels as well.

DN: They would. Of course they would. Absolutely.

SJC: If you had your life over, would you do the same sort of things?

DN: Mostly, I think, yes.

SJC: You have no regrets?

DN: No. I certainly have no regrets. I am at *edem* with Edith Piaf, *Je ne regrette rien*!

SJC: Will you write a novel?

DN: I'd love to. I might. I probably would have to start with short stories. It was always my wish to be a great writer. I'm an orderly person in some ways and I felt that I had to tidy my own nest and solve all this stuff about homosexuality and now I might do it. I do write now every Friday. I'm a tabloid journalist for the *Evening Herald*. I spend my time subverting inside what they put on the cover about the immigrants and asylum seekers and so on. I also tell my indecent stories. And I've just been made a member of the NUJ, which I'm very pleased about, so the discipline of writing a column might make it easier to write a book.

SJC: You are quite left wing, then. Are you a socialist?

DN: Yes. I certainly believe in the ideals of socialism. I'm not party political because parties have to appeal to the lowest common denominator and they become doctrinaire. As a result of that, all kinds of impurities seep in. That's why socialism and communism have never succeeded. It's a tragedy. It could have worked, especially in Nicaragua, but the United States and the Vatican combined to do in what was the most significant political experiment of the twentieth century — finding a third way, which is where we are going to have to go. Capitalism is bound for a crash in my opinion, because it's predicated on an infinitely expanding market. You've got to find a melding of the two.

SJC: Whom do you most admire in Irish political life and how would you describe yourself politically?

DN: Michael D. Higgins here. I mean he has as silly a voice as I do and he managed to overcome that and become a cabinet minister. You hear him squeaking away. He wouldn't get away with it in England. They kicked out Heath because of his laugh. The English are so stupid. They have absolutely no political awareness or consciousness. Michael D. wouldn't stand a chance. I loved Noel Browne. I like people like Tony Benn. I don't always agree with him. He's often wrong about Ireland, with his uncritical acceptance of the Republican agenda, which is all guilt and compensation, which a lot of decent English people feel towards Ireland. But then, on the Peace Train, so many people sucked up to the bloody Orangemen because they were southern Catholics with republican backgrounds, whereas I was kneeing them in the balls.

SJC: You're not a nationalist?

DN: Me? I used to quote Seamus Heaney's line: "I'm a nationalist meself right enough. I believe in a united Ireland but I draw the line when I hear the gunmen goin' on about dying for the people whereas it's the people who are dyin' for the gunmen." I'm not particularly nationalist. I don't give a shit. I don't. What difference is it going to make to me? Right, you have a little stamp with the whole island on it. If it would make the sun rise an hour earlier or the grass a bit greener or give people a better income or make people happy, but it's a complete illusion. We are so interconnected, England, Northern Ireland, the South, Europe. I really think it's mad. I find the English view of us terribly irritating, even though I'm half-English myself so there is a knee-jerk reaction. If I were in the company of diehard republicans I'd make sure to come across as English. On the other hand, if I was in England and I got this snotty approach, then I would be a rabid republican. It depends on the context. I have situational politics!

SJC: Is there anyone special in your life at present?

DN: Ezra really. That's it.

SJC: So what's going on with him?

DN: Well, it's the same bizarre relationship. I speak to him on the telephone every night. Isaac's gone now. I'd like to be in touch with him. He's terribly complex. And the good side of him is just beautiful and interesting and cultivated, but if I were in touch, he'd just explode because he's just looking for people that he can attack.

SJC: Why don't you look for someone else here?

DN: It's a bit late to start, to be quite honest with you.

SJC: Are you happy?

DN: Yes, I am. Definitely. Mostly. I mean, nobody is absolutely happy all of the time. When my poor aunt, whom I am seeing this evening (she's 102) goes, I'll be shattered by it, but that will pass, as everything does. As long as I can find things to enjoy, to amuse me, to engage my interest, then I will get a lot of happiness out of life, which I do. I enjoy just looking at things. There was a dark day recently and people were complaining about it but it depends on what you're looking for. I mean, what's the point in looking for sunshine on a dark day? Let's look for something else. If you leave yourself open to positive things, they will come to you but if you keep looking for something that isn't there . . . On one of these awful days I was going down Marlborough Street, Tyrone House, where there's a building site and there were these huge trees, underneath of which was this wild grass and weeds and nettles, and the sheer luminosity of the foliage under the trees was absolutely beautiful. But you wouldn't have seen it if it were a bright sunny day. You needed that grey ceiling of cloud to see it. So there's always something.

SJC: In your post-mortem existence, whom would you most like to meet?

DN: Oh, I don't know. I think probably some quite ordinary people. What's the point in being a star-fucker on a cloud as well as everywhere else? I would like to see Ezra really. I've no great desire to be sitting with Mozart or Beethoven or Einstein or Joyce or these sort of people. No. None.

DANIEL O'DONNELL
Singer

Daniel O'Donnell has been in the entertainment business since leaving school. He is one of the country's most popular and successful singers with a host of best-selling albums/CDs and videos to his credit. He has won a number of awards, including "Irish Entertainment Personality of the Year", "Donegal Person of the Year" and "British [sic] Male Country Singer", amongst others. He is not only a singer with a huge and devoted following; he is also a tireless campaigner on behalf of Romanian orphanages. We spoke in my home, where he displayed an old-fashioned civility and quiet courtesy. He struck me as sincere but private, not wholly at odds with his public persona.

SJC: What does music mean to you?

DOD: Well, I suppose music is my life. For me, music is about getting great happiness and fulfilment in life. Certainly, it's a way of communicating. There are no barriers with music. You either like the type of music or you don't. If you like it, it doesn't matter where it's coming from or to whom it's going.

SJC: How do you feel when you are singing?

DOD: I suppose I feel in control. I don't think anything could faze me. I'm comfortable. I get nervous going out — everyone does — but it's not an uncontrollable feeling. It's good to be a bit nervous.

SJC: Kris Kristoffersen and Willie Nelson are all great singers and songwriters. Who has influenced your style of music?

DOD: I don't know if I've ever been influenced as such by singers. My favourite singer is a lady called Loretta Lynn, who sings very much from a woman's point of view (so there's very few of her songs that I would sing), but I've never really wanted to be like anybody. I would have a great admiration for Cliff Richard. In the music business, if there is a secret or formula for success, it's to be an individual. That's the most important thing. I don't know if I always knew or thought that, but I certainly never wanted to sing like anyone else. I never tried to copy anybody. There was nobody I aspired to.

SJC: What's your view of up-and-coming artists compared to the likes of Tammy Wynette and your great friend Loretta Lynn?

DOD: I suppose there are very few now who are instantly recognisable. When Tammy sang, there was an instant recognition. Randy Travis has that. But there are a lot of the newer singers who are the same. They could be anybody. But I suppose there's always something in a voice that's recognisable. To be recognised, there has to be a difference.

SJC: Your sister, Margo, was very big in the seventies. Was music always part of your family?

DOD: I can never remember not singing. My cousins all sang and my grandparents and uncles and aunts. They don't and didn't sing like I sing, but they could all sing. I was the youngest of five. My father was the youngest of eleven. I have cousins who would be in their sixties — twenty years older than me. There's a few my age but there's only one cousin of mine younger than me.

SJC: The music business is very tough. How have you managed?

DOD: It's tough, but I would have to say that I have no feeling of being hard done by. I haven't felt that. I don't feel it and I don't want to feel that either. I won't allow myself to have it. I've been lucky with the manager I have, John Reilly, who has been everything, who has looked after me better than even a father could. He is for me as a person, rather than me as a product.

SJC: Your public persona is one of sweetness and light, some might say saccharine. Is that the real Daniel O'Donnell?

DOD: Well, I mean, I just think I'm very normal as a person. I don't think I'm better than good or worse than bad. I'm just normal. I think the general run-of-the-mill person in this world is just a good person. And I think I would fall into that category, I hope.

SJC: Do you find that family is so very important, especially considering you must be cautious in making friends?

DOD: Yes. You grow up with your family and my family have been supportive of what I'm doing. I don't make friends easily with people. Maybe people in general are like that. I wouldn't be wary of people and look at them and ask, "What do they want?", but I don't just rush into things. If you meet people over a period, you are able to see who's who and what's what. The genuine person will shine through over time.

SJC: You are known for your charitable work with Romanian orphanages. That must give you a sense of purpose.

DOD: Yes, I think it's great to be able to use the fact that I would be well known in that way so that people get to know about the situation. I got to know about it through a neighbour of mine. The fact that I have this public situation is good. If my neighbour speaks and a hundred people listen, it's a lot, but if I speak, it could be thousands, so it makes a big difference. When Eileen, my neighbour, came back and was so disturbed by what she saw, and she's a very realistic person, I felt that there was something I could do. I could sing. It's about as much as I could do. I had this song given to me, "Give a Little Love"; but when I looked at pictures of the children, it was as if it was written for them. I recorded it so the proceeds could go to them. I went to Romania to make a video to promote it and see for myself. There was a Thomas in me, though I knew Eileen would be telling the truth. I wanted to see and be sure for myself but not with the intention of getting involved myself. When I got there and saw the situation and realised the enormity of the task, to try to rehouse them, I felt it wasn't my problem. It wasn't hers either, but it's very difficult to walk away and say that. So that's how I got involved.

SJC: Has music a political function? Should it have a social role?

DOD: I don't know that I would like to get involved in that side of things. I'm not interested in that. I'd like to think that when I sing, it's for a feel-good factor, not trying to persuade people to do this, that or the other.

SJC: So you're not political then?

DOD: I wouldn't say I'm political.

SJC: What is the role of the artist in society?

DOD: From my situation, I would say it's that good feeling. I feel it when I sing in a theatre or wherever and I think it makes people forget for a period. And that's good enough for me.

SJC: What do you think of Ireland in the year 2001 and the Celtic Tiger?

DOD: There's positive and negative to everything. I think many people have bene-fited from it. The downside is for the youth. Because when you're starting out, it's difficult. I feel it's more difficult now, to get started in your first home. I'm not mar-ried, but I think for a young couple who get married . . . Years ago, people were happy to go into a flat, to start with a house and do one room. Now it's a case of doing everything. To keep up with others is difficult and that's a sad situation. I think that the prosperity this Celtic Tiger has brought creates a lot of tension and stress for the youth. Life goes on. Ireland, especially Dublin, is very cosmopolitan. When I walked up Grafton Street there I felt I could be anywhere. I went into a card shop in the Stephen's Green Centre and this fella put his head in the door while I was get-ting served and the girl, who looked Irish to me, spoke to him and I didn't under-stand what they were saying and I said to her: "Is he speaking in another language?" and she said, "Yes." I said, "What is it?" and she said "Swedish." I felt it's incredible for Ireland. How do I feel about it? I don't know if I have any feelings on it. Maybe I feel that eventually any tiger, if it's pursued too much, will eventually turn and I would imagine the Celtic Tiger will turn and whoever is closest at the time will get hurt. Some will have benefited and be far enough away from it, but others will suffer. I absolutely love Ireland and I love Donegal more than I love anywhere else.

SJC: So she still has soul?

DOD: Oh absolutely, and the people in Ireland still have it without a shadow of a doubt.

SJC: In the light of one pop star taking "holy orders", would you ever consider something like that?!

DOD: No, I don't think so. No.

SJC: Are you a spiritual person?

DOD: I was brought up Catholic and still would be a practising Catholic. It's important for me to go to Mass. You are closer to God when things aren't going right. I always feel that if something isn't right in my life, that I'm almost living with God, and if everything's flying you can forget about calling someone. It's a bit like that. I don't like to miss Mass at the weekend. I feel that connection with God.

SJC: What's your relationship with God? And what is God?

DOD: He has us here to reach some sort of situation so we would be ready to go to wherever He is. I don't know. I can't say. It's a never-ending Being.

SJC: Do you believe in angels?

DOD: I do, yes. I think there have to be Guardian Angels. I thing you are saved from bad things happening. They weren't there yesterday when I walked into the door!

SJC: Yes, I noticed the bruise on your eye. Do you believe in the Devil?

DOD: I think, yes, there is badness in the world, evil.

SJC: Do you fear death?

DOD: No, I don't fear death at all. I look forward to it.

SJC: Why?

DOD: I don't look forward to the actual dying. I enjoy life, but I just think it will be nothing compared to what's to come. I have nothing more to do, though I will do plenty, I suppose. I won't feel I have to stay here for anything. Whenever the time comes, I will be ready to go.

SJC: What is soul?

DOD: What is soul? It's hard to say what I think soul is. I suppose if I meet someone who has soul, I think they impress me. I think they believe in themselves and in what they're doing. There's goodness there. Soul is the part that goes on, it's that part of me that will go to wherever we go. I don't quite know how to answer it.

SJC: A lot of country music is sad and soulful. Does the music ever affect your mood?

DOD: It wouldn't bring me down. Occasionally, a song will make you think that that's a very sad situation. That would happen with songs. I don't know how it would affect me. It depends. But I don't write, so I don't sing my own songs. They can strike a chord and then you will feel the emotion.

SJC: What's your favourite song?

DOD: I don't know that I have a favourite song. I like different songs at different times.

SJC: Do you think country music is maligned by the more mainstream music industry? I'm thinking of Whitney Houston singing Dolly Parton's "I Will Always Love You". I feel Dolly sings it with real, raw emotion.

SJC: Yes, I would say that too. Whitney does a super job on it, but you know where it's going to go. It's like seeing a straight line and knowing it's going to continue straight. It goes to where it has to get. With Dolly, the delivery is not as important as the actual message. Do you understand? Whereas with Houston, with Whitney, delivery is what's important. There will always be a market for country, for that type of music.

SJC: What are your interests outside music?

DOD: I love golf. And I like being with people I like and being just very normal.

SJC: Have you found your soul mate?

DOD: No. No.

SJC: What do you look for in a partner?

DOD: I really don't know, to tell you the truth. Personally, I don't know if I'll ever find . . . I'm not looking, number one. I'm not searching for anybody, so therefore it's not a priority with me and if it's not a priority . . . It's a bit like going shopping for nothing but if you see it you find it. I don't know what I'd look for. I suppose you know it when you find it. But as far as looking for it, I can't tell you.

SJC: Love isn't a lack in your life?

DOD: Not really. I couldn't say I am unhappy because I don't have a partner. I like not having to be anywhere at a particular time or be answerable to anybody.

SJC: Do you ever get lonely or depressed amid all the clamour and attention?

DOD: There are times you get . . . I don't know if depressed is the right word. You can get lonely in a room full of people, but not generally. I'm not that type of person. I like my own company. People who like their own company don't get as lonely so much.

SJC: Are you happy?

DOD: Yeah, I'm happy. I'm a happy person. If I had to imagine my life, I could never imagine it as it is. I love what I'm doing. I love singing. I don't feel I work. What more can I say about it?

Micheál Ó Muircheartaigh
Broadcaster

For years the voice of Micheál Ó Muircheartaigh has been synonymous with the voice of the GAA. His infectious enthusiasm for Gaelic games and his unique turn of phrase have ignited the interest of thousands who tune in to the radio to hear his remarkable commentary. Micheál Ó Muircheartaigh has made broadcasting into a fine art. His style is inimitable. We met and chatted in a private room in the Burlington Hotel with a brilliant view of Dublin below us. He was gracious with his time and generous with his helpful suggestions. After an unhurried interview, we spent some more time continuing the discussion about sport, politics and Ireland. Micheál Ó Muircheartaigh is utterly dedicated, not only to sports; he also takes a keen and lively interest in the state of contemporary Ireland. This Kerryman, with his magical accent, embodies an archetypal Irishness.

SJC: What is it about Gaelic games that has you so enthused?

MOM: I think intrinsically they are good games in themselves, especially hurling. I have seen a lot of games all over the world and I think hurling would compare with any game I have ever seen. Gaelic football might not be of the same high standard as football but I think properly played it is still a very attractive game but I suppose the basic thing is that they are Irish games and we in Ireland, like every other nationality, should try to preserve our own. I would have nothing against soccer or rugby or cricket — they are all wonderful games — and we should take an interest in all of them. But I think every country has an obligation to ensure that the principal features of their own culture are preserved. That's why I would have a leaning toward Irish games. But they are good games in themselves.

SJC: When did you begin your career as a broadcaster of the sport and how did you get into it?

MOM: I was always very interested in it and then the opportunity came up by chance. I began in 1949 in Radio Eireann — there was no television then. Since the year of its inception in 1926, they had been broadcasting Gaelic games, and then other games, so I was familiar with the radio and games, principally Micheal Ó Hehir. It was the custom to broadcast two games a year *as gaeilge*. I was a student at St Patrick's College in Drumcondra and word came to the college that they were giving auditions in Croke Park the following Sunday for a commentator *as gaeilge*. This appealed to me, so about ten of us went for the audition and as a result of pure chance I was asked would I be willing to broadcast the Railway Cup Final the following week, which I did. It started by accident.

SJC: And what were you studying in Pats?

MOM: To be a teacher.

SJC: And you qualified and taught?

MOM: I taught for a number of years, both in primary and secondary schools, but I gave up teaching, which I liked very much, to concentrate on being a sports broadcaster.

SJC: Did you grow up in a prominent GAA family? Presumably you played the sport?

MOM: I did, yes. And I went to school in Cork, where everything was through the medium of Irish and we played the Gaelic games. We spoke nothing but Irish and we had students from all over the country. We had nothing against other games — we were familiar with them from listening to the radio and hearing people talk about them but for us the number one was the native culture.

SJC: Did you play soccer or rugby?

MOM: No, there was no such thing as soccer, just Gaelic football. There was no hurling in the college. It was very small — just 80 pupils in all, and all were geared to becoming teachers. It was a preparatory college for a teacher training college but we had students from Cork, Kerry and Limerick — from every county in Munster. We had them from Donegal, Mayo, Galway, Kilkenny, Louth and Dublin and we even had one from Monaghan and Cavan as well. So it was like a university though it was small. We had a very broad outlook and a mixture of the dialects and cultures. We had an appreciation of all, though a practice only in our own.

SJC: What's your favourite sporting memory? What was your favourite All-Ireland final?

MOM: Something that will never leave my mind was my first visit to Croke Park. I came to Dublin in September 1948 and Croke Park was 20 minutes walk from the teachers' training college. In those days you didn't need a ticket to get into an All-Ireland final, though maybe you did if you wanted to go into the Hogan stand, which at that time only held about 2,000 people. The Cusack stand held another 6,000. But there would be at least 75,000 people who could gain admittance on the day by turning up, so naturally we drifted to Croke Park for the All-Ireland final of 1948, between Cavan and Mayo. I still can see it. We went towards Hill 16 — it was cheap, and a very windy day with a perfect view of the whole match. We could see Micheál Ó Hehir's box, which was a bonus as he was a famous man to us and I still can see his box on stilts between the old Hogan and Long stand. Mayo didn't score at all in the first half and they almost won it in the end, so that always made an impression on me. I have seen every single All-Ireland since then, but I have a special *grá* for something that happens for the first time, like when County Down won the All-Ireland in 1960. I think there was something magical about that. They were an unusual team. They were the first team to arrive in Croke Park wearing tracksuits. They were a flamboyant team. I would naturally be a follower of Kerry and Kerry had a tradition of ambling out on to the field, very casual, but the Down team bound out on to the field and maybe do a lap before the game, wearing tracksuits, which we thought was alien, but it made an impression. As well as that, they were a terrific footballing team — they beat Kerry in the final of 1960. They were the first team to carry the Sam Maguire Cup across the border. I will never forget the excitement when thousands spilled on to the field when the game was over. I think that was a fantastic occasion. I think of other firsts, years later, when Donegal won their first All-Ireland in 1992, something that would have been incredible five years before. I remember seeing the Offaly hurlers make the breakthrough. I like the birth of some-thing new.

SJC: You mentioned Micheál O'Hehir. How did you regard his style of commentat-ing? Had that any effect or influence on your own style?

MOM: I wouldn't say he had any effect on the way I broadcast, because I started off broadcasting through the medium of Irish, but he was the man that created this great interest. He always had this great enthusiasm for the game and knew every-thing about the players on the team, which would encourage you to do research all the time and try to have more and more information.

SJC: That's your style.

MOM: I am lucky in that I know a lot of the players. I trained some of the players. I would know their ambitions and the great effort they were putting in. I would know their feelings when they would win and lose. I think that's a help to anyone — knowing the players, the managers, the trainers, the followers and the people in the media as well.

SJC: What's your view of the GAA's position on prohibiting so-called "foreign games" from being played in Croke Park? Is that policy still sustainable, in the light of the present political climate?

MOM: I will answer that by going about it in a roundabout way. Bans have been ap-plied to sport for a long time back I found it unbelievable when I discovered that there was an overall ban on any sport by statute from 1345 until about 1845 — ex-cept archery. They thought that the pursuit of any other sport was detrimental to the welfare of archery. There was a ban on any organised sport for 500 years, so there was a ban mentality — which didn't mean that the games weren't being played, but they weren't organised. If you look up the foundation dates for any of the sports' bodies, be it the GAA or rugby or tennis, they are all post-1845 because the Act was repealed then. I would often compare the GAA ban originally to what was in vogue when Ireland became an independent state in the 1920s, when there was no industry in Ireland on account of all the Manufacturing Acts over the centuries. So the infant Irish state put up a barrier of tariffs and the like to protect infant industry. The same thing came into the games. Soccer and rugby had started before the Gaelic games — the GAA was founded in 1884 and rugby and soccer had been founded in the 1860s, so they had a headstart. So I think the initial bans were a form of industrial protection.

But I would never favour bans and I don't think that any of them did any good. I think there were political motives as well. It's long gone past its sell-by date. I don't think the essence of sport lends itself to bans of any description. To come back to the question you asked about the GAA and not allowing any games other than Gaelic games to be played in Croke Park: I would like to see that go as well. I don't think it has any meaning nowadays. When Croke Park is finished it will be a magnificent stadium — it was always a magnificent stadium and the finest one in Ireland. Regardless of what activities will be played in Croke Park, I think that in the minds of the people of Ireland Croke Park will be associated with Gaelic games. I would see nothing wrong with renting it out, at an economic rent, provided that everyone understands that it is the property of the GAA and they decide what the conditions are, and I think that day will come.

SJC: You play golf.

MOM: Yes, all sports are good, if you take them from the health aspect alone, which makes them a good investment by the government. It creates a healthier people especially for those who aren't competitive or over the age of thirty. It keeps them more involved in sport and we would save in terms of medical bills. It also channels the energy of young people and keeps them away from idle pursuits and crime, etc. Money spent on sport is a good investment.

SJC: You're renowned for your turn of phrase. How do you come up with sentences such as 'Is the ref. going to blow his whistle? . . . No, he's going to blow his nose!"?

MOM: I doubt if I ever said that! It reminds me of a story: at an early Sunday Mass, someone who had been out late the night before fell asleep and woke up as the priest was yelling: "As Saint Paul said . . ."; this person was alleged to have stood up and said: "He never said that, it was said for him!" It could be the same for some of my sayings. They were said for me!

SJC: But do you practise them beforehand?

MOM: Not really. If I am speaking to aspiring young commentators, I say to them, "There is one crime: silence." You have to keep talking and if the play stops that doesn't mean that you should be restricted in any way. If you cast your eyes about away from the play, you will always see something that merits a comment or that inspires a thought. There's a lot more happening than the game itself. Look at the spectators, the players, the sky, the trees or anything. I just keep talking. I remember one time taking someone to Bord Na Gaeilge when I was chairman and I brought a tape and microphone and I said, "We'll look out the window", and told him to start talking. He said, "I can't see anything." So I said, "Well, there's a bus passing and there are cars and you can see Merrion Square", and so on. Then he started off and you couldn't stop him! You just keep talking about what comes into vision. It needn't be connected with the primary duty at a match, which is to describe that. There are many stoppages and I think some listeners are interested in the peripheral things as well.

SJC: Gaelic games have historically and traditionally been associated with Irish nationalism. How would you describe your political position?

MOM: I was never aligned to any particular party, deliberately, because I think if you are in sports broadcasting you will be talking to and meeting people who have different shades of political opinion, to which they are entitled and I wouldn't like to be perceived by any one of those as belonging to another. Some people try to figure out what my politics are. I take all politicians as I meet them. There was a time when it was heresy to praise politicians of one party in the presence of those from another party. I think that day is gone. I take them as they are. I remember one time being at a ploughing match and a certain political party had a stand there and I was with another stand. Some people from this party wandered over to the farmers' stand and were talking to me, and one of them said, "You wouldn't be one of us at all, I think." I said, "I would be very interested to find out how you came to that conclusion!" He said, "Well, you are a little bit too close to the Irish." He meant the language, and I told him there were as many people in his party interested in the language as any other party. People's perceptions can often be wrong. I treat them all as individuals and take them on merit.

SJC: But you would probably identify yourself as an Irish nationalist?

MOM: Oh yes. "Nationalist", though, can have the wrong meaning as well. Some people equate nationalism with being anti-everything else. I think there should be a certain Irishness about all of us, regardless of our political leanings, and that would apply to unionists as well as to nationalists. The English people should also be proud of their Englishness. That's their nationalism. That doesn't mean you should look down on others. I would treat them all as equals. I am very much associated with the Irish language, but the English, French and Japanese languages are all wonderful languages. I would like everyone in Ireland to be at least bilingual — fluent in Irish and English and in as many other languages as they can manage. I think that is the way of the future.

SJC: You mentioned that you are a Gaeilgeoir. Do you think the Irish language will survive?

MOM: I am absolutely certain. I was never despondent about it. I walked into a shop yesterday morning to get a paper and straight away the woman behind the counter started to speak in Irish and then she called to the husband and said that he had a little bit of Irish as well and I felt he was delighted to show me he had a little bit. That would not have happened twenty years ago. People who had Irish hid it and spoke it among themselves. If you wander into UCD or Trinity, you'll meet several hundred young people who would be willing to speak Irish with you and do it openly in the pubs and on the streets. I am very hopeful that Irish will always survive.

SJC: Do you ever feel when you are speaking English that you are alienated from yourself in any way, that it isn't as natural, that there's something awkward about it?

MOM: I wouldn't say so. I grew up on the edges of the Gaeltacht and we had Irish, but it was an area where Irish was dying out. I grew up speaking both Irish and English in school and college. I would speak Irish with those who speak Irish, and English with those who speak English. If the Galway football team walked through the door now, I would automatically speak Irish to some of them who come from the Gaeltacht, and to the Kerry team as well, but when I meet players who come from counties where there is little Irish, I would be just as much at ease speaking English.

SJC: Which county and people have the most soul, do you think, and what is soul?

MOM: It wouldn't be confined to any county. I think it's a personal thing. I think Clare people have a lot of it. They won the All-Ireland hurling final in 1914 and they didn't win again until 1995. I saw them having harrowing defeats during the years and I remember being at a function in Clare and making an extraordinary statement: "I hope you never win an All-Ireland!" I was half-joking. The reason was that I know no county in Ireland that look forward so much to the day when they'll win. They keep coming back, defeat after defeat. And I said, "Maybe you'll be disillusioned when it finally happens and maybe you're a happier people looking forward all the time." I would say that's what soul is, the people who have belief all the time, even though they weren't achieving anything. The will was there, the determination was there and the dream was there. I'm sure they were envious of Tipperary and Cork and Kilkenny. But if we keep trying, our day will come as well. For that reason, I think there might be more of what you call "soul" in the people of Clare. But you'll get it anywhere. I think it's everywhere. It's very strong in Kerry. They say football is the number one religion in Kerry, ever since they played in their first All-Ireland final in 1892. They lost that one, but won thirty-two of them since then. I think soul also means that you put a little bit of the past behind you — you appreciate what it did for you — but the important one is always the next one.

SJC: You mentioned Kerry and you're a Kerryman. Why is it called the Kingdom of Kerry?

MOM: It depends on the type of Kerryman you meet. The theory put forward most often is that it goes back to the time that there was a king called Ciar, said to be an outstanding person, and the territory was named after him. Now that's an explanation that pleases Kerry people. But there's another one that Kerry people never accept, which is that some time in history the Viceroy who reported to the King of England went over to report an insurrection and rebellion going on in Ireland against His Majesty's powers. He painted a very bad picture for the king, and when the king asked was it widespread, he was told that it was — except in Kerry! At that stage it was said that the king filled two glasses and said, "Let's drink a toast to the loyal kingdom of Kerry." It may be true — they may have abdicated from insurrections at times — but nobody will know. I would be more inclined to accept the Ciar Rí explanation, because almost every place name in Ireland can be traced back to the Irish language. Cork can be traced back to Corcaigh, meaning the marshy territory at the mouth of the river, which is what it was before it was developed. Interestingly, St Patrick was never in Kerry and there's no church or mountain, stream or well named after St Patrick. You have places connected with Patrick everywhere in Ireland except Kerry. It is said that he looked toward Kerry and said, "I bless you westward but I'm not going in there", and he took a shortcut to Cork. He didn't go,

Kerry people will say, because the religion was already there. Another story is that his donkey was stolen from him in Limerick and it was too long to walk so he took the shorter road to Cork.

SJC: Are Kerry people more individualistic than people from other counties? I'm thinking of the fact that it has produced people like John B. Keane, Brendan Kennelly and yourself, amongst others?

MOM: I think more independent than individualistic, and maybe they both go hand in hand. I always thought Kerry people were independent — and I think it's a good thing to be — and study things as they are and come to their own conclusions. I think Kerry people are slow to accept other people's interpretations of anything. I don't know whether the mountains or the sea would breed that.

SJC: The Kerry and Cork accents have people enthralled. Do you consider your magical accent to have been an asset in your success as a commentator; after all, it is the voice of the GAA?

MOM: I never gave it any consideration. That's the accent I have. I had Kerry Irish but was exposed to different dialects and accents and we used to mimic and imitate each other, but we always liked to keep our own and I think it would be a very dull Ireland if everyone had the same accent. I like when Niall Tóibín does the different accents. It's something I would never have been conscious of.

SJC: In your view, who is or was the best footballer and hurler the games have produced?

MOM: I was listening to Mick O'Connell, a famous Kerry footballer, speaking the other day and he was asked that question. He said you couldn't answer that, because a goalie is very skilled in a special aspect of the game, which is totally different to the skill of a midfielder and a full back, so it is very difficult to compare. I have always been steadfast in my belief that the greatest Gaelic footballer that I ever saw was the Galway man, Sean Purcell. It might be that I saw him early in my career and first impressions last. He was the first really big star that I saw and he went to school with me and was in St Patrick's training college when I was there and we did teaching practice together. So all that might have influenced me, but still it's amazing how many other people from all over the country say it too. But then, where do you leave Mick O'Connell and Jack O'Shea, Mickey Sheehy, Jimmy Keaveney, Brian Mullins and others and the great County Down players from the 60s like Sean O'Neill and Paddy Docherty? But if I were limited to one, I would still say Sean Purcell of Galway.

SJC: What is it that he has that others don't?

MOM: Mick O'Connell said you should never judge a player by the number of All-Ireland medals he has. He said some of the greatest players never won anything. To me, Sean Purcell was absolutely expert in all the skills of the game. He could kick and solo with the right and left. He could kick and was very stylish in kicking from the hand. He was a wonderful catcher; he could play in any position. He starred as a midfielder, centre back, fullback, full forward, centre forward, and he was equally proficient in all positions and he lasted a long time, but above all he was a team man. When it comes to hurling, I suppose longevity is a factor and I always go back to Christy Ring of Cork. I often ask hurlers who are twenty-seven years of age and thinking of giving up after playing for their county for ten years, "Could you see yourself being Hurler of the Year in twelve years' time?" They say, "God, you're crazy — it couldn't happen!" And I say, "Well, a man I knew did that — Christy Ring." He was voted Texaco Hurler of the Year at the age of thirty-nine! And I ask them can they imagine playing for their province in seventeen years' time and still winning medals. Christy Ring did all that. He played for Cork non-stop from 1939 to 1965. He was regarded as the complete hurler and for years he maintained that level. Even at the age of 41, he was the top scorer in the country. Based on individual skill, I would say that the current exploits of D.J. Carey would match anything I ever saw. He has all the skills. He practises and perfects things. He doesn't foul; I have great time for people who achieve the ultimate just by sticking to the rules of the game and not fouling others. If you play according to the rules, referees will never bother you. I think also of Eddy Kerr, who in All-Ireland finals alone scored seven goals and seventy-seven points. He started in 1959 and finished in 1977. I think the number of years a player puts in to it must be taken into account.

SJC: You have mentioned famous sportsmen, but who has stood out for you as an archetypal Irishman, perhaps a politician, someone exemplifying Irish soul?

MOM: I would say Ken Whitaker, whom I got to know principally through my connections with the Irish language. Ken, as a lot of people know, was born in Belfast and came South. When his studies were completed, he joined the civil service and he eventually became the Secretary of the Department of Finance. He was interested in the Irish games and language but also in the economy of the country. His aim and attitude was to make Ireland the equal of other countries. In the 1950s, he was the first to bring out a programme for economic expansion. I still have the document at home; it was revolutionary for its time. It advocated more state influence on the development of industry. He got that across to the government. I would say that the tiger of today had its roots back in the mid-50s. He was later Governor of the Central Bank and was respected the world over. He had this level approach to everything. Ireland didn't just mean the Irish language for him or the Irish games, but the economy, the outlook of the people, the involvement of the state. It was like the books of old of the philosophers — it was for the "common good". I would say that on any shortlist of famous Irish people who contributed a lot to making the state what it is today, I would put Ken Whitaker very high.

SJC: What about Seán MacBride — he was always seen as a statesman?

MOM: Seán MacBride kept other aspects alive. His mother was the famous Maud Gonne and his father was Major John MacBride, of international notoriety. When I was young I used to hear people talk about the time Maud Gonne came to the Dingle races. She was supposed to have been a very beautiful woman and people spoke about seeing her and hearing her talk about the time when self-government would come and she was promising the people that they would live longer and have better education, health and housing. All these things have come to pass. I would have a great *grá* for the likes of Maud Gonne, and of course Seán MacBride was her son, who contributed to the nationalist point of view and keeping that alive, which was important. Once he became a Minister in the inter-party government of 1948, he proved also that he could be an international statesman as well. There are many, depending on what angle you take.

SJC: What's your view of contemporary Ireland and the Celtic Tiger?

MOM: It's wonderful to see it. I remember when I was going to school the mainspring of the Irish economy was agriculture. The number of people who were involved in industry was infinitesimally small. The change has taken place gradually and Ireland has changed. The standard of living for everyone has risen immeasurably over the years. Great advances have been made. Most people complete their second-level education and a very high percentage go on to third level. They are all very positive and I think they are bringing a change of attitude as well. Maybe not all sectors are being treated the way they should be. Maybe there isn't enough concentration on bringing the people on the bottom of the rung up. I don't think the value of education is being stressed enough. Something should be started to give education to people in their forties, because some of them didn't get it. You start with educating the parents first, if they need it, rather than the children. Irish society needs to make adjustments at the moment.

SJC: Do you think Ireland still has soul?

MOM: Certainly. You need only talk to the people in the universities and especially if you go abroad, and I have been all over the world. When you are abroad and meet Irish people, you realise that they have this soul for what Ireland means. I have a son in America and he rang me and said, "I'm looking at the Patrick's Day parade in Stanford", which was a week ahead of time, and I asked him what's in it and he said, "A few fire engines and floats with Irish dancers and musicians." I think little things like that give soul to it. We Irish have something that makes us different to the ordinary people of Stanford, who have other traditions, which we should respect, but we have our own. The greatest proof is the growth in the number of Irish schools. A fortnight ago, I was down opening an Irish school in Roscommon. It was the first in Roscommon — and this is the year 2001. In 1973, we had a list of schools teaching through the medium of Irish outside the Gaeltacht — the number was 14. It's now 157. That is proof that the parents of today felt they missed something and they would like to see their children have it. It's not a question of superiority, but of equality and choice. There are people who wouldn't like it, and that's fine with me.

SJC: What are your interests outside sport?

MOM: I'm very interested in politics and economics. I studied economics and I like the ramifications and applications of economics. I am genuinely interested in people and I think if you are interested in people you have to be interested in politics. I know it's very fashionable to run down politicians nowadays, but I think they are a group that works extraordinarily hard. Of all the groups in Ireland they need PR more than any other group. I like politics and I have great regard for people who work for communities. They get no recognition and they don't seek it either.

SJC: Who has impressed you most in politics?

MOM: Jack Lynch. I got to know Jack the sportsman. People all over the country didn't look at Jack Lynch principally as a Fianna Fáil man but as a politician and sportsman. He used say himself that on account of his sport he could go anywhere in Ireland that belonged to the opposition politically and there was a great welcome for him. Another one would be Séan Lemass. He was the practical man. He had a view that if Ireland was to survive as a nation equal to all the others, then we had to do something about the industry of the country. Lemass and Whitaker understood each other. He was in the Department of Industry and Commerce for many years and contributed an awful lot to the development of modern Ireland.

SJC: Are you a spiritual person?

MOM: I would be a practising Catholic. I would be a spiritual person more than a religious person. I think, thankfully, the day has come when all religions are looked upon as equals and they have validity. Over the generations when the priest and the teacher were the only people with any real education, they played a noble part in bringing Ireland towards what it is today.

SJC: Finally, are you happy?

MOM: I'm as happy as I can be. I was never a worrier. I take and enjoy every day and that's always my advice to players. I used to tell them to enjoy the preparation and the day when it comes because the day will come when we won't be able to be involved. That is my philosophy— to make the most of everything. When players are thinking of giving up, I say to them the time will come when nobody will ask you to play for them. Sport isn't meant to be taken too seriously. That is still my outlook.

DANA ROSEMARY SCALLON MEP

"Dana" Rosemary Scallon represents Connacht-Ulster as a Member of the European Parliament. She ran unsuccessfully for the Presidency of Ireland in 1997. She is probably best known as the singer who won the Eurovision Song Contest for Ireland, for the first time, in 1970 with the song "All Kinds of Everything", which subsequently became Number 1 throughout Europe. She is known for her strong pro-family stance and for her conservative Catholicism. She spent time in the United States where she hosted an evangelical programme, Say Yes, on the Catholic Cable Network. I met with her in Galway. I found her to be a straightforward, capable woman with strong right-wing convictions who is not easily swayed. It is hard to avoid the impression that she is driven by a messianic mission, on behalf of her particular brand of religion.

SJC: You began your career as a singer, winning the Eurovision Song Contest for Ireland in 1970 with "All Kinds of Everything". What was that whole period of your life like?

DS: By the time I sang in the Eurovision I had decided I didn't want to be a singer and I had harboured an ambition that had been there since the age of ten, to be a teacher. Initially it was ballet and then music — I had studied piano since I was six years old — and then I wanted to teach music and English. I was particularly interested in dealing with the mentally handicapped because they have a great love for music and a natural rhythm and the Eurovision was a last fling, so it was a huge shock to the system when I won it. I really didn't think I had a chance of winning — Ireland had never won before and I certainly didn't think they were going to win with me! I was so close to sitting my exams. Initially, I found it very hard to adjust to being a pop star. It wasn't a dream come true. It was completely unexpected.

SJC: You have done recordings, TV series and a film, *The Flight of the Doves*. Which aspect of your life then did you most enjoy?

DS: I had been on the stage in competitions, in ballet and music and singing and I was raised with those, so I was used to being on the stage. I studied classical music and was always more comfortable working backstage with the musicians. I really enjoyed the preparation work — preparing for the recording of an album and working with the arrangers. I didn't enjoy the idea, in filming, that you could invest perhaps six months of your life and have no control on the outcome because once it's recorded it's in the hands of other people. I got quite good reviews for that in America and I was offered management in that area, to continue looking for film work, but I really wasn't interested in handing over all that control.

SJC: You became a presidential candidate in 1997, losing to Mary McAleese, who was elected President of Ireland. And you were elected as a Member of the European Parliament in 1999. What brought you from singing into politics? As far as I know, Nana Mouskouri was the only other Eurovision singer to make the same transition.

DS: I think the end product of entertainment is your relationship with the people and for me all through my career I would often spend more time talking with people after the gig than I invested in the gig, sometimes until two or three in the morning. Through the days, it was a constant round of visiting people and care centres and hospitals and I was a part of a number of charitable organisations dealing with the mentally handicapped and the elderly. It wasn't that my whole life was about singing and I needed the response to survive. It was never like that for me — I knew I would survive if I never sang again because it wasn't my life force. It was always my relationship with people that was important to me. My moving in to the presidential election wasn't motivated because I wanted to be the President, but rather was motivated by what I saw as an injustice to the people. I had a unique, international platform where I could speak. I felt there was a conspiracy of silence, a consensus of opinion within the country whereby they could just keep you silent. I knew if I could use an international platform, I could shine a light in on what was happening. I took the platform to speak. Does that make sense?

SJC: Presumably you felt that the consensus was a liberal agenda?

DS: Yes. I think there has to be balance in everything. It was a time of political change and it eased the change if you silenced or discredited an organisation that could bypass the media and the politics and speak directly to the people. It is seen as dangerous if that organisation isn't saying exactly what you're saying and isn't in agreement with how you want the country to develop. If you can undermine that authority, then you are able to ensure that what you want is heard and followed. It played into the political and media consensus, to undermine the authority of the Catholic Church. If you don't have balance, there is generally a political reason why you don't. I think that was the situation in Ireland and for many it still exists.

SJC: Do you feel you were badly treated by the media or the political establishment, by liberal Ireland?

DS: I never thought of it as being badly treated. I think that, after a while, people can forget why they are doing something and in turn they become part of the system. We are what we are not just because of what we think but what we see reflected around us. This consensus was there and in place from the time of the Bishop Casey situation. And if you are only moving in circles where people are thinking the same as you are, how are you going to know what anybody else is thinking? There are people who think differently and who have a right to think differently. I think what my presidential run did, initially, was to challenge the consensus. When someone does that, they are seen as a threat. It didn't worry me, though sometimes it embarrassed me, but I knew it would happen. That was my choice, knowing it would happen, to have the guts to take it. Was it worth it? Yes. Did I enjoy it? No. It had to happen. Then it was a challenge: to challenge the people to look at themselves. I think it was a challenge to Irish society.

It was 1995 when I first became aware of the fact that there were a huge number of people who felt totally isolated in their own country because they couldn't see what they believed reflected back anywhere in the media, television, on the radio, or even in their own churches. I was not at all thinking of politics at the time. I was promoting a twenty-fifth anniversary album and RTE did a documentary, a small part of which was on myself and my family at home; they filmed the meal and we said our Grace before meals with the children, which was just part of our normal everyday life. It wasn't a huge statement about anything — it was just what we did. And the reaction to that when I did a tour around Ireland was huge. I actually had people moved to tears, who told me how much it meant. I was shocked at the reaction. Then I realised that these people had been marginalised, and that's a terrible thing.

SJC: So that crystallised it for you?

DS: That and the referenda, where a court in Europe can say that our government is acting unlawfully, illegally and unconstitutionally. This bullying and intimidation of the people in a democracy, where the people have the last say, was so blatant, and yet people felt helpless. They couldn't break the status quo. They didn't know that other people felt the same as they did and they couldn't see any way of breaking this stronghold. Neither could I, but I saw I couldn't do nothing and just sit there, because that would be defeatist.

SJC: The majority of people voted in favour of divorce. The abortion issue is still unresolved.

DS: It was a small majority, after the government had used five hundred thousand pounds of taxpayers' money to promote a "Yes" vote.

SJC: Until Patricia McKenna took it to the courts, even though she favoured divorce.

DS: Yes. The content of the referenda isn't as important as the way it's carried out, and the fact that one member of the Oireachtas stood with almost 50 per cent of the people of this country is, in itself, telling.

SJC: Presumably you think it's a scandal that there is some kind of legalised abortion available in Ireland, despite the overwhelming majority being against it, and you must obviously favour a referendum?

DS: I favour a properly worded referendum.

SJC: And do you think that will happen?

DS: I have great doubts. If we sit long enough and do nothing for long enough, then by that time the constitution of Europe will be firmly in place and the Court of Justice will decide over our Constitution and over the will of the people. So if we do nothing for long enough, we can say, "I never wanted this but it's now out of my hands." I think it's disgraceful that the wishes of the Irish people, who are the last voice and the final deciders on anything to do with our Constitution, are being betrayed.

SJC: One example of the European courts' ruling that the Irish Constitution needed changing was the court case that Senator Norris took to have the law liberalised in relation to homosexuality. What was your view of all that when it occurred?

DS: Ireland was the first to lower the age to sixteen, the lowest in Europe, and the rest of Europe had to follow suit. Again, the Catholic Church never condemns whoever the individual is. I was raised in a business that had many homosexual people working in it and I have to say that, as a woman in that business, I found them to be the greatest of friends and the kindest of people, talented and gifted. I would have a deep respect for the homosexual friends that I have. What we are talking about is a society that is undermining the family unit. In some cases it's being done out of a sense of compassion for other family units. Everybody wants to be loved and to love but we have a society here within our Constitution that is based on the unit of the family, which is the fundamental unit. It's nothing new — it's recognised throughout the world as the most stable unit within society, which makes society stable, and if it's weakened it makes society weaker. It's well documented. In every sector, be it in communications or IT or industrial relations, we are encouraged to search for best practice, for what works and gives long-term security and stability. And within relationships, for the family, for the parents, for the children, for the woman in particular, the best practice is the family unit where the husband and wife are committed for life to the raising of the children, and there's well documented research in America to say that when that breaks down it affects the children and throws the woman into poverty.

SJC: How does that affect two men living together who can't adopt or marry, according to the laws of this country? How do two guys who want to live in a long-term, monogamous relationship of love undermine the family?

DS: We have within the European Community the situation whereby if one country moves in one direction, it puts pressure on other countries to move in the same direction. As I say, everyone wants to love and be loved. The question is: what do we as a society regard as best practice or the common good? In the Netherlands, they have just had marriages for homosexuals, and because of advances in genetic engineering you can now have homosexual couples adopting children through surrogacy. How do you measure that against a man and a woman committed for life and raising their children? What research do we have which says there's no difference for the child? We have seen again in the States, who have gone down the road thirty years before us, the effects upon children, especially the male child, of not having a father. How do we see what is best for the child? We don't have that information. What we do now is what works. It sometimes breaks down, but does that mean we scrap it altogether? Does that mean that any kind of relationship is all right? If my dogs and I decide together, and I really love my dogs though we don't have a sexual relationship, that we're very special, what then? A stable society rests on a stable family unit and that has to support best practice.

SJC: So would you find it difficult to tell those friends that how they love should still be outlawed?

DS: I didn't say that anyone should be condemned or thrown into prison. And, yes, I do have homosexual friends who are deeply hurt. That's why I say, everyone wants to love and be loved, but what do we as a society promote and support for the common good of that society?

SJC: On that note, what do you think of Dana International who recently won the Eurovision, who is a great fan of yours and who created a huge controversy among the Orthodox Jews in Israel because he is a transsexual?

DS: I wasn't in the country at the time. I was quite upset that he was better looking than me! I suppose I didn't think a whole lot about it. I am a Catholic, a Roman Catholic and try to live by the teachings of my church and my church teaches me that I must have the deepest respect for homosexual people, but the church upholds the family unit as the basic unit of society.

SJC: How do you enjoy being an MEP for Connacht-Ulster and what legislation have you been involved in?

DS: I particularly chose Connacht-Ulster because I felt it was seeing neglect. It has suffered deliberate political neglect. It hasn't had its fair share of European funding. I felt a tremendous sense of identification and I've always loved the West. My roots are in Donegal but I was raised in Derry. I am involved in two main committees.

One is regional policy, transport and tourism, which I felt was to tailor to the needs of the area, and it also covered the small farmer who was never meant to be helped by the Common Agricultural Policy. The other committee is youth, education, culture, media and sport. I really wanted those two committees and I got them. We're dealing with a lot of different reports. One is the abuse of alcohol by children and adolescents and the sexual exploitation of children and adolescents on the Internet. There is so much going on within regional policy, especially transport. We have a moral obligation to invest money. I vote on about fourteen reports a month — it's a huge volume of work.

SJC: You hosted an evangelical programme, *Say Yes*, on EWTN, the Catholic Cable Network in the States, attracting thirty million viewers worldwide. And now you're involved in ethical dilemmas and religious debates. Would you say that you driven by a religious agenda?

DS: No. I don't think it falls into religion. What I have been taught within my religious community is a tremendous basis because it centres on respect for the human being. When I did that programme, most of the crew and staff weren't Catholic and about 70 per cent of my guests weren't Catholic. Then, as I got to know more Catholics, it balanced out a bit more.

SJC: Do you miss singing? I know you wrote and sang "We are One Body" for the Papal visit to Denver in 1993.

DS: I would like to keep my hand in singing. It's a bit like keeping in touch with who you are. I now enjoy singing. Sometimes, when it's your job, it's different. I love working with youth and with pro-life people because they are the most joyful and rooted people. I may go and sing but I get more than I give. It's like visiting somebody in hospital — you think you're giving something but you come out of there glad you went.

SJC: Being raised in Derry, how do you view the Republican movement, Sinn Féin, and Gerry Adams?

DS: I have always been non-violent. We're obviously talking about the IRA, and Sinn Féin are the political wing of the IRA. I didn't go the political route — I went the grassroots way. I was a spokesperson for Co-operation North. I did my work at grassroots level.

SJC: You chose to become an Independent. Would you ever consider joining a political party or setting up one?

DS: If I could find a political party that was in tune with me. There are certain advantages to being in a political party. But I haven't found that. I am an associate member of the European People's Party. It's a federalist group and I am not a federalist. I find I tend to vote with the Greens on environmental issues, the Socialists on economic issues, and I vote with my own group on other issues, particularly on the protection of the family and life, because the EU has a very anti-family and anti-life thrust, which I obviously wouldn't be in tune with.

SJC: Would you agree that all the political parties are singing from the same hymn sheet and are clustered at the centre, and that the electorate don't have a real choice, though now there is the National Party and the Christian Centrist party, which may suit you?

DS: No; I would very much respect them but I wouldn't want a connection with them. I don't know who the Christian Centrist party are. But the National Party and Family Solidarity were there battling along before I ran for the presidential election. I have a lot of respect for them.

SJC: What's your view of contemporary Ireland and the Celtic Tiger?

DS: Not a lot different to what a lot of people feel. There's a great anxiety about the pace of change in the country and I think that there's been such an unbalanced presentation of Christian values. You can't remove something and have nothing there in its place. We are a deeply spiritual people and for me the whole person is physical, mental and spiritual. If you only take of the physical or the intellectual you push away the spiritual and you don't have a balance in the person or in society, and I think that robs us of who we are.

SJC: Does Ireland still have soul?

DS: Oh yes, but people are disturbed. They are not sure how to adjust. There is definite unease. We're basically individualistic in Ireland — we like to make up our own minds. For many years, in relation to the EU, we have been anaesthetised by money and that has resulted in an acceptance of lots of things. There hasn't been a deep discussion about what we've been signing up to. Now we are at a point when we're looking around and there's a deep unease about what's happening. [*This interview took place before the Nice Treaty was rejected by referendum in Ireland.*] There is a murder a day and more on weekends. It's at an epidemic. We are now number one for binge drinking. It's a symptom of something wrong. We have an epidemic of suicides among beautiful young people. A suicide is not a material loss — it's a despair on the spiritual level.

SJC: How would you define soul?

DS: I can only define it for myself. I was raised in a Catholic home that had a lot of close connections and respect for other religions. I was raised to be very open and I am glad of that. For me, the recognition of the fact that there was a God and that that God created me and loved me and therefore knew me more intimately than I knew me, despite all my imperfections, gave me a deep peace.

SJC: And sustained you?

DS: Yes, absolutely.

SJC: Have you ever had your faith severely tested?

DS: Oh yes. In my middle teens I remember waking one morning and knowing there was no God, that God was the great escape who would make you feel better. I didn't want that. But if He did exist, it dawned on me that to live the Christian life was the easiest way. But to live the Christian life is probably the most challenging for the individual. That was the beginning of my journey and the next step was to be vulnerable, because if you accept there is a God who has the best road for you, you have to be vulnerable and not take all the decisions yourself.

SJC: And if you believe in God, do you also believe in the Devil?

DS: Yes. I think we have always have opposites, don't we, like good and bad?

SJC: How do you pray?

DS: I pray in varied ways. I try when I wake up to offer the whole day. I try to get to Mass when I can, daily. It took me a while to cop on to that, but I think the Eucharist is a strength, for me. I try also to pray the Daily Office, which is a profound prayer. It's also the prayer of the universal church. I am hooking into a wellspring of spiritual strength.

SJC: Do you ever get depressed?

DS: I think everyone gets down. I certainly get down, but depressed to the point of despair, no.

SJC: Finally, are you happy?

DS: I am basically at peace, which doesn't mean I am always happy. I have a very good husband who would be very spiritually in tune with where I am and I with he. Life can hit you some very hard knocks and when you are in the middle of it, trying to keep your head above water, to have someone there who says, "Let's pray about this", because there's no human answer, is really wonderful. And I have four beauti-ful children, who are all healthy. I have people who love me irrespective of what I do and I have people whom I love. That's happiness in itself.

About the Author

Dr Stephen J. Costello was born in Dublin and educated at St Gerard's School, Castleknock College and University College Dublin, where he read philosophy and Spanish. He holds an MA and PhD in philosophy. He subsequently trained in psychoanalysis. He has been lecturing in philosophy and psychoanalysis for over ten years at University College Dublin, Trinity College Dublin and at a number of psychotherapy training institutes. He has been published widely in leading academic journals and is the author of a forthcoming book entitled *The Pale Criminal: Psychoanalytic Perspectives*. He is a member of the Association for Psychoanalysis and Psychotherapy in Ireland. Apart from his intellectual interests in philosophy, religion and psychoanalysis, Dr Costello practises the Japanese martial art of Aikido and is a member of the Irish Aikido Association.